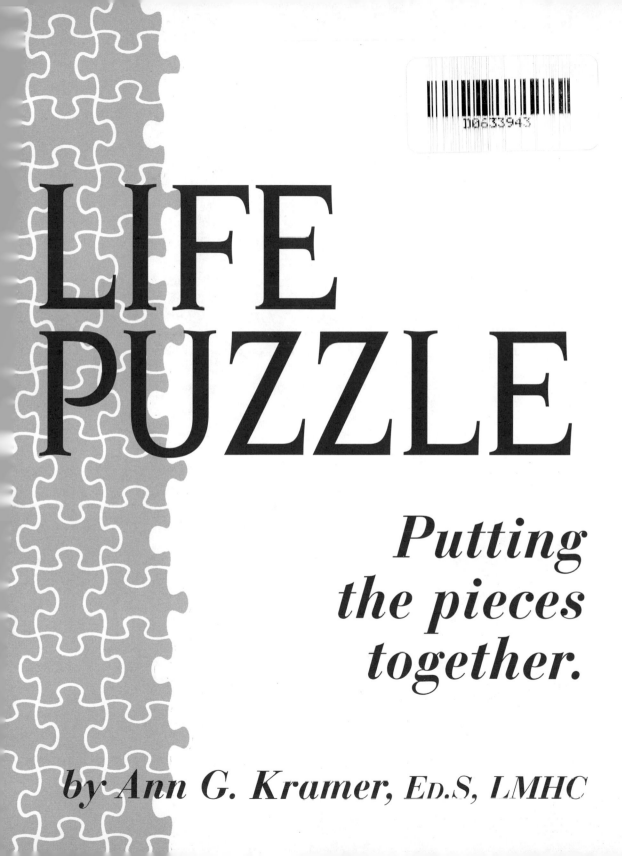

# LIFE PUZZLE

*Putting the pieces together.*

*by Ann G. Kramer, Ed.S, LMHC*

# Acknowledgments

To all those who created this book...my friends, clients, chance encounters, other authors I've read (and recommend in this book!) I give my greatest thanks. Without you *Life Puzzle... Putting the pieces together*, would be a boring treatise. Instead, it is a book of living people and their ideas, dreams, problems and visions.

Special thanks to my loving husband who has been supportive and encouraging me in this endeavor.

ISBN 0-9659-426-0-0

©2002, Second edition, Ann G. Kramer

*Printed in the United States of America*

# *The search for your Life Puzzle...*

**A**s a child growing up you are constantly asked "Well, what are you going to 'do' when you grow up?" Little children give answers such as a fireman, a doctor, a nurse or a mommy because they are the choices they see in their world. The subtle message we all learn is that we're supposed to grow up and 'do' something. The focus through our school years is to complete them so we can 'do' some type of work example. This is reinforced in our adult lives as one of the very first questions we ask someone we've just met is "Well, what do you do?"

This is such a constant question is it any wonder we come to the belief that our goal in life is to 'do' the one major role we've selected for ourselves? And we trust that if we're the best mom, doctor, lawyer, or Indian chief, our lives will be complete—a smooth ride for the rest of one's life. It's a rude awakening for many young adults when it doesn't actually happen like this.

But what if you had grown up in a world that asked, "How's your Life Puzzle coming along?" And with this question, you understood that there were many pieces of your life and it would take a life time to complete. Would you have designed your life differently? Yes, you would.

The premise of this book is that you are much, much more than the role you play each day. You are a person who is in the process of putting together a whole Life Puzzle that goes far beyond the one piece of "What do you do?"

We grew up in a world that we believed and trusted was showing us the right way to become an adult. We believed that it was a good system and it would provide us with the knowledge we needed to be whole. If we did what we were told and followed what those ahead of us did, the promise was we would grow to be a good, successful adult. We followed somewhat blindly, hoping one day all the confusion, fear and insecurity we felt as children would melt away once we were adults.

But the reality? Adulthood arrives and we discover we are still filled with confusion, fear and insecurity! We work hard at getting jobs under our belt and being good at "doing" something with the hope that the stress and anxiety we feel inside will go away. Only it doesn't quite go away, because we are operating from a picture of ourselves that is too small and limited to ever give us a feeling of balance and wholeness.

It's time to expand our view. Instead of focusing our lives on the limited "what you do is what you are," you need to redefine your life into a whole picture: Your Life Puzzle.

Your life is like a gigantic puzzle and it is up to you to put all the pieces together. It is a tricky puzzle to work on but it can also be lots of fun. It's much like someone handing you a box filled with 10,000 puzzle pieces and asking "what is this going to be when it's put together?" Alas, there's no picture on the outside of this box! So you're standing there staring at lots of cut up pieces with no idea what this puzzle will look like. Your response is "I don't know, I'll tell you when I'm done working on it."

Working on it…that's what making your Life Puzzle is about and every single human being has to do it. Just as you could not put a 10,000 piece puzzle together overnight, your own Life Puzzle will take a lifetime to complete.

There are 16 primary sections to your Life Puzzle as you will see within the book. And within each of these 16 primary sections are lots of smaller pieces that you will pick up and place into your whole Life Puzzle during your life.

When you shift from the limited view you were taught to one that explores the fullness of making your Life Puzzle, life will take on an entirely new picture. Instead of the rush to get one or two major roles under your belt with the illusion that it will make you feel whole, making your Life Puzzle shows you a picture of yourself that will take a lifetime to complete but will give you peace throughout the journey.

A puzzle requires lots of thinking, pondering and often trying out a few pieces here and there before finally getting it right. The same goes for you.

To make you the best you can be— think, ponder, try out a few pieces here and there.

Making a puzzle requires patience, persistence, humor and sometimes frustration (where is that piece!!!!!!) so does making your Life Puzzle. Little by little, you'll find your "self" coming together. Be patient, keep trying, laugh at yourself a little more and eventually you'll find that piece that takes you on to the next stage of putting together your Life Puzzle.

## A couple of tips about making your Life Puzzle:

*1. No gurus are necessary in order for you to create your Life Puzzle.*

You and only you can decide how to put your Life Puzzle together. Others can offer advice, but be careful. Often when your own Life Puzzle-making is in its early stages, it is tempting to let someone else who appears to or perhaps even does have more of their Life Puzzle made, tell you the best way to make yours. Advice is useful, but not when you give up listening to your own inner voice in exchange.

*2. Do not be afraid to rework an earlier section of your Life Puzzle when it appears that the pieces aren't coming together in the way you thought they would.*

Remember when you were a young child putting together a puzzle? You were often tempted to stick a piece into the puzzle, even though it seemed a little tight. After convincing (fooling?) your-self this was the right piece, you continued to add more pieces until about 18 pieces later it became obvious that the earlier piece wasn't the right one after all. Of course, you had two choices: keep it there and mess up the puzzle or take the incorrect piece out and rework it.

Well, Life Puzzles are like that too. There will be times you choose one thing but down the road it becomes obvious that if you keep that piece in place, a lot of other pieces are going to get misplaced too. In making your Life Puzzle, the sooner you accept you've made a mistake and correct it, the better. There is no shame in this…everyone makes mistakes. Fix it and get going again.

## What does a Life Puzzle look like? What do I use as a role model?

It is hard for many of us to picture our whole self because we've rarely met other people who have worked on and built a healthy Life Puzzle. This is a bit of a dilemma.

Human beings are notorious copycats! Since our very early days we've been copying other human beings in order to figure out how to do things for ourselves. Young babies watch adult faces and learn to respond in kind. Thus, a baby who sees his parent laughing and smiling will copy this and try to smile too. Even learning to walk is an action we copy by watching everyone around us walk. Our parents clap and smile at our first step and we know we're doing something right!

As we grow, we copy our schoolmates or our brothers and sisters and their actions. It's amazing to watch a three year old try to do the very things her six year old sister is doing, even though she doesn't have the motors skills necessary to be successful. A little older and we start using actors in television or movies as examples of what we want to look like. As we head into high school and the push to "do" something becomes stronger, we try to copy older siblings who have left home or other adults that look like they're doing okay.

Through most of this copying the drive is to "be like everyone else." We do this to overcome the feelings of inadequacy that are so prevalent in our young years.

## Don't copy others: Make your own!

Why keep copying when those you're copying aren't that happy? Why would you want to repeat this? Stop a moment and think of the people you know. Are they in balance? Or are their lives frazzled, running after one thing or another, constantly tired and anxious in their quest to "do" with the hope that when they finally "get there" it will be worth it?

I hear again and again the frustration that occurs in adults when they do get to that supposed "there". As one of my clients said, *"I have been telling myself since I was a teenager that the thing I most wanted to do was be a great mother. I was sure that if I did everything necessary, i.e., find the right husband, set up the beautiful home, and then have my babies I would finally find the peace I had never felt while growing up. But now I have all of these things and I'm still depressed and confused. What did I do wrong?"*

It's not that she did anything wrong. It's just that the view she picked for herself misses too many of the other pieces of her Life Puzzle and she ends up feeling depressed, confused and empty. She, like most of us, had nobody to show her these other Life Puzzle pieces. But the good news is she can teach herself—and so can you.

And that's what this book is about—how to build your Life Puzzle—piece by piece.

Unlike traditional puzzle-making where we use the picture on the cover of the box to help us put the pieces in the right place, making your Life Puzzle requires you to put the pieces down and trust that as you do, the picture that develops is right for you. Initially this may feel strange and awkward, but what most people discover as they move into this process is that it is great not to have to copy a preset picture of themselves but to design their own unique picture that becomes their Life Puzzle.

Remember too, Life Puzzles are not finished until the day you die. There is time to change almost any section of your Life Puzzle if you do not like the picture that begins to emerge. The one exception to this comes after you have added children to your Life Puzzle. This is the only area of your Life Puzzle in which you cannot say, "Oops, I don't think I want this after all." So, as you'll see in chapter 14, I encourage you to think long and hard before you add children to your Life Puzzle to be sure it is what you want to do because you can't give them back!

You can change your work, your partner, your financial situation, your nutrition, your exercise and even your sexuality, but once you've added a child, that is a part of your Life Puzzle forever. You may learn to be a better, more dynamic parent, but you can never choose to not to be a parent once that child has arrived on Earth. Even if you divorce and move out of state…you are still a parent

and it is still a part of your total Life Puzzle.

## Piece by Piece…here you go.

The 19 chapters will each cover one of the Life Puzzle pieces. You will notice that some of the chapters are quite long and others considerably shorter. In order to keep this book within a reasonable number of pages, I've decided to focus more fully on nine sections while touching lightly on the other seven.

The nine I've chosen are the foundation for a healthy Life Puzzle and I think you need to first explore these areas to get a good start. If all of this is new to you, these nine areas will give you plenty to work on.

There will be a follow up book to this one and it will focus on the first nine again and then expand the information to a fuller view of the other seven. Considering that making your Life Puzzle is an on-going process, I think doing it this way will offer the most effective way for you to use this book. You can only take in so much at one time without feeling overwhelmed.

I want you to use this book and I'm concerned if it is too big you will find it intimidating and convince yourself it will take too long to get through it all. Because we have been taught to be taskmasters, often when we read a book like this we want to absorb the information quickly, put it to use, and then get on to the next task.

However, I am hoping to break you of this habit. This quick, get it all done obsession leads us to create lives that care little about the process of how we get there…just get there. In this quick-fix habit we lose our true selves. This is not the way to create a healthy, well-balanced Life Puzzle.

So as you read this book, realize that this is not a quick fix book. You will not be a miraculous new you after using this information for a week or two. The goal of reading and using this book is to come to the realization that you do not need to rush your life just to get it done. The goal is to read this and use it for the rest of your life journey through a process that is good for you.

I encourage you to read this book slowly. You might go through the whole book, but then return to the section that you feel is most important for you to explore more fully. Re-read it and do the exercises, read the books suggested and take your time as you put to active use the information you have gathered.

Remember: piece by piece, enjoy the process while you're in it. As you do, your Life Puzzle will become whole.

**The primary areas that will be explored in this book include:**

Self Responsibility
Nutrition
Communication
Feelings
Thinking
Working
Partner/Relationships
Parenting/Family Building
Spirituality

**The secondary areas are:**

Exercise
Sexuality
Financial Responsibility
Play & Recreation
Special Challenges
Community & Environment
Finding Meaning

# Life

Life is a challenge…meet it

Life is a gift…accept it

Life is an adventure…dare it

Life is a sorrow…overcome it

Life is a tragedy…face it

Life is a duty…perform it

Life is a game…play it

Life is a mystery…unfold it

Life is a song…sing it

Life is an opportunity…take it

Life is a journey…complete it

Life is a promise…fulfill it

Life is a beauty…praise it

Life is a struggle…fight it

Life is a goal…achieve it

Life is a puzzle…solve it.

*~Author unknown*

# Table of Contents

# Pieces
# of Your
# Life Puzzle

# Life Puzzle

We all have the same 16 core areas, 5 edges that create the SELF, yet no two of us will put them together in exactly the same way. Thus we all have a common bond while maintaining our own unique SELF.

# *Piece by piece to make the whole.*

**A**s you can see there are quite a number of different pieces that go into making your Life Puzzle. There are 16 distinct sections that merge together to make a whole.

There's plenty of time to work on this Life Puzzle...your whole life! The problem for so many of us is that we're in such a rush to make our Life Puzzles as quickly as we can and be done with it. But a dynamic, terrific, creative Life Puzzle can't be rushed. What's the point of getting it all done as quickly as we can? Why are we trying to complete our Life Puzzle by the time we're 21, 25, or 32?

## Take your time!

It's helpful to look at the pieces of your Life Puzzle on the previous page. Don't panic, you don't work on them all at the same time or for equal amounts of time! At different times of your life certain pieces are much more important than others. Obviously parenting and financial responsibility aren't top priorities for a 14 year old. Work is a major focus in the years 25-65, but is less important at 87.

It's important to realize that each area will require awareness, changing, growing and then a renewed awareness that continues on throughout your life. Our lives are not static, repetitive,

boring day-in, day-out processes. (Well, not if you get involved in creating your Life Puzzle!) Yes, there are many people with dull lives but even these people could, by understanding that they have a choice in developing their Life Puzzle, take a dull life and turn it around.

All the pieces make a whole. All pieces are equally important to your wholeness, even though they don't all require the same amount of time on either a daily basis or life long sense.

For instance, in your 20 to 60's you are quite focused on your "work" piece. Work does require quite a bit of a day's time in comparison with daily nutrition or exercise. But if the work piece is developed while excluding other pieces overall, your whole Life Puzzle is going to be unbalanced.

Look again at the puzzle pieces: each is an important part of your Life Puzzle. Too often we get caught up in one or two pieces that consume huge portions of our lives. Work is one of these, especially for men.

I remember teaching a seminar using this Life Puzzle as a stress management tool. A gentleman came up after class, he was about 47 years old. He said to me, *"I spent 27 years, 6 days a week with 15 hour days working, until one day, 3 months ago, I was forced to quit when the family-held* *company I worked for changed hands. Tonight I realize that I have lived a Life Puzzle where work took up 15/16's of the puzzle. These last three months have been almost enough to kill me because I have been so out of control without work to fill up my every waking moment. But I see now I have much to live for. There are 15 other pieces that I'm going to take the time to work on. I'm going to put my Life Puzzle together and make it come out balanced."* *

## Why do we get so few lessons on Life Puzzle making?

If you look at the different areas of your Life Puzzle, stop and ask yourself:

When were you taught:

1. **Good nutrition** as a daily lifestyle?
2. To **exercise** on a regular basis... for life?
3. **Good communication skills** that encourage honesty and good listening?
4. **Parenting skills** and family building?
5. **Thinking skills**....how to be a positive, pro-active thinker?
6. How to **create meaningful work** beyond the paycheck?
7. **Spirituality and religion**...did you get lessons or was it pushed on you?
8. **Sexuality**...to have a healthy respect for your body and sex?
9. **To earn money, manage it, save it,** etc.?
10. **Feelings**...Were you allowed to express feelings such as anger or fears so you could manage them effectively for your life?

### How about you?

In most of these areas you received few lessons on how to make the best choices in your life. How then do you take full responsibility for your Life Puzzle? It is a dilemma. If you are going to create a healthy, dynamic self, you might first feel like throwing up your hands, screaming "no fair" and getting mad at all those who didn't teach you these lessons, but after that...then what?

Here's the bottom line: the system we all trusted to provide us with the necessary lessons so we would be able to take responsibility and create a whole Life Puzzle...does not exist. It never has. Human beings have been "making it up as we go along," plodding through and doing the best we can with what we've got at the moment. And for most of man's history, basic survival was about as much as we were interested in. Food on the table, roof over our head was about all there was time to get done each day.

From this basic survival "get through the day lifestyle," we have suddenly emerged, in just the last 40 years, into a country that has gone from surviving to thriving. No longer is it get food, any food, on the table. Now we have the ability to make food choices that are the best for good health, good nourishment and great taste.

In this quick shift there has been little time to set up a system to address this and begin providing these lessons,

---

*I'm happy to tell you that this man has created a much happier life for himself. He does work, but he leaves at 5:00 p.m., takes time to vacation, has a much better relationship with his wife and children and continues to explore new areas of his life.

be it through schools, parents, church etc. Thus, it is now up to you!

The human race is in a tremendous process of change as we shift from the old "just get through the day" lifestyle to one of making a Life Puzzle. You are a part of this shift. You are the transition generation. You are the new creator. Just like the caveman who learned to use fire for his benefit, you too can learn to use what's available around you and within you to create a healthy Life Puzzle. It will be well worth it!

## Choosing to Build Your Life Puzzle:

### Welcome to the Adventure of Your Life!

# *Where are you on the Choosing Continuum?*

The Choosing Continuum is an excellent tool to help you determine your commitment to building your Life Puzzle. It gives you a reference to go back to time and time again. In all the areas of your life, which we will begin concentrating on in the next chapters, the Choosing Continuum is a handy reminder of where you are now and where you're headed next.

Repeatedly asking yourself, "Where am I on the Choosing Continuum and in what direction am I headed?" helps you stay more centered and balanced. It also helps you focus on living your life pro-actively.

As you will notice on the Choosing Continuum, on the left side, life is not one of choice, it's a matter of reaction to the world around you. It is the "wait till a problem arises, then do something about it" way of life.

Whether you are talking about your health, your feelings, your sexuality, your family, your kids…do you find yourself constantly doing things after a problem arises instead of taking action long ahead of a problem coming to the forefront? If you do, welcome to the crowd!

Most people run their lives this way because they don't really understand that there is another possibility. They watch everyone else doing it so why would they think it is abnormal?

The reaction most people have to the Choosing Continuum, after they really examine it, is to realize that yes, they are living on the left side. After this realization they are confronted with a choice. They either accept that they are going to continue living this way or they are going to have to make another choice.

Choice: that's the difference between the two sides of the continuum. Life Puzzle-making is the choice to become pro-active. It is a conscious way of meeting the outside world by taking responsibility for the purposeful reaction you give to it in all the dimensions of your life, so in all the areas of your life, you are aware of your responsibility and take steps to make choices that will be useful to your life.

For example, you become aware that your health isn't just something that happens to you but instead is a result of many daily choices: exercise, nutrition, thinking, feelings etc. As a result, you make choices in these areas with the knowledge that each choice impacts your whole life.

That's what making your Life Puzzle is all about: your whole life. Not just getting through, birth to death, with as few dents as possible but creating a whole life that makes for a dynamic journey.

# THE CHOOSING CONTINUUM

### Use it to help you determine your commitment to creating your Life Puzzle.

**Making your Life Puzzle is a haphazard process.**

**Making your Life Puzzle is an active, conscious process throughout life.**

| 0 | 1 | 2 | 3 | 4 | **5** | 6 | 7 | 8 | 9 | 10 |

**LIFE THREATENING ILLNESS. PROBLEMS THAT CANNOT BE IGNORED.**

**SYMPTOMS OR PROBLEMS ARE CONTROLLING YOUR LIFE. CONSUMED WITH MANAGING THESE ISSUES.**

**DISCOMFORT, FAIRLY CONSTANT ANXIETY**

**AWARE OF ONE'S PHYSICAL, EMOTIONAL, INTELLECTUAL, SEXUAL AND SPIRITUAL ISSUES AND IMPACT ON YOUR LIFE.**

**LIVE A DAILY PROCESS OF INTEGRATING ALL DIMENSIONS OF SELF TO ACHIEVE OPTIMAL HEALTH AND LIFE. ON-GOING LEARNING AND GROWING EXPERIENCE.**

- Doing enough to get by in life. Get up, do the day, go to bed, do it again.
- Neutral health: no noticeable health complaints, take health for granted.
- Maintain status quo.
- Do what everyone else is doing.
- Accumulate material possessions.

*Wait until it's broke, then fix it. Only get active in your life when the discomfort or problem is more than you can ignore. Unaware of your Life Puzzle.*

*Practice a daily lifestyle to prevent illness and create a healthy, well-balanced lifestyle by choice: Making your Life Puzzle.*

Re-Active
Passive
Unconscious
Victim

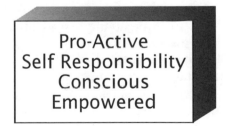

Pro-Active
Self Responsibility
Conscious
Empowered

**In all the areas of your Life Puzzle, ask yourself: Where am I on the Choosing Continuum and what direction am I heading…in my nutrition, partnering, parenting, spirituality, communication, etc.? Am I pro-active or reactive?**

## The Choosing Continuum

It is just a tool to help you see the choices you have to make in your life. As you will see, the Continuum runs from 0 to 10. The way most of us have been taught (or not taught!) to live our lives is to assume that if we're at 5, where we don't have any major health complaints, life is okay, nothing spectacular but not too bad either, then we figure..hey we're okay, good enough. And we go on living our life like this until a problem arises and we are forced to do something about it.

That's the 0-4 range. We are pretty good at "doing something" when we have problems, signs, symptoms, etc. to manage. Alas, once we get back to the 5 stage we go back to living pretty much like we did before the earlier problem.

Look at the issue of dieting: You're at 5 when you're okay with your current weight level. You're not dieting, you're eating pretty much whatever comes along. At 4 on the Continuum, you notice you've put on 10 lbs., which for some is enough to start watching what they're eating again…a small diet. However, for a lot of people, it's not till they reach 40 lbs, down around 2 on the Continuum, that they really hunker down to do anything about their weight…and then they intensively diet to lose 40 lbs. as quickly as possible. Usually they do something radical like a pineapple and pretzels diet and they stay on it for eight weeks, lose the weight. Then they're back at 5 and they revert to their earlier eating habits and the weight creeps back on.

Whether it's dieting, marriage, family building, choosing work you like or whatever, the question is: Are you choosing or reacting?

Now, with Life Puzzle-making as the model, the cycle is quite different; 5 is not the end point…5 is the starting point. Instead of living life just to get by, Life Puzzle making is a lifestyle that is pro-active in creating health in all the dimensions of your life: physical, emotional, intellectual, spiritual, sexual and the community. It is based in self-responsibility and the realization that you are a wonderful, unique human being that can achieve a dynamic life by choosing to actively be aware of and be creative in the design of your life. Making your Life Puzzle is a daily process of being conscious of yourself in the fullest dimension.

Using the issue of dieting as an example, starting at 5, you accept where your weight currently is, even if you're overweight! Then you begin to design a lifestyle that will bring you towards your ideal…not quickly, but through the process of living healthfully each day to the best of your present ability.

## Which direction are you heading?

Even someone with a life threatening illness can be building a dynamic Life Puzzle if they are headed in the direction of taking responsibility for their Life Puzzle pieces despite their illness. On the other hand, often people who have no obvious illness will rate themselves an eight on the Continuum while they are living irresponsibly—eating too much, drinking too much, and are workaholics with poor personal relationships. What direction are they headed? Reactive or pro-active? This is the key to using the Choosing Continuum.

## Seem too overwhelming?

As you're reading this do you find yourself saying "Yeah, well I would take better care of myself but I don't have time, what with the job, the kids, the spouse, I'm too tired, I don't have enough money, I would if I could, but I can't."?

All of those responses are fine but you still have to make a choice…will you make your Life Puzzle or just let it happen? Only you can decide. And it isn't the spouse, the kids, the money, etc. that will make that decision. Only you can.

You might convince yourself that, well the changes required will upset my partner, therefore, I'd best not rock the boat because it will make him/her angry, irritable or uncomfortable.

What you're really saying to yourself is this; you're willing to accept years of sharing your life with a person who says they love you, but in order for you to share your life with them you can't make healthful lifestyle choices because it might bother them. What does this leave you with? A "do enough to just get by" marriage. What side of the Continuum does this put you on…and what direction? Is that what you were planning on the day you walked down the aisle?

Poor marriages don't just happen, mediocre lives don't just happen….they are a result of not choosing to do something about them.

You say you did try to do something about your marriage, health, nutrition, and exercise but you didn't see any results. And why bother anyway if you're not going to see immediate results?

## Wake Up Call

Life Puzzle-making is not for the faint at heart, give me the quick fix, don't ask me to make much effort in my life kind of person. Making your Life Puzzle is a daily

*It takes so much to be a full human being that there are very few who have the enlightenment or the courage to pay the price. One has to abandon altogether the search for security and reach out to the risk of living with both arms. One has to embrace the world like a lover. One has to accept pain as a condition of existence. One has to court doubt and darkness as the cost of knowing. One needs a will stubborn in conflict, but apt always to total acceptance of every consequence of living and dying.*

Morris L. West
**The Shoes of the Fisherman**

process that never ends. It is for those who can accept that they may see no tangible results of their actions for a long period of time but they continue on anyway. It is for those who know that if they are going to have a dynamic life they will have to make it happen.

This book is written for all those people who would like to live a full and exciting life from start to finish. You might be thinking, well doesn't everyone want a full life? Perhaps, but wanting it and believing you can have it are two different things.

Everyone wants it, but most of us were raised on the left side of the Choosing Continuum. We know how to react, but we are much less comfortable with making choices. Yet the only way you can have a dynamic life is to choose to do so. It won't just happen.

## DON'T MAKE EXCUSES, MAKE CHOICES.
### Welcome to your Life Puzzle

In the next chapters, we will be covering all the pieces of your Life Puzzle. There will be lots of helpful suggestions, ideas and challenges to the current way you may be living your life. Some of the ideas will work for you, others won't. Some of those that won't work now may work in a few years.

Making a Life Puzzle is a process of everyday living. In the beginning stages, it seems like every area of your life requires more awareness, new choices and lots of changes. On the one hand this can be very exciting, on the other hand it can seem so overwhelming that we completely shut down and ignore it all.

The beginning stages of anything new we are learning often results in frustration because it brings up a lot of fear and vulnerability. We don't like being unsure of ourselves and we avoid learning many things if we think it will leave us looking funny and feeling uncomfortable.

Remember when you were learning to ride a bike? There's probably not a kid that at one point didn't scream at the parent or big brother who was trying so hard to be helpful… "I hate this stupid bike! I don't even care if I never learn to ride this dumb bike. Who cares anyway, I don't need to know how to ride a bike."

And of course, big brother or mom said, "Come on, give it another try or we'll do it again tomorrow, maybe it'll be a better day for it." Eventually, you did learn to ride that stupid bike because the reward of knowing how to ride a bike and being able to ride with your friends greatly outweighed the frustration that the earlier attempts created.

Making your Life Puzzle is learning to ride the bike of life. (I know…kind of a corny analogy.) You will encounter many frustrations and there will be days you just want to quit and go back to sitting on the curb and watch life go by. It is a choice you can make, but you are going to have to accept at this point that you choose, no one else does.

Making your Life Puzzle is an on-going process of awareness of where you are now, adding pieces to your Life Puzzle by choice, allowing these new pieces to become part of you and then starting all over again.

It is a never ending but ever growing and challenging process. The longer you work at it, the easier it gets at one level but it takes you into ever deeper dimensions of your life which brings up more choices in the long run!

Are you game? If not, stop reading now…it'll be a waste of time. If you are… get ready for a heck of a ride!

# Life Puzzle making
# is *not*
# about perfection!

It is about

SELF ACCEPTANCE

of where you are now,

who you are now

and the Life Puzzle you are

creating each day.

**Let go of "being perfect" and discover that
building a healthy Life Puzzle is a process
that can only be lived one day at a time.**

# *Life Puzzle under construction! What's it look like so far?*

**A** healthy Life Puzzle is an ever growing process, but it's helpful to review the different areas and see how your Life Puzzle is coming along so far.

On the next few pages, you will see a series of questions that cover the different areas that merge to make a healthy Life Puzzle. Only you will see the outcome and it is important to be realistic and honest so that the picture that will emerge on the scoring sheet gives you an accurate reflection of where you are today.

**Read each of the questions. When scoring, keep the Choosing Continuum in mind, then choose where you think you would land on the Choosing Continuum. A scale of 0-10 is provided to give you assistance.**

## THE CHOOSING CONTINUUM

| 0 | 1 | 2 | 3 | 4 | 5 | 6 | 7 | 8 | 9 | 10 |
|---|---|---|---|---|---|---|---|---|---|----|

REACTIVE
UNCONSCIOUS
PASSIVE
VICTIM

DOING JUST ENOUGH
TO GET BY

PROACTIVE
CONSCIOUS
SELF RESPONSIBLE
EMPOWERED

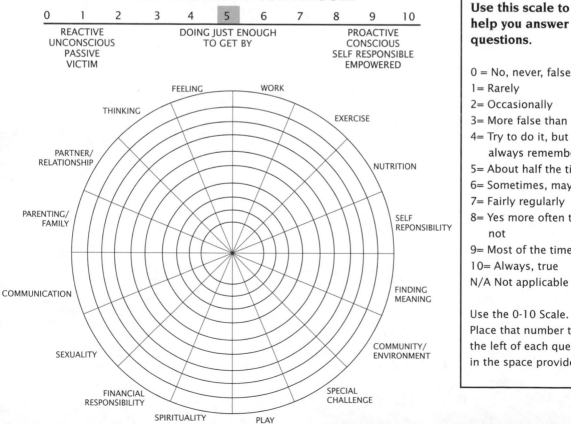

THINKING · FEELING · WORK · EXERCISE · NUTRITION · SELF REPONSIBILITY · FINDING MEANING · COMMUNITY/ENVIRONMENT · SPECIAL CHALLENGE · PLAY · SPIRITUALITY · FINANCIAL RESPONSIBILITY · SEXUALITY · COMMUNICATION · PARENTING/FAMILY · PARTNER/RELATIONSHIP

**Use this scale to help you answer the questions.**

0 = No, never, false
1= Rarely
2= Occasionally
3= More false than true
4= Try to do it, but don't always remember
5= About half the time
6= Sometimes, maybe
7= Fairly regularly
8= Yes more often than not
9= Most of the time
10= Always, true
N/A Not applicable

Use the 0-10 Scale. Place that number to the left of each question in the space provided.

## Self Responsibility

_____ 1. When I make decisions I keep possible consequences uppermost in my mind.

_____ 2. I practice a preventive health lifestyle by eating well and exercising regularly.

_____ 3. I feel confident that my life is in balance due to the choices I've made.

_____ 4. I know my happiness in life is a direct result of the effort I make to grow in the various areas of my life.

_____ 5. When driving, I use my seatbelt.

_____ 6. I actively seek ways to reduce stress in my life.

_____ 7. I am comfortable with my body. I am comfortable looking at myself naked in a mirror. I like what I see.

_____ 8. I feel that my current state of health is a result of my daily lifestyle.

_____ 9. I wake up ready to face each day.

_____ 10. On the whole, daily living is a pleasurable experience.

_____ TOTAL SCORE

## Nutrition

_____ 1. Each day I consciously eat foods for my health.

_____ 2. I drink at least 4 glasses of water per day.

_____ 3. I limit my fat intake by eating a limited amount of beef and pork.

_____ 4. I eat five, 1/2 cup servings of vegetables each day.

_____ 5. I eat one piece of fresh fruit each day.

_____ 6. I am consciously aware of the amount of fiber my body needs and seek to eat this amount each day.

_____ 7. I am pleased with my daily diet and its nutritional quality.

_____ 8. When grocery shopping, I choose foods that provide health benefits.

_____ 9. I limit the amount of coffee, tea, colas, or other caffeine drinks to no more than 2 per day.

_____ 10. I limit the amount of alcohol I drink to no more than 1 drink per day.

_____ TOTAL SCORE

## Exercise/Physical care

_____ 1. I use exercise to help me prevent illness.

_____ 2. I use physical exercise to help me improve my emotional state.

_____ 3. I have taken active steps to ensure my body will function well for 80 or more years.

_____ 4. I am aware of my body every day. I treat it with respect.

_____ 5. I understand that many physical pains are a signal from my body to add more exercise.

_____ 6. I choose not to smoke.

_____ 7. I regularly exercise at least three times a week for twenty minutes or more.

_____ 8. I regularly use massage to help relieve stress in my body.

_____ 9. I regularly stretch and move my body to release tension.

_____ 10. I use breathing exercises to manage stress and my mood.

_____ TOTAL SCORE

## Work

_____ 1.  I have consciously explored and chosen the work I do.

_____ 2.  I do not consider myself a workaholic.

_____ 3.  What work I do, I take responsibility for doing my best (even if I don't currently enjoy it.)

_____ 4.  I know that I am responsible, not my employer, for increasing my work skills, knowledge etc.

_____ 5.  I seek to work in harmony with my co-workers.

_____ 6.  I seek to resolve conflicts at work to everyone's mutual satisfaction.

_____ 7.  The work I do I would do even if they didn't pay me.

_____ 8.  I keep myself open to learning news skills to improve myself, my company and my work.

_____ 9.  I am committed to adding value to the world through the quality of the work and effort I give.

_____ 10. I do not see myself trapped in life because of the work and money I make.

_____ TOTAL SCORE

## Feelings

_____ 1.  I feel comfortable acknowledging my feelings and sharing them with others.

_____ 2.  I am conscious of my feelings.

_____ 3.  I am aware that my face reflects my feeling state: I know what my face is "saying" right now.

_____ 4.  When experiencing negative feelings such as anger, frustration and fear, I am able to recognize them and manage them appropriately.

_____ 5.  When feeling overwhelmed with sadness, anger, jealousy or anxiety, I would seek outside help (counselor, minister, friends, etc.)

_____ 6.  I am okay with letting my anger, sadness or frustration show.

_____ 7.  I think it's okay to cry.

_____ 8.  When I have a problem I am unable to manage, I can ask for help without feeling anxious or vulnerable.

_____ 9.  I think that all feelings are valuable and don't try to hide from negative feelings, like anger or jealousy.

_____ 10. I am okay with looking silly or foolish in front of my friends.

_____ TOTAL SCORE

## Thinking

_____ 1. I see myself as an open minded, creative thinker.

_____ 2. As a thinking stimulation exercise, I try to look at issues from more than one angle before making a decision.

_____ 3. I actively pursue creative thinking through writing, art, brainstorming exercises etc.

_____ 4. I continuously read, take classes, listen to training tapes, etc. to increase my learning.

_____ 5. When worrying about a problem, I am able to step away from it for a while to give myself a chance to relax.

_____ 6. I am aware that the way I respond to other people makes my life pleasant or more difficult.

_____ 7. I am aware that the way I am thinking about a problem can be changed.

_____ 8. I continuously look to learn new things to improve my life.

_____ 9. I am conscious of using positive methods to release stress and let off steam.

_____ 10. I am aware of the connection between my thinking and my body's physical response (blood pressure, sweating, rapid breathing etc.)

_____ TOTAL SCORE

## Partner/ Relationships

_____ 1. I am aware of the model my parents may have shown me for creating a partnership and how that may effect my current relationship.

_____ 2. I know a healthy relationship starts with self-love.

_____ 3. My partner and I have discussed individual goals as well as partnership goals.

_____ 4. My partner is as committed to growing this relationship as I am. I believe this based on his/her actions.

_____ 5. My partner and I can discuss issues of conflict with open hearts that seek to understand each other's view.

_____ 6. When issues of conflict arise, I communicate directly to my partner in a timely manner, instead of discussing it first with others.

_____ 7. I actively work on my relationship to avoid taking the person I love for granted.

_____ 8. I support and encourage my partner to deal with personal growth issues.

_____ 9. I experience love for many people and actively build my friendships.

_____ 10. I do not expect my partner to give up things that are important to him or her to make me and the relationship happy.

_____ TOTAL SCORE

## Parenting/Family

_____ 1. I have taken parenting classes.

_____ 2. I have studied child development before producing a child.

_____ 3. I understand my children are depending on me to teach them how to be healthy, self-confident people.

_____ 4. I am teaching my children to build their own healthy Life Puzzle.

_____ 5. I am actively involved with my children's schooling.

_____ 6. We have a regular discussion time to foster good, open communication with our children.

_____ 7. Everyone in our family shares responsibility for making a healthy family group.

_____ 8. We use exercise as a source for family bonding.

_____ 9. My family and I are working to make our household a pleasurable place for all members to be.

_____ 10. Parenting (or not parenting) a child is a conscious decision I make each day, both for me and the child.

_____ TOTAL SCORE

## Communication

_____ 1. I understand that my body "hears" every word, positive or negative, that I say and it reacts to this self-talk.

_____ 2. My inner self-talk is mainly positive.

_____ 3. In reviewing my communication with others, it is focused first on seeking to understand others.

_____ 4. When becoming defensive in a discussion, I am able to stop myself, re-focus and open myself to healthier communication.

_____ 5. I am aware that my self talk affects the way I see the world.

_____ 6. When negative self-talk occurs, I am able to stop myself, explore what is going on inside and then deal with it so it doesn't cripple my life.

_____ 7. When I make a mistake, I am able to take responsibility for it without resorting to negative self-talk.

_____ 8. I am a good listener.

_____ 9. When a topic is being discussed, I have no problem stating my views, even if they aren't the popular view.

_____ 10. I voice my needs instead of stuffing them inside me.

_____ TOTAL SCORE

## Sexuality

_____ 1. I understand fully my biological sexual self and treat my body with respect.

_____ 2. I understand fully the opposite sex's biological sexual self and treat their body with respect.

_____ 3. I can talk openly about sex with my partner.

_____ 4. I am comfortable masturbating.

_____ 5. I share myself sexually with respect for myself and my partner's needs.

_____ 6. I practice safe, responsible sex.

_____ 7. I am comfortable with my body and treat it with love and gentleness.

_____ 8. I have confronted and explored the mixed sexual messages I learned while growing up.

_____ 9. I feel sex is a natural aspect of my whole Life Puzzle.

_____ 10. In lovemaking, I concentrate on all the sexual areas: physical, emotional and spiritual, and not just the orgasm.

_____ TOTAL SCORE

## Financial responsibility

_____ 1. I take full responsibility for all my personal finances and financial obligations.

_____ 2. I maintain a balanced household budget, keeping debt at a manageable level.

_____ 3. I review my financial status annually.

_____ 4. I am not constantly worried about money because of financial obligations I have made beyond my means.

_____ 5. I continue to learn about financial management for me and my family.

_____ 6. I plan for the future needs of me and my family through sound financial planning.

_____ 7. I have explored my relationship with money: the importance I place on it, the early lessons I learned as a child.

_____ 8. My partner and I openly discuss money. We do not let money issues undermine our relationship.

_____ 9. I have a savings account.

_____ 10. Except in the case of emergencies, I charge credit cards only to the amount that I can pay off fully each month.

_____ TOTAL SCORE

## Spirituality

_____ 1. I am actively involved in my spiritual development.

_____ 2. I live my spirituality each day.

_____ 3. I bring my spiritual principles with me to work and family encounters.

_____ 4. When under pressure to act outside my spiritual beliefs, I am able to stand up for them.

_____ 5. I honor and respect other spiritual doctrines.

_____ 6. My spirituality provides me with a peace to help me through difficult times.

_____ 7. Even when tragedy occurs, I remain peaceful in my spiritual focus.

_____ 8. I have examined traditional religions and their doctrines and have made a conscious choice of what is right for me and my spiritual growth.

_____ 9. I am actively involved with others in my spiritual quests, we are comfortable sharing ideas in this arena.

_____ 10. Daily I try to live love for all.

_____ TOTAL SCORE

## Play

_____ 1. I laugh at myself with joy.

_____ 2. I am open to trying new activities without having to be good at them.

_____ 3. I enjoy music, art, theater, games and dance as a regular part of my life.

_____ 4. As I play with children, I become a child again.

_____ 5. I can goof off and relax in the midst of a very busy schedule.

_____ 6. I don't always have to be doing something constructive to be okay.

_____ 7. I enjoy being with friends who I trust and love.

_____ 8. I maintain some form of playful relaxation in my life as a necessary part of my health.

_____ 9. I enjoy leisure activities without experiencing guilt.

_____ 10. I can sit down and enjoy a magazine or book even when there are other things that need to be done.

_____ TOTAL SCORE

## Special Challenge

_____ 1. I feel my life is in balance.

_____ 2. I do not let any aspect of my physical body (health, body shape, weight etc.) control my belief in having a healthy, well-balanced, pleasurable life.

_____ 3. I like who I am and I am happy to be me, just the way I am.

_____ 4. I feel I am equal to others.

_____ 5. Where I live, the car I drive, the clothes I wear do not make me more or less than other people.

_____ 6. I do not believe that my life is limited because of the family I grew up in.

_____ 7. I do not believe that my current personal circumstances are controlled or limited by life's circumstances such as my family, marriage, job or kids.

_____ 8. I feel capable of achieving any goal I set for myself.

_____ 9. In reviewing a trauma that occurred in my life (death, rape, physical violence, emotional abuse, etc.) I do not feel it defines the future for me.

_____ 10. I see myself as a survivor instead of a victim.

_____ TOTAL SCORE

## Community and Environment

_____ 1. I participate in my community through volunteer work or contributing to charity.

_____ 2. I vote in all elections.

_____ 3. I limit my driving as a method of improving air quality.

_____ 4. I teach children to respect and honor the environment.

_____ 5. I feel businesses should support employees participating in volunteer community projects.

_____ 6. I am actively involved in my community, church, etc.

_____ 7. I try to recycle and conserve energy wherever possible.

_____ 8. I am aware of local, national and world events.

_____ 9. I feel it's important to honor the environment and my daily actions support this belief.

_____ 10. I regularly read the local newspaper to be aware of local issues in which I might involve myself.

_____ TOTAL SCORE

## Finding Meaning

_____ 1. I am conscious of death in my life, especially my own.

_____ 2. I see death as a natural process to be honored instead of feared.

_____ 3. I am conscious of my entire life journey in relation to my impending death.

_____ 4. I see the meaning of my life as an ever-changing process at different stages of my life.

_____ 5. I am open to changing my goals and direction of my life, even if it requires intense effort.

_____ 6. The meaning of my life comes from inner rewards instead of external ones: money, status, material possessions, fame, etc.

_____ 7. I have taken steps to prepare for my death, ( such as writing a will and discussing burial choices with loved ones.)

_____ 8. I see my life as a continuous process of growing up.

_____ 9. I have goals in my life and am working and playing towards them with balance.

_____ 10. I see a purpose and value to my life.

_____ TOTAL SCORE

## ADDING IT ALL UP:

Each section will have its own "Total Score".

(1) Go back through the questionnaire and transfer that number to the appropriate section under "Total score".

|  | TOTAL SCORE |  | ACTUAL SCORE |
|---|---|---|---|
| Self Responsibility | _____ | (2) Divide each of | _____ |
| Nutrition | _____ | these "Total | _____ |
| Exercise | _____ | Scores" by the | _____ |
| Work | _____ | # of questions | _____ |
| Feeling | _____ | that you | _____ |
| Thinking | _____ | answered in | _____ |
| Partner/Relationship | _____ | each section. | _____ |
| Parenting/Family | _____ | *(This accounts for the* | _____ |
| Communication | _____ | *"not-applicable" questions.* | _____ |
| Sexuality | _____ | *Most sections you'll divide* | _____ |
| Financial Responsibility | _____ | *by 10 but some you'll* | _____ |
| Spirituality | _____ | *divide by less since some* | _____ |
| Play | _____ | *questions weren't* | _____ |
| Special Challenge | _____ | *answerable—for example,* | _____ |
| Community/Environment | _____ | *if you have no children* | _____ |
| Finding Meaning | _____ | *you'll answer just a few questions under parenting/family.)* | _____ |

(3) Now, return to the first page of this Life Puzzle assessment and look at your Life Puzzle diagram. You will notice that each section has been divided into ten divisions. For each section above, take your Actual Score and color in the appropriate number, starting at the center of the circle and moving out. When you are finished, you will see a visual picture of your Life Puzzle.

*Look at the completed diagram:*
Which pieces of your Life Puzzle are the most filled in? Which pieces of your Life Puzzle are you not aware of in the daily building of your Life Puzzle? Are you surprised by what you see? Can you see areas that are so out of balance that they may be causing problems for your life?

## Time to work on making your Life Puzzle!

Wish it was all filled in? It can't be! We're so conditioned to taking tests that we want to get all the answers right or filled in. But in building your Life Puzzle, the Puzzle won't be finished until you die. Until then, there's plenty of time to fill in the Life Puzzle pieces by being actively involved in your life.

# Building a Healthy Life Puzzle:

## *Start with the edge first!*

# Good edges make the rest of building your Life Puzzle so much easier.

## How do you make a puzzle?

Give a young child a puzzle and the first thing they'll usually do is lay down the corners. Then they look for the other flat edge pieces to fill out the rest of the outer boundary of the puzzle. Once this is completed they'll fill in the inside pieces. This is a very logical way to build a puzzle and almost every child does it this way. Even young children understand that if you start with the outer edges, it protects the puzzle and makes it easier to add the inner pieces after having this base or foundation to work from. Rarely will you find a child looking for the center pieces and then building outwards. Children quickly realize they will build a puzzle much faster and effectively starting with the edges first.

The same goes with making your Life Puzzle. It makes much more sense to start with your edges, too. This is known as a boundary. Boundaries are your way of saying to the world: This is where I start and end. Without boundaries, others can push you around, moving or changing the pieces of your Life Puzzle to fit their needs. We all need good edges.

If your Life Puzzle is ever going to stand on its own, it is vitally important that you have strong edges. Without them, you will always be at the mercy of the world around you. Other people will be able to invade your Life Puzzle, break it apart, mess it up or…and this is the worst…they will end up building your Life Puzzle to make it work best for them.

There are several different edges that you will need to build. On the following pages these edges are discussed. As you read about these edges, ask yourself: Do you respect your own edges? Do you respect other people's edges too?

## The 5 edges of your Life Puzzle.

The edges of your Life Puzzle allow you to stand as a whole and separate SELF. There are five edges:
- Physical
- Emotional
- Thinking
- Sexual
- Spiritual

You must develop your edges in each of these areas. This occurs from the time you are a baby, when you have none of these edges, through your full adult years when (if all has gone well!) you will have completed a strong edge in each of these areas and stand confident and ready to take full responsibility for running your life.

You start with your physical edge, gaining the knowledge that your body belongs to you and no one has the right to physically hurt it, attack or abuse it. This would seem so obvious that of course you have a physical edge, and of course no one should invade your body. But look at the large number of child abuse cases—these children do not understand they can say no to an adult that is abusing them. They endure years of this physical invasion only to arrive at adulthood completely unaware that others do not have the right to hurt them. Add to this domestic abuse, where women stay in marriages for years, receiving black eyes and broken arms but totally unable to walk away without feeling guilty that they "made him do it".

If your physical edge is incomplete, it is next to impossible to have a strong edge in any of the other areas. If you can't stop someone from hitting you, how are you going to stand up for your creative ideas or your feelings?

We build our edges while growing up. If our parents were knowledgeable, they would work towards helping us in this process. But when you consider how few people study child development or take parenting classes before they bring a child into this world, is it any wonder parents rarely know to help their children build strong edges?

This is beginning to change, but for now you are going to have to go back and look at your own life to determine if the edges of your Life Puzzle are in place and strong. Strong edges will give you the foundation for your Life Puzzle.

## Do you have strong edges?

Do you trust yourself? Do you like yourself just as you are today? These are signs of someone with a healthy edge. Do others and their opinions control you? Do you spend a lot of your life trying to please others with the underlying feeling that once everyone else is happy (spouse, children, parents, grandparents, co-workers), then you'll feel happy? These are signs of incomplete edges.

Don't misunderstand, people with strong edges do work to please others and are aware of other people's opinions, but not to such a degree that their lives and their happiness depend on it. They can accept that others may not like them and still feel quite content inside. That's because they run their lives from a strong foundation of their physical, emotional, thinking, sexual and spiritual self.

## Are your edges strong? A simple test.

Stop for a moment and ask yourself this question:
1. What is the focus of your relation-ship with other people? Do you:
A. Put yourself first and others second?
B. Put others first and yourself second?

If you picked B...then you are operating from weak edges. You may find yourself running your life ragged pleasing others and are often a victim to others and their cruelty. You'll find yourself constantly resentful and angry that others aren't appreciating all you've done for them. It is a vicious cycle and if you are going to build a healthy Life Puzzle you will need to break away from it.

> *Edges seem kind of obvious, don't they just show up at birth? NO, and that's the big problem because we're born without any edges. We develop our edges during the different stages of our childhood.*

• • • • • • • • • • • • • • • • • • • • • • • • • • • • • • • • • • • • • • • • • • • •

## DEVELOPING EDGES IN STAGES

| Baby | Toddler | Child | Early Adolescent | Teenager | Adult |
|------|---------|-------|------------------|----------|-------|
| No edges | | Testing edges, often runs back to adult for security | | Beginning to have own identity, separate from others | Full edges |
| TOTALLY DEPENDENT | | INTERDEPENDENT WITH OTHERS | | | INTRADEPENDENT |

• • • • • • • • • • • • • • • • • • • • • • • • • • • • • • • • • • • • • • • • • • • •

**Baby:** Totally dependent on others for all needs. Babies don't see themselves as separate from the adults in their lives because they can't. A baby has no separate identity from the adult it needs for total survival.

**Toddlers & Children:** Between the ages of 2 to 11 a child is constantly attempting to take on some level of self-definition and begins breaking away from needing others all the time. During this time children have to trust that as they separate themselves from the adult, the adult will still be there if necessary. When a child's attempts to establish a separate SELF results in rejection, punishment or abandonment from parents or other loved ones, problems in edge development arise. The child will stop these early separa-tion attempts if it feels that abandon-ment, punishment or rejection will result.

**Early adolescent/teenager.** Begin-ning to push away from parents' edges to establish SELF. This is a very crucial stage of edge development and many pitfalls can occur in our society. Teenag-ers are establishing many competing parts of the self during this time. Not only are their bodies raging with hor-mones that affect them mentally and physically, but they are trying to make sense of the schoolbook information that they've learned over the last 14 years. They're asked to make decisions in the sexual arena, they are dealing with a world gone crazy, and some parents mistakenly give them more credit or freedom than they actually know how to manage. At the same time that they desperately want their parents to help them with all the confusing issues going on in their life, they also feel like they can't have their parents' help; otherwise, how will they be making their own decisions? Quite a Catch-22! So, if they can't use their parents for help, who is there for them? Peers? Well, that's what they'll use, but frankly....talk about the blind leading the blind! Why would you use as a role model someone who is just as confused? Don't know why, but we all did it!

The competing and conflicting messages that teenagers receive make it very overwhelming. If there is not an adult available (not necessarily a parent) to whom this teenager can go for guidance and balance, the teenager is at high risk of arriving into adulthood with many pieces missing in the edge of their Life Puzzle.

---

There are so many issues that threaten a teenager's development that getting through them with even moderately strong edges is quite amazing.

---

**Family Breakdown:** Divorce, single parent families, abusive families...all of these impact a child's ability to build strong edges.

**Television:** Think of the role models available for teenagers that come from television: Soap operas, Roseanne, Beverly Hills 90210, etc. Very few shows provide healthy, strong-boundaried teenagers as a role model. Perhaps the writers and producers can say that they did not create these shows for those reasons, but nonetheless, teenagers (all children actually) use characters on TV as role models, whether they are aware of it or not. Face it, the days of Leave it to Beaver and the Brady Bunch are over!

**Street Violence:** It's a scary world out there.

**Teenage pregnancy:** Everyone loses when a teenager becomes pregnant. The girl's edge-building time is interrupted by the birth of a child who demands constant attention. For many girls, their personal development is stopped at this level and they arrive at adulthood without strong edges. At 25, 35, 45...they do not have a full definition of themselves. The baby also loses because a teenage mom and dad can not provide the necessary emotional and intellectual strength to help children develop their own edges. You can't teach your child to be whole if you aren't!

**Peers:** We usually attract friends and people who are like us. Thus, if you have a poor definition of self, you'll usually find as friends people who also have a poor definition of self.

**Schools:** Overcrowding, poor programs, violence, lack of funds, etc. are commonplace. Whereas schools were once a haven for teenagers, for many school is nothing more than a waste of time. Some schools are great, but too many are spending more time trying to discipline unboundaried children than acting as learning centers.

**Churches:** Reports of priest abuse, the Jimmy Swaggert/PTL scandals, cults, rich money making schemes...church and religion have become so separated from the spiritual message that teenagers no longer find solace or direction from them.

---

Time marches on...whether or not a teenager develops strong boundaries, adulthood is going to show up.

---

**Adult:** If all has gone well, an adult has arrived with a strong definition of self— all 5 edges complete, SELF in charge. Attention everyone: this doesn't happen very often! Many adults show up physically in a big body but still feeling unsure of who they are and where they fit into the world. They don't feel confident to accept full responsibility for designing and creating their own lives. They are still dependent on others for approval, they have little confidence and satisfaction (self-esteem).

If you are reading this and feel that you have arrived in adulthood and your edges are not well formed, don't panic. You can still build them. Let's get going.

## Weak Edges:

- Giving your life away.
- Self- esteem is fragile.
- Others and their needs determine your day.

When your edges are weak, it becomes very easy for other people to overpower your life. You let them in! This results in your Life Puzzle becoming constantly tangled up in their lives instead of focusing on making choices that are right for you.

Weak edges are a two-edged sword. Some people with weak edges are pushed around and life becomes a process of serving others. The second type of person with a weak edge is the one who abuses others with fists or their vile, mean words. Both of these people are not focused on making healthy life choices while they are acting this way.

Nobody wins when your edges are weak. Your life becomes either a jumbled mess of trying to please others or one of manipulating others so you can get through your life. It is a life filled with anxiety and stress. The next crisis is just around the corner waiting to get you.

## Strong Edges:

- Taking responsibility for your whole Life Puzzle.
- Self-esteem grows.

People with strong edges are not hardened people who don't let anyone get near them! On the contrary, people with strong edges are quite involved with others but out of a genuine desire to be with the people in their life, not out of fear of abandonment or guilt.

When you have strong edges you operate from a point of self-love, self-trust and self-respect. From this vantage point, your relationship to other people is one of respect and honor instead of manipulation and control. It is a healthy vibrant way to live your life.

When your physical edge is strong, you respect, honor and care for the body you live in. You wouldn't agree to letting someone else hurt it without standing up for yourself. When your emotional edge is strong you're in touch with your feelings and manage them appropriately. And as all your edges become stronger, you trust that you are the best person to run your own life; not your mother, father, spouse or best friend. It takes daily courage to remind yourself of this and consistently practice living this strong self.

## Building the edges, creating the SELF

At birth, we have no SELF! We have a potential for SELF. But if we were born and then stuck in a corner for 25 years, we're not likely to realize much of that potential. It's much like a regular puzzle—when you open the box, there's the potential for a great puzzle to be completed. But if you never take out the pieces and put them together what do you have? A puzzle? No, you have the potential for a puzzle.

If you think about it, the first thing we do after pouring all the pieces out of the box is to begin working on the edges. Once we get the last piece of the edges together, we know we're serious about making this unique puzzle! It's potential is beginning to take shape.

This is true in Life Puzzles too. You have to put down the edges in order to

establish a separate SELF that is all your own and in this way the potential of your SELF begins to be realized. Unfortunately there are millions of adults walking around who really aren't much more than all those scrambled pieces still sitting in the box! Their edges were poorly formed throughout their childhoods and they launch into their adulthood still unsure of what or who they are.

Here's the good news—you may discover that one or more of your edges is still missing pieces, but it's never too late to get started on making your edges! Next we'll explore the 5 primary edges that must come together in order to allow your SELF to become whole and stand on its own for your unique life journey.

# PHYSICAL EDGE

This edge is complete when you have full respect for your body and its care and total respect for other's bodies.

The first edge we begin building is the physical edge. We start this around age 2 and if all goes well, complete it sometime around age 15. When this edge is complete, we know that our body is our body and that no one has the right to touch our body unless we give permission AND, we do not have the right to touch someone else's body unless they give us permission. When these two conditions are in place: awareness of our own, and respect for others, we live with honor and love for our own bodies and care and concern for others.

Before the age of two, a baby doesn't see itself as a separate SELF. It can't! It's 100% dependent on everyone else. But around age two, the baby can now walk, talk and one of its most favorite words is NO! The baby is beginning to establish that their SELF is now in charge and they're going to do it their way. Of course, at age 2, they're not really in charge—it's a testing time, but over the next 15 years, more and more this child will know that their SELF has to make choices over where their body will go, what it will do, and how it will be respected both personally and by others.

By the time a child is 15 or so, appreciation of one's physical body—its height, weight, shape, ability to get you around in life and understanding that its something you have to take care of for a lifetime should be a part of one's consciousness. Unfortunately, it isn't for lots and lots of folks. General awareness of our bodies seems to get lost in the process of growing up. Most of us take our bodies for granted, figuring they'll do what they're going to do no matter what we do.

This lack of awareness translates finally into a lack of responsibility for taking care of our body's health throughout our lifetime. The physical edge is incomplete when we ignore our bodies, its health and care. Clearly, our SELF is not in charge if we're unaware of our bodies!

Another 'invader' that disrupts building the physical edge of our Life Puzzle is the media. As young children, we are presented with a very warped view of what physical beauty is. Through magazines, television, and even billboards, we are constantly bombarded with the 'look'. It is defined as ultra thin, tall and well-shaped for girls and muscled, tall and firm for boys. To live up to this definition, only about 1% of the population even has a shot at it! But children don't know this, so they try desperately to achieve it. Thus, they become obsessed with achieving a "look".

We see girls as young as 9 starting to diet to achieve it, and then little by little coming to hate their bodies. The media is coming through their physical edge and shaping the SELF. Thus, the edge does not complete, the SELF does not fully form and this child will walk into adulthood wondering who she is, believing she's not good enough, has an ugly body etc. Boys are less likely to go to this extreme though this is beginning to change as the media has recently begun targeting this population too.

Many adults spend a lifetime running after this image, never realizing that all these outside influences are controlling their SELF. Of course, that's because at such a young, developmental age, their Life Puzzle was invaded by this media picture and they weren't yet mature enough (developed enough SELF) to reject this invading image. But you can also see how this can have lifelong consequences.

So ask your SELF: are you in love with your body? Do you respect it, care for it and honor it through healthy eating, exercise etc. Do you allow others to hit you, or do you hit others? Are you constantly trying to live up to a media image of your body and when unable to look like the (airbrushed) models in the latest magazine, find your SELF depressed? Do you respect other people's edges as well? It is an important insight into your own edge whether or not you respect other people's edge too.

Remember: the physical edge is complete when we know that no one has the right to touch our body unless we give permission and we do not have the right to touch someone else, unless they give permission. And we know to love, honor, nurture and care for our bodies for a lifetime.

---

Physical abuse is rampant in this country. Many children are raised in physically violent homes where they or their mother/father are constantly being hit. Children raised in this situation do not learn even the most basic edge: respect for one's body. They do not know that their body is their body and no one has the right to touch them without their permission. Thus, they grow up to become involved in relationships that repeat the pattern they saw as a child. Typically, women become abused, men become the batterers but actually both are involved in the same thing: lack of physical edge and little or no development of a true SELF. When this edge is missing, the SELF doesn't form completely and thus, these adults make choices that are not healthy, proactive Life Puzzle-making, but instead, Life Puzzle-jamming.

It's easy to see when a woman is being beaten up that her physical edge is missing and her SELF is being 'shaped' by her partner. But what about him? Does he have a completed physical edge and strong SELF. NO! The batterer is missing his physical edge too.

Domestic violence doesn't work for either partner, yet right now, we typically approach only the victim/survivor to intervene. We will take her out of the home, protect her and then work on building her SELF-esteem, building the edge. What do we do for him? Almost nothing—we approach him as a criminal. Now don't get me wrong, we do need to hold him accountable. But behind that we have to realize that the batterer is missing his physical edge, has a poorly formed SELF and is acting out his confusion in a Life Puzzle-jamming fashion. If we are going to finally break the cycle of domestic violence, we need to help both partners build their physical edge and develop a strong SELF. Otherwise, he will just find another victim and continue to perpetuate his own confusion.

# FEELING/EMOTIONAL EDGE

The emotional edge is complete when we are fully aware of what we are feeling and our SELF is managing the feeling instead of the feeling managing our SELF.

We begin building the emotional edge around age 7. Oh yes, we're emotional long before age 7—heck we're emotional from the moment we get here. But up until around age 7, we're not very good at managing our emotions. From birth to about age 7, we can be mad one moment, sad the next, glad the next or afraid two seconds later. Emotions come and go on a whim. During this time, we're beginning to learn what things are scary, what things make us happy or sad etc. It's a very big exploring time. Many times a child really doesn't know which emotion to pick, so it's a testing time—sometimes we get it right, sometimes we don't!

In an ideal world, we would complete this edge around age 21, but in truth, this is the hardest edge of all to complete and very few of us accomplish this by age 21! But if we did complete it by then, we would consciously know what we're feeling at all times—mad, sad, glad or fear—and then have the ability to act appropriately on those feelings. Unfortunately, the journey of our childhood often results in our learning to block our awareness of feelings—sometimes because the pain or fear is too much for us to deal with or in other cases, we just completely confuse ourselves and then lock on to feelings that are misapplied to the situation.

For example, recall the first time you saw a jack-in-the-box. For a 2 or 3-year old child, the first time they have this experience, their normal reaction is to CRY! Why? Because they have no idea whether or not that stupid clown is going to hurt them! Now all the adults watching this are so surprised that the 2-year old doesn't get it, but hey, how would a 2-year old know? What experience do they have of clowns popping out of seemingly docile boxes that make pretty music? (I always wonder how many children have a fear of clowns because of this experience!!!) And so it goes.

Every day as children we are exposed to new experiences, all requiring us to respond out of either joy or fear and it gets quite confusing. We can misjudge things, develop fears out of nowhere. These fears can still be overwhelming us when we're adults. For example, a client shared that when she was 7 years old, she suddenly started having nightmares in bed. Scared the dickens out of her and she'd cry and scream until her parents came and got her. Eventually, they let her sleep in their room and she stayed there until age 13. Then they moved and she got a separate room in the new house. But this 'fear of being alone at night' translated into a lifelong fear of being alone. She married right out of her parent's home and her husband and she were inseparable. But comes a time when her always-present husband suddenly had to be out of the house more and more. She suddenly found herself an emotional wreck and couldn't figure out why. We finally traced it back to her childhood fear, worked to clear out the old misperception of 'fear of being alone in the dark' before her SELF could get back on track with her Life Puzzle-making. Initially, fear was managing her SELF, now her SELF knows how to manage the fear.

The tricky thing about the emotional edge is that we're building it in the midst of discovering our emotions. That's sort of like trying to put together the puzzle at the same moment you're pulling the pieces out of the box! Is it any wonder so many of us don't complete this edge! Add to this growing up in abusive environments, schools that are often not supportive environments, a society that has little time to trouble itself to care for children's emotional needs and its not unsurprising at all.

Let me give you an example. I had a client who came to me at age 32. Though successful in the corporate world, her personal life was extremely fragile. As a child, she had been emotionally abused by her mother and father. They ruled her world and she was desperately afraid of them. She could not stand up to either of them, and any encounter with them sent her into a tailspin of depression and high anxiety.

As we talked and discussed edges it was very apparent to her that they were violating her emotional and thinking edges. Though she was better educated and more successful than either of her parents, they had convinced her that they were superior to her. We worked on her edges and over time she was able to assert her edges with almost everyone…but her father pushed a button that wiped out the boundary growth, time and again.

About two years later, when our therapy sessions had become very intermittent, I received a call from her. She was elated! She had finally confronted her father and stood up to him. This had taken great courage on her part and she had fretted over it for weeks before the event. Because she was so sure he would verbally attack her, she arranged to meet him in a very public place in the hope that it would prevent him from becoming out of control. At an amusement park, she sat him down and started to talk. She told him of all the pain his behavior had given her; all the years of screaming, yelling and put downs. She was there to tell him that she no longer would allow him to do this to her. From this day forward, he was not welcome in her home unless she invited him first (he regularly let himself into her home at his discretion and then he'd call her and yell at her if her house wasn't spotlessly cleaned). He also was not allowed to yell, scream or put her down. If he didn't like the way she was doing something he was not free to tell her. This was her life and she felt quite capable of running it without his constant attack.

My client was shaking through this entire encounter. She was waiting for him to explode and attack her—verbally and physically. But you know what happened instead? Whether it was the total shock of her standing up for herself, or he was just too exhausted to continue this abusive relationship, he broke. And there in the middle of the amusement park, he sat and cried. And to my client's greater shock, he apologized and asked to be forgiven. He said he never realized that she remembered all of the chaos of her childhood years and the violent divorce with her mother. Then he talked about his own childhood and the pain and incredible abuse he had survived at the hand of his mother (who was still alive and to whom he had never stood up and told her to stop violating his edges!).

For my client, her life changed dramatically when she stopped allowing others to violate her edge. It taught her self-respect and helped her relate much better to her parents. Life isn't picture perfect and yes, her parents still slip back into their old patterns. But now she either tells them to stop, leave her home or not to call her until they treat her with respect.

Another 'invader' to your feeling edge, just as in the physical edge is the Media and it's power to manipulate your SELF through your emotions. The advertising industry specifically targets coming through your emotional edge to shape your SELF so you will buy their products. They especially hit your fears and inadequacies—showing you that by buying their product you can remove these fears or inadequacies. Feeling a little powerless—buy a fancy sports car—that's a sign of power! Of course, it doesn't really make your SELF powerful, what it does is help you mask the fear of powerlessness by diverting attention away from you and onto the car. And it works, people buy stuff every day that they neither need or want, but which they hope will make their SELF feel whole. But after the fancy car doesn't work, then what next? Complete the edge and form a true SELF!

*To complete this edge ask your SELF:*

Are you consciously aware of what you are feeling (mad, sad, glad, fear)? Are you able to choose how to respond to a situation so that SELF is in charge of the feelings instead of the feelings being in charge of the SELF? (Ex. Someone says, "Looks like you're having a bad hair day", and you feel 'hurt'. Now, do you acknowledge the hurt and then let it go, knowing a bad hair day isn't that big a deal. Or do you feel the hurt and then let this feeling have you running to the bathroom to check the mirror all day? SELF managing feeling or feeling managing SELF?) Do you know that no one has the right to tell you how to feel or to manipulate your feelings so you will do what they want. And you do not have the right to tell others how to feel or manipulate their feelings so they do what you want.

If you're thinking that this edge needs work, don't be surprised or disappointed with your SELF. Most of us do! There are exercises in this book that can help with this, and you might also consider counseling too. Often times, missing or jammed pieces in our feeling edge are hard to find on our own. A few sessions with a good counselor (try to find someone who comes from a holistic perspective) can speed up the ability and effectiveness of building this edge.

To recoup: The feeling edge is complete when you are fully aware of what you are feeling (mad, sad, glad, fear) and the SELF is managing that feeling instead of the feeling managing the SELF.

# THINKING EDGE

The Thinking edge is complete when:

1. We know that we are responsible for all our choices and their consequences; we are able to stand up for our choices without being influenced or controlled by others to do as they wish but against our choices.

2. We respect that others have the right to make choices that are right for them, even if they wouldn't work for us. And they too must be responsible for the consequences of their choices.

We begin the thinking edge around age 9 and hopefully complete around age 21. Now, of course, we clearly think before age 9, but up until about this age, the 'logic' center of our brain is still in formation. Logic requires facts/data. How much data does a 2 year-old have? Not much, thus, we can't hold them responsible for many of their choices. But starting around age 9 and on, we're collecting tons and tons of facts/data and we can use this to help us make conscious choices. Are we very good at it at age 9? No, but hopefully, as we keep adding more facts/data, we get better and better at it. So, by the time we're in our late teens, early 20's, we are taking responsibility to make the choices we need to build our unique Life Puzzle and fully accept the consequences of those choices.

Most of us have our thinking edges invaded and smashed when we are quite young. That's why, as adults, we proceed to do the same thing to many others that we encounter. It seems normal because everyone is doing it all the time.

In our first five years of life most of us can manage to deal with others telling us that we aren't "thinking right" because everything we're doing is brand new. Most parents are tolerant of the mistakes. But by the time we get to school, watch out, thinking edges are about to come under siege! Children are very vulnerable during their early school years; this is when their thinking skills are being developed. As you'll see in Chapter 6, thinking doesn't just happen, it must be developed through a series of processes that takes us to our highest thinking skill level. In theory, schools should be an open environment for experimenting and learning to think well, but the reality is that it doesn't take a child very long before he realizes that his way of thinking is not as good as the other children. Thinking edge development gets lost here. Because the child perceives that some think better than him and others don't, he quickly places himself in an artificial hierarchy. This early perception locks our minds into a *misinterpretation about our thinking selves.* With this misinterpretation firmly in place, children create lives that live up to it!

The system focuses on what you got wrong, not what you got right. The natural curiosity that you had as a child is obliterated by the time you get to third grade! Those who excel in school continue to work on their thinking edge, growing in their strength and trust of their thinking self. But for far too many others the school experience convinces them that they aren't as capable as the next guy and they begin developing a self-attitude that allows everyone to cross their thinking edge. This is the great portion of children, those who just "get through" school and can't wait to get out and away from the abusive condition that leaves them viewing themselves as inferior to others.

Certainly this thinking edge violation doesn't happen in a vacuum at school. At home, if you're told you're stupid, if you're told to be "more like your smart brother", or you have a parent who has low self-esteem and is jealous that you might be smarter or more capable, you'll often find they'll undermine your own thinking edges in very subtle ways in order to control you. In addition, if other edges such as your feeling edge are also being attacked, it only increases the destruction of self-esteem.

You can begin to see how these different edge violations add up and determine whether or not you enter into your adulthood with strong edges. These weak edges affect the confidence and satisfaction you have in yourself: self-love and self-esteem. And this of course, affects the quality of your Life Puzzle overall.

Stop a moment and think; do you have strong thinking edges? Do you take responsibility for your life by making choices to build your Life Puzzle? Do you stand up for those choices even though others may challenge you to change your mind? Do you respect others and their choices and don't try to change their choices to fit your needs?

When you have strong thinking edges you'll discover that you approach people much more openly. You spend less time in judgement and more time in trying to understand their point of view, how they might have come to it, etc. It opens communication channels, allowing more depth as you come to appreciate the wide variety of thinking skills that one problem can have applied to it.

Remember, the Thinking edge is complete when:

1. We know that we are responsible for all our choices and their consequences; we are able to stand up for our choices without being influenced or controlled by others to do as they wish but against our choices.

2. We respect that others have the right to make choices that are right for them, even if they wouldn't work for us. And they too must be responsible for the consequences of their choices.

# SEXUAL EDGE

The Sexual edge is complete when:

1. Our other edges: physical, emotional and thinking edges arc firmly in place.
2. We are consciously aware of our body, feelings and thinking choices before we engage in any sexual activity. We respect our partners' body, feelings and thinking choices before we engage in sexual activity.

We begin building our sexual edge around puberty and hopefully complete it by our early 20's. The sexual edge is not about whether or not you're a good lover! It is about the SELF being in full charge of creating a healthy, sexual identity. It is dependent on the first three edges—we must first know, love and respect our bodies and our partner's body, be fully aware of our feelings and conscious of our choice to become sexually active with SELF (masturbation) or others (intercourse).

You can see it becomes imperative to build strong physical, emotional and thinking edges in order to become a sexual being that is in charge of blossoming a true Sexual SELF. Think about it: if your physical edge is incomplete and your partner uses your body in ways that make you uncomfortable but you can't seem to say no, then your sexual edge isn't going to be complete. Or if your partner manipulates your emotions, 'tricking' you into saying yes, even though you want to say no, again the SELF is not in charge of your sexuality; your partner is invading your edges and using your SELF for his/her gratification.

The adults of this world have a major conflict in the development of sexual edges for our children (and since all of us adults were once children, we need to acknowledge that we were products of this societal conflict too!). We talk abstinence at one level, while letting our 12 year-old girls wear skin-tight outfits that have sex written all over them. We talk responsible sex, but to this day, despite the sexual revolution, the majority of parents cannot and do not discuss sex and sexuality with their teenage children. How can we help our children develop healthy, well-balanced responsible sexual edges—physical, emotional and thinking—if we send them a message of discomfort, unease and secrecy about this topic? This adult confusion results in risking our children's lives because without helping them to form healthy edges, we open them up to a world of AIDS and STD's (sexually transmitted diseases—including herpes, chlamydia, gonorrhea, syphilis and a host of others), without the knowledge and respect they need for their sexual edge.

Start by asking yourself: Do I have a healthy sexual edge? Am I comfortable with my physical sexual self? If not, why not? What messages have I absorbed that leave me uncomfortable with my physical sexual self? Next, am I comfortable with my emotional and thinking sexual self? Do I know what I like? Do I accept it or do I attack myself with guilt and shame over these sexual feelings like, "nice girls shouldn't feel this", or "a man shouldn't have these types of desires for his wife—get them out of your head?"

Very few of us have healthy sexual edges. Our society sends such mixed messages that, in total bewilderment, most of us stick our head in the sand on the entire issue. This results in poor sexual relationships with others because we don't make the effort to know ourselves. This makes it impossible to share our best sexual self with a partner—and vice versa. This definitely affects your total Life Puzzle.

The other problem with poor sexual edge development is sexual abuse. When we don't have a clear respect for our sexual SELF, we can sexually violate or be violated sexually by others. Usually this goes hand in hand with other parts of our edge being fragile. For example, someone whose emotional edge is weak is very easy to manipulate. Mix this in with sex and the person may find himself or herself using sex to feel better. Thus young girls, hoping to feel more confident and loved, give sex to boys with the hope that this will make them feel better about themselves emotionally. Unfortunately, this usually results in the girl being tossed aside as the boy casually uses her and then moves on. The end result: she feels worse about herself, not better. But typically she'll do it all over again with another boy, hoping this one will be the one that makes her feel good about herself.

Boys also misuse sex as a way to build up a fragile self-esteem and self-love. Unsure of who they are, sex becomes a way to give them an illusion of power and strength. Thus, a boy whose thinking edge is weak can mistakenly convince himself that he's pretty tough stuff when scoring through sex. But it usually leaves the boy feeling rather empty when the sex act is over.

It is easy to violate another's sexual edge when your own edges are not secure. Unfortunately for boys, this illusion of power and sex becomes fused, and sex becomes a false sense of security for thinking, feeling or spiritual edges that are weak. Everyone loses when this happens. This boy will go through life with a warped sexual edge, it will affect his relationships and it will affect his other edge development.

Most of us need to look at this aspect of ourselves and question how it is affecting us as a result of our childhood development. These are not easy questions to ask ourselves (and most of us remain too afraid to bring it up in polite conversation!). However there are lots of books and videos to help you confront this issue. It is worth exploring— for you, your partner and your children.

It is vital that you explore this aspect of your edge development. Chapter 13 goes into it a little bit more.

Another key issue that needs to be addressed is homosexuality. This book is written from the premise that homosexuality is a normal development in about 10% of the population. It is within one's genetic make-up and one's desires that being gay or lesbian emerges.

Unfortunately, in our society, there is still a great deal of conflict on this issue, but from a Life Puzzle-making perspective, homosexuality is understood as a personal choice. Here's what must be acknowledged; if you are a Life Puzzle maker, then you must honor and respect that others can make choices in their Life Puzzle that you do not agree with. As we've said throughout, every human has the same 16 core areas, 5 edges to create the SELF, yet no two of us will put them together in exactly the same way. Thus, for some, homosexuality is the piece they're putting into their Life Puzzle and it is the right piece for them, even if you don't agree with it

For a homosexually oriented individual, your physical and emotional sexual edge is the same as a heterosexual one; no one has the right to cross your sexual edge unless you give them permission and vice versa. Your physical and emotional sexual desires are right for you and no one has the right to tell you they aren't.

You too will need to do the personal work to strengthen your sexual edges. This is tough work but worth it. It is one thing to accept that you are homosexual, but you must ask what are the messages from your childhood that are affecting your total sexual self-development. If you are at peace within your sexual self-definition... terrific! If you are not, your edges need strengthening. Almost all of us in this country have work to do in this area of our Life Puzzle development.

Remember, the Sexual edge is complete when:
1. Our other edges: physical, emotional and thinking edges are firmly in place.
2. We are consciously aware of our body, feelings and thinking choices before we engage in any sexual activity. We respect our partners' body, feelings and thinking choices before we engage in sexual activity.

## SPIRITUAL EDGE

The Spiritual edge is complete when you can operate your daily life from this perspective:

I am greater than no one; no one is greater than me. In everyone shines love or light (or God's love or light), and as I can see it in me, I can see it in thee (and when I can't see it in thee, its probably because I can't see it in me).

The Spiritual edge is not about how you practice a religion. The spiritual edge is the last piece in the formation in a truly loving SELF. You accept your body, your emotions, your choice-making, your sexuality and finally come to peace with your SELF. At this point, you accept your SELF, all the good and the not so good, as you take full responsibility for creating your Life Puzzle.

If you look at the above statement: I am greater than no one, no one is greater than me—stop and ask your SELF, do you operate your life from this angle, or is it more "I am better than some, some are better than me?". Most of us are so caught up in comparing our SELF to others, that our spiritual edge never quite forms. But with a completed spiritual edge, you come to realize that everyone you meet is a Life Puzzle under construction—with the same 16 core areas, 5 edges that create the SELF. Thus, everyone you meet is just like you—not better, not worse—but trying to put their pieces together!!!!

Yes, you may have more pieces in some areas than they do, or they have more in another area than you—but it's not a better than or less than—it's a realization that we're all in this together. Thus, you can look at a homeless wino on the street and realize that he too is a Life Puzzle under construction and while he's clearly missing many pieces, ultimately he's just like you. Now look… can you see the love or light inside? He might not be able to right now, but if your edges are complete and your SELF is in the process of 'practicing only love', then you can see that it is potentially in this person too. This allows you to approach him from understanding and love instead of confusion, judgment and fear.

A strong spiritual edge is essential for a healthy, well-balanced Life Puzzle. For most of us, it will require us to do some very hard work. First we ensure that our other edges are intact, then we must examine the current state of our spiritual edge and decide what is necessary to rebuild it pro-actively as a part of our Life Puzzle.

As I was writing this book, I had discussions with numerous people. One of these discussions centered around the importance of spirituality and God to one's Life Puzzle. My friend was urging me to focus more on this area as she felt that it is with strong spiritual development that one should start Life Puzzle building.

I do agree that when one has achieved a strong spiritual edge—where each day you walk and live your spirituality and you see it in all that you meet— your Life Puzzle building will become much easier in all the other areas. However, I don't believe you can start here. As I said to my friend, "You are excited about your spirituality and what it does for your life, your relationship and your family, but that's because you have already done the intensive, life-long work to bring you to this process. You're in your late 30's and feel this. Would you have been able to bring this enthusiasm towards spirituality when you were 16?"

Her reply was, "Well no, but I wished I had, it would have been much easier for me to deal with all the other issues that I had to deal with at that time."

And my response to her was, "Yes, I agree it would have been easier to have answered all those questions we have at 16 if you'd had the spiritual edge you now have (as in: hindsight is 20/20!) but wasn't it in the process of learning to know your own feelings, learning to assert yourself and your way of thinking, learning to get in touch with your sexual self, that you were also able to explore your spiritual issues? You had to have a strong physical, feeling, thinking and sexual edge well underway before you could reach out and strengthen your spiritual."

It has been my experience that when we try to convince ourselves that we've determined our spiritual selves in our early 20's while still very insecure about our feelings, our thinking and are conflicted about our sexual self and unaware of our physical bodies, what we actually do is confuse our spiritual edge within the mask of religious rigidity. At this age, we will lock onto a particular religious dogma that fills in all our answers of right and wrong on the spiritual questions. It can be fundamentalism, born-again Christian, mystical Eastern, Judaism or some New Age hodgepodge of all of the above. But when we connect to this in our very early years, it is so easy for us to have all our other edges overwhelmed by the religious rules and regulations. We lose ourselves to this religious devotion and making our Life Puzzle takes a back seat. We mistakenly believe that religious doctrine is the same as one's spirituality and lose our true selves in the process.

Your spiritual edge will be vitally important to your Life Puzzle but it can't be rushed. If you are in your teens reading this book, this is a wonderful time for exploring and learning about the great religions while you are getting in touch with your thinking and feelings and starting to understand your body. If you are in your 20's and 30's, hopefully you are finding that your feeling, thinking, physical and sexual edges are firming up and strengthening towards a balance so that your spiritual self can now be more fully explored from a point of self-love. And I think it is probably not until you are in your 40's that your spiritual edges are fully formed. At this point you move from "practicing a religion" to living your spirituality every day as part of your Life Puzzle.

Again, your spiritual edge is complete when you can operate your life from this belief: "I am greater than no one; no one is greater than me. In everyone shines love and as I can see it in me, I can see it in thee."

# What stage of edge development are you in?

**A**s noted before, edge development is an on-going process from childhood throughout adulthood. As you can see, each edge builds on the other as you grow. If your physical edge is still fragile—that others invade you by physically attacking you—then your feeling, thinking, sexual and spiritual edges are affected too.

Remember: all edges are a two way street. If you want others to respect your edges you must also respect theirs. If you believe you have strong edges but find yourself invading others—through physically hurting others, emotionally hurting others by laughing, mocking, gossiping, being sexually distant from your partner and not respecting his or her needs—it is a sign that your own edges are still weak.

## What happens when we don't have respect for each other's edges?

When we don't operate our lives from the understanding that *every human being is a unique and separate self with the right to walk this earth,* we end up creating a lot of different problems:

**Abuse:** Physical, sexual and emotional abuse are a result of both parties not understanding about edges. For those being abused, their edge is being violated by a person who is not respecting their separateness. Often this happens because the person being violated does not know he or she can say, "No, don't do that," as in the case of a child being physically or sexually abused. Abusers are without edges, too. Think about it: How could anyone physically, sexually or emotionally hurt another person if he had a good, strong edge or definition of self? Because once you have developed a good edge of self it naturally comes with the *understanding and respect that others have edges too.*

**Self-Abuse:** If you are unaware of your own edge it is possible for you to become self-abusive—physically and mentally abusing yourself in response to a feeling that you aren't good enough, you don't fit in the world, that you're hopeless, etc. This self-abuse is a misinterpretation of your right to make mistakes, i.e., be human.

**Racism:** If you don't respect each human being as having a separate and equal right to be on this planet it is very easy to look at a particular group of people and say....they're no good. This is an institutionalized form of abuse.

**Violence:** Physically violent people, whether they use their fists or guns, operate from a lack of knowledge about edges. They do not respect their own edges and they do not respect the lives of others. Physically hurting another person has no meaning to them because they have no feeling for themselves or others. (I'm not talking about self defense.)

**Drug and Alcohol abuse:** Ask most drug or alcohol abusers and at the heart of the abuse is a lack of self-definition....they have no knowledge or understanding of their unique, separate self. The seed of drug and alcohol problems usually start young, when our edge development is in a very fragile stage. Feeling unsure of our unique self, we suddenly discover that while high we feel more "solid" than we do when we're not high. This is a false sense of edge that feels very real to someone who is unaware of better methods for building his own true edges. The need for this feeling becomes all-consuming. As a result, we mess up the edge-building stage during these years. Until we stop the alcohol or drug abuse, then go back and do the personal edge work necessary to get knowledge of our separate, unique self, we will find ourselves repeatedly battling with the bottle or the drug. Drugs and alcohol are not the problem...it is definition of one's self edges.

**All addictions:** Food, gambling...anything we do compulsively, even when we know it is not good for us, is rooted in poor edge development.

• • • • • • • • • • • • • • • • • • • • • • • •

**Strong Edges = High Self Esteem:**
the confidence and satisfaction in **oneself**.

Self Esteem is not a result of:
- How you look ▪ Success in your job
- The amount of money you have
- The number of friends you have
  - Talent ▪ Fame ▪ Love

Self esteem can't
be found, can't be
earned from
others. *The confidence
and satisfaction
you have in yourself*
comes from within...
Self-love.

NOBODY LIKES ME,
EVERYBODY HATES ME,
I'M GOING TO EAT SOME WORMS

WORMS

• • • • • • • • • • • • • • • • • • • • • • • •

## Self-esteem is at the very core of building a healthy Life Puzzle.

Every human being who walks this earth has an inherent right to high self-esteem. The person responsible for creating this is you.

Simply by knowing that *confidence and satisfaction* in oneself comes from within, you can accept yourself with love—today— just as you are. Once you accept your life as yours to design and create, then you can get on with making your Life Puzzle.

But if you continue to place your "self" in other people's hands, by letting them judge you, (i.e., are you thin enough, smart enough, rich enough, lovable enough) it will be impossible to truly create your own genuine Life Puzzle.

*Well, if everyone has the inherent right to high self-esteem, how come I don't have it?*

## Breaking the cycle of low SELF esteem.

The confidence and satisfaction we have in ourselves, self-esteem, could be easily developed throughout our child-hoods if the adults in the world that we grew up in were filled with their own high self-esteem. Unfortunately, most adults—including your parents, teachers, ministers, priest, the boss—do not possess high self-esteem. That's not because they don't want it…it's because they too were raised by adults with low self-esteem. The cycle of low self-esteem has been repeat-ing itself generation after generation.

You can only "gently lead" a child towards the development of high self-esteem by assisting the child in develop-ing the healthy edges that define a self. Through the years, as your children grow, you gradually show them how to trust in themselves. But you can only teach what you know, and if, as an adult, your own self-esteem is fragile at best, it will be next to impossible to create an environment for your children where high self-esteem can flourish in a trusting, open environ-ment.

The low self-esteem cycle can be broken for you and your family. But it will require work on your part. First and foremost, you will need to do the inner work of finding out where your own self-esteem got bruised and battered while growing up. And then you'll have to do some forgiving of the people that created those bruises. You'll have to come to a point of accepting that, though you were hurt and your self-esteem was crushed, rarely did the people who did this to you do it with malicious intent. More often than not it is strictly an act of their own low self-esteem screaming out. You just happened to be on the receiving end of it and as a child you did not know what to do.

Typically, children who grow up in environments that are chaotic, abusive and lack trust and support from the adults around them interpret this process by blaming themselves, assuming that they are at fault or no good. They arrive into adulthood as the walking wounded, carrying around years of *misinterpretations of actions* of the adults in their early, young life. This is the heart of low self-esteem.

Despite being an adult, when you have low self-esteem, you are often just as confused and conflicted as you were as a child. Only now, because you're an adult, the rule book says you're *supposed to have your act together.* When you realize you don't, you do the same thing you did as a child...blame yourself and assume you are no good. It's a vicious cycle.

It's time to break this cycle. Let's begin to undo years of misinterpretation and negative self-talk. Let's begin to see yourself as a whole human being who has the ability to build your own *confidence and satisfaction* in yourself: high self-esteem.

## Resentment and Intimidation: Your edges need strengthening.

If you find yourself resenting others needing you, demanding of your time and expecting you to just be there for them, it is a clear signal that you have weak edges. When we truly choose to give of ourselves, no resentment is possible. When resentment arises it is a sign that you have tied your self-esteem to giving to others as a means of getting approval for yourself. It is a sign that you have weak edges.

It also means that you are violating someone else's edge because when we resent another person it is because they are not giving to us in exchange for what we've given them (i.e., you owe me). When you put someone in this position, everyone loses, all edges become weak and vulnerable. No one is living from a self-responsible model.

Wouldn't it be better for you to take care of your own needs directly? If in reading this section you are coming to the conclusion that you need to strengthen your own edges, that's okay. Very few people grew up in environments that taught them to have strong edges or a strong definition of the self.

## Are *you* giving your power away?

Your Life Puzzle is just that: yours. You own it, nobody else, and you don't have to apologize or make excuses for being...you. Yet many people are forever forgetting that they are in charge of making their own Life Puzzle!

How often do you find yourself intimidated in the process of meeting other people? Do you find yourself nervous, unsure, out of sorts, wondering what the other person is thinking about you?

What's happening when this is going on? Has the other person actually done

# Use the Choosing Continuum:

· · · · · · · · · · · · · · · · · · · · · · · · · · · · · · · · · · · · · · · · · · · · · · · · ·

## Are your edges weak or strong?

*Can you see how this will affect the rest of your Life Puzzle?*

| Weak Boundaries | Strong Boundaries |
|---|---|
| ■ External focus of control | ■ Internal focus of control |
| ■ Poor self-identity | ■ Strong self-identity |
| ■ Looking outside self for identity | ■ Look within self for source of identity |
| ■ VICTIM | ■ I CHOOSE |
| ■ OTHERS CHOOSE FOR YOU | ■ I TAKE RESPONSIBILITY |

### Who are the "others"?

MEDIA
FAMILY
CHURCH
SOCIETY
FRIENDS/PEERS
WORKPLACE
$$$$$$
MONEY
??????

There will always be outside influences telling you who to be. Why do they know better than you how to run your life?
*They don't!*

To achieve high self-esteem...*confidence and satisfaction within yourself*...you must begin to trust that you can make the best choices for your life based on your desires and decisions. Self-esteem building is a process of reducing the power that outside (external) influences have over your life and replacing it with a life based on choices that are consciously controlled from within (internal). It is an empowering process based in self-love and self-trust. Everyone has the right (and responsibility!) to do this.

anything? And even if they did, why would this make you give up your power of self?

Let me give you an example: I was talking to a client and she was sharing what was happening in her marriage. This woman had spent her entire life doing everything for everyone, especially her family. She had supported her husband during an unexpected job lay-off and had worked herself to the bone. But now that her husband was back at work their relationship had deteriorated for a variety of reasons. They now argued often and she was recalling the last argument she'd had with him. As a result of stress she'd put on a little extra weight, though she was still quite attractive. Her husband however had screamed at her "Don't you ever look in the mirror? You're disgusting!" This phrase had been haunting her for weeks, to the point of serious depression and instant tears. As she was explaining the situation she kept saying, "Well, I know I need to lose a little, but I think I still present myself quite well."

I said to her "Why do you give your power away like that?" Her answer was to explain all over again what he was doing to her that was ruining her life. So, I repeated the question, "Why do you give your power away like that?"

It took her a while to realize that *she was empowering him* with the ability to hurt her. If she stood firm with owning her own Life Puzzle then she would spend her time taking care of herself and not allowing others to shape her Life Puzzle by "breaking her edge" and shaping her SELF.

Become aware of your own power of self because it is a vital component in the strengthening of your Life Puzzle. It is also a statement of the strength of your edges. Watch yourself during the day…how often to you give your power away? To the boss, spouse, co-workers… the store clerk? Work on firming up your edges and you will discover your Life Puzzle takes on a strength so you can feel the power of self-love.

## Do your weak edges leave you feeling guilty?

Many people go through life feeling constantly guilty that they are not doing enough for others, that they said or did the wrong thing and have therefore hurt another and they feel so guilty about it. Everything they do makes them feel guilty. If they take a day off from work to take care of personal things they feel guilty that they are hurting the corporation, their boss, their fellow employees. If they take the last available sale item off the rack, if they can't make fresh cookies for their child's classroom, they spend the day haunted with the feeling of guilt. Everything they do becomes attached to guilt.

We can be so consumed with this belief of guilt that our lives become paralyzed and we manage to accomplish little. Often this "guilt" is actually not guilt at all, it's remorse. But this confusion and mislabeling gets its foundation in weak edges.

Understanding guilt and the proper role it plays in your self esteem is central to your Life Puzzle making. When you come to understand that you aren't really as guilty as you thought you were, you will discover this lifts a tremendous burden from your life. Living under the yoke of guilt that we mistakenly attach to our actions limits your Life Puzzle. So busy berating ourselves for all the stupid, silly mistakes we make throughout our day, there is little time left over to focus on the positive steps we've accomplished, all the good things we've done. Our lives get caught up in patching up this "guilt", making amends, watching that we not do it again, kicking ourselves…how could we have said, done, thought that…how, how, how!???

Most guilt is actually remorse. Yes, humans do things that are hurtful to others, but often these behaviors are not intended to inflict pain or hurt others.

There are times you just can't do everything and yes, you feel badly (remorse) that this hurt her, but this isn't guilt!

That's the difference between guilt and remorse. Now ask yourself, are you guilty or remorseful? Most likely, its remorse.

This mislabeling of our actions as guilt becomes an all consuming process. When your edges are weak, you find yourself constantly putting other's needs ahead of yours, even when they cause conflict for you. Quickly you find yourself feeling anxious anytime that you can't do for another and you mislabel it guilt.

## Remorse = Behavior

Accept that your actions hurt another though you did not intend it to do so. Accept that you are not happy with it. Make amends for this behavior.

## Guilt = Morals, Inferiority, Worthlessness

Guilt = badness. Your actions violate personal morals/ethics/law. Seek to hurt others despite violating your moral or ethical standards.

No one enjoys feeling guilty and it inevitably leads to a downward spiral of negative feelings about oneself. Such as, "I'm not good enough—if I was more organized I could take on being coach of my son's soccer team, be my daughter's Brownie troop leader and still manage the church bazaar." Or "No one will want to be my friend if I tell them no, I can't drive them wherever they want to go." On and on it goes until you find yourself going crazy to please others in order to avoid feeling guilty.

This has to stop. This mislabeled guilt is a thinking error! As a healthy, well-balanced human being that is busy building one's Life Puzzle, it is not your responsibility to please everyone else in

Ask yourself, is it guilt? For example, if you took the day off from work, are you really morally wrong? Are you inferior and worthless because of this action? Of course not! You may not be comfortable taking time off from work, but this doesn't equate to moral inferiority. Same thing with not making cookies for your child…this action doesn't make you worthless!

Did you sit around and think, "I won't make those cookies because I intend to hurt her?" Of course not.

order to be okay within yourself. Tying this "lack of pleasing everyone else" with guilt is illogical thinking that is self-destructive. Breaking this cycle is necessary if you are going to move forward and build a healthy Life Puzzle.

## But don't we need guilt?

Yes, we do. Guilt is necessary for a moral society. We must set standards of behavior that protect us all. Violating these laws and standards should produce guilt. For issues such as murder, theft, adultery, conscious deceit of people, etc., guilt is appropriate. Guilt plays a strong role in defining human interactions with others. It is good that guilt (along with a long jail sentence!) prevents me from murdering my friend when we argue over the last cookie on the plate. It is good that guilt prevents me from breaking into my neighbor's garage and stealing his new car. Participating in these types of action, I should assume blame for them. This is guilt because I've broken the moral or ethical code.

But assuming blame for saying no to taking on the church bazaar chairmanship? What moral law have you broken? Beating your spouse needs guilt—you are violating moral law.

But feeling guilty for not going to every function of a particular social group, that's a thinking error. It isn't guilt. If you make a conscious decision to meet your needs but it happens to conflict with someone else's, you do not have to feel guilty. If the other person tries to make you feel guilty, what are they doing? Breaking your edge, not respecting your right to feel as you do or make a choice that is right for you.

Ready to give up guilt? There are several wonderful books that can help you do this—one I highly recommend: *When I Say No, I Feel Guilty*, by Manuel Smith.

A simple way to start breaking the guilt habit is whenever you feel guilty, stop and ask yourself two questions:
*1. What moral law have I broken?*
*2. If I've broken no moral law, then why am I uncomfortable accepting my conscious decision for this action?*

Remember, not pleasing the rest of the world at all times is not a moral law! Do not apply guilt to this action. We may all endeavor to help our fellow man in many wonderful ways, but on the day that we can't, accept it and move on!

## You don't have to do all this work alone.

Strengthening your edges is a vital part of your Life Puzzle building process. If you have been a victim of abuse, grew up in a home where alcohol or drugs were present, if school was a negative experience that continues to haunt you, it is very probable that your self-esteem, and your ability for self-love, have become impaired.

Please consider counseling. Though many feel that going to a counselor is a sign of weakness, in truth, it is just the opposite. People who choose to work with a counselor exhibit true signs of inner strength. They realize they have issues that are impairing them from building their healthiest Life Puzzle. Instead of running from themselves, they pro-actively choose to confront these issues and work with a counselor. It is one of the most powerful and courageous steps we can take.

How do you find a good counselor? First, ask friends or colleagues for a referral. If you know someone who has had good success with a counselor, it is great to have this feedback. Second, call several counseling offices and ask to talk with one of their counselors (they'll probably have to call you back). When you talk to them, share with them a general description of the key issues you feel you need to confront in therapy. Then ask what type of therapy they work with—what is their style of therapy? Some run groups, some do short term cognitive therapy, some work with

Biofeedback—you want to get a good understanding of their outlook. After talking with several, choose one and set an appointment. After your second appointment, review your feelings. Do you feel comfortable with this counselor or is there something that just doesn't click for you? If deep down you aren't comfortable with this counselor, then try another—don't just give up. Usually you'll find the right counselor for you within two or three tries, and many times on the first.

*Understand, the counselor works for you,* so it is vitally important that you feel confident and comfortable with the counselor. If these things are missing, it is better to spend a little more time looking for a different counselor than it is to keep working with someone that you aren't comfortable with or quitting all together.

# ACTION PLAN

## Exercise #1. The mirror exercise.

Go to a mirror and stand in front of it. Look at yourself, straight in the eye and repeat the following out loud:

**I love me**      **I like me**      **I care for me.**

Do this three times each day. Record your feelings about doing this exercise in a journal. This exercise may seem very simple, but it causes much distress for people. Doing this exercise will help you confront the comfort zone you have or do not have with yourself. Do you love your *self*? Are you caring for your *self*? Do you like the *self* you are becoming? What is making this so difficult? What inner issues prevent you from loving, like and truly caring for yourself?

## Exercise #2. Your edges: how strong are they?

On a scale of 1 (low) to 10 (high), how strong are your edges?

Physical edges:      _____
    Respect and care for your body.
    Don't allow anyone (including yourself) to hurt, abuse or touch your body
    inappropriately.

Feeling edges:      _____
    Are aware of and take responsibility for your feelings.
    Can share your feelings openly.
    Don't allow others to violate your feelings with putdowns or guilt.

Thinking edges:      _____
    Have respect for your thinking skills.
    Feel capable of expressing your thoughts in a crowd without fear of ridicule.
    Don't allow others to intimidate you.

Sexual edges:      _____
    Have respect for your physical and emotional sexual self.
    Express your sexual desires with your partner, openly and honestly.
    Don't allow others to use you and you don't use others through sexual encounters.

Spiritual edges:      _____
    Have explored your spiritual self, consciously.
    Live your spirituality each day: I am no greater than another, no one is greater than me.
    Don't allow others to make you feel inferior.

How does it all add up? _____

*Only you will see the results of this exercise. Be honest with yourself. It is more important to realize that you have weak edges than to pretend to yourself they are strong. There is no shame in a low score. It can be wonderful to finally confront this in concrete terms and then begin the growth work on your edges which will lead to self-love.*

*With your edges in place you can work on putting the pieces of the puzzle together.*

# The Core Piece: Self-Responsibility

# # 1. Self-Responsibility

**Y**ou can't make a great Life Puzzle by having someone else make it for you. At the same time, you can't use other people as an excuse for why you aren't working on your own Life Puzzle ("Sure I'd work on my Life Puzzle if my mom wasn't always bugging me to do things for her or my sister wasn't so much prettier than me that I can't ever be as good, so why bother?") Self-responsibility is the key to creating a terrific Life Puzzle for yourself. No one else can do it for you. You can ask for help and many times it's good to ask for help but only you can put that help into action.
**No decision *is* a decision…**

Many of us try to ignore the issue of self-responsibility by just not thinking about it. We sort of hope it will go away or we pretend to ourselves that we just haven't gotten mature enough for it or next year we'll be better prepared for it—then we'll do it. Actually, by the time you are 10 or 12 years old, you are already able to make the decision to accept responsibility for your life.

Unfortunately, avoidance of the decision to take responsibility becomes a life-long process for many people. They just pretend they haven't made the decision! But to *not make the choice* is a choice.

So you need to stop now and ask

yourself, do you accept full responsibility for creating your Life Puzzle? There are some responsibilities in life that we like, others we wish we could pass off to others. In making the **Puzzle that is You,** eventually, you need to accept that if you are going to create your best self, as you grow into your adulthood you will need to accept full responsibility for your life. It's worth it!

At the heart of yo[ur] Life Puzzle:
**Self-Responsibili[ty]**
It is the number o[ne] step and from it al[l] the other parts of your Life Puzzle wi[ll] be affected.

**Okay, I'll take these.**

Exercise
Feelings
Environment
Playing
Partnering
Community
Spirituality

**Someone else can have these**

Nutrition
Thinking
Working
Parenting
Finding Meaning
Financial

*Nope, you've got to take them all!*

*But all those responsibilities are a drag! I want the right to be free, come and go as I please, do what I want to do. Why do I have to take on all these responsibilities in my Life Puzzle?*

So you can be truly free.

What? We often confuse taking responsibility for our lives with limiting our lives. But the truth is, NOT TAKING RESPONSIBILITY for our lives is the most limiting action you can make in your life.

To be truly free in your life is to be fully conscious of your life and its daily choices. This conscious act of living is filled with vibrancy, energy and joy. This is freedom to live. It does not mean that your life will be blissful and easy at every moment. Many of the challenges you will be confronted with will force you to do inner searching, hard work, make sacrifices and will at times be frustrating. But when done in the context of choice and self-responsibility, even these times will have meaning in your life.

NOT TAKING RESPONSIBILITY means a life that is not conscious. It is limiting to your life because when you are avoiding making choices life becomes painful, uncertain, and numbing. You let events of the moment determine your life without conscious decision-making.

For example, in just one area of your Life Puzzle, let's look at how taking or not taking responsibility can affect the freedom of your life.

**Nutrition:** "I want to eat what I want to eat without having to make responsible choices." I hear this all the time when I give classes on nutrition and healthy eating. As I show people what the best foods are that affect their body and mind, invariably someone pipes up and says, "Well, yeah, but I like my burger and fries and I don't want to give them up for veggies and pasta. I want to be free to eat what I feel like without thinking about the choices I'm making."

Well, that's fine. You can eat unconsciously on a day-to-day basis. However, we know that poor nutrition over a lifetime leads to heart disease, obesity, Type II diabetes, cancers, digestive problems, and poorer mental judgement. Poor nutrition depletes your body of necessary energy, leaves you tired, irritable, and as one client said to me, "I was so tired, I could barely drag my butt through life."

Whether you are feeling it now or will feel it in the future, inevitably eating unconsciously, (i.e., without taking responsibility for the choices you make), will limit your life. Some of these limits will be dramatic. Heart disease that requires by-pass surgery is pretty limiting, others will be more subtle, such as feeling too tired to read to your kids at night because you've eaten so little food of quality during the day that your body can barely function.

Want true freedom?

GET CONSCIOUS. Take responsibility for your life!

## Don't Call Home

My father dropped me off at college on my 18th birthday. I was excited and scared. On the one hand, I couldn't wait until he got back in the car. On the other, I wanted to hold on to him and never let go!

As the time came, my father pulled me aside from the hustle and bustle of the dorm room and took me outside for a little talk. It is a talk I will never forget.

"Well, honey, it's finally arrived. Your day of freedom. For the last 18 years, I've tried to teach you everything I know and overall I think I've covered just about everything I think you'll need to get you through life. For the things you'll need that I didn't know about, well, I did the best with what I knew.

"I want you to know, that from today forward, you are free to make any decision you want in life. You don't need to choose something because it's what I might have told you to do. You can do anything you want to do. If you want to do drugs that's your choice. If you want to drink again, your choice. Study hard, don't study hard—your choice. I just want you to keep one thing in mind, as you make your choices. If any of your decisions get you in trouble, you find yourself flunking out of school, getting thrown in the slammer, find yourself pregnant… whatever it is, just remember, don't call home.

"Because with freedom of choice comes one catch: responsibility for the consequences. So before you make a decision, take a moment to think through the consequences. If you are unwilling to accept the potential consequence, then you'd best make a different decision. For I will not be held responsible for your decisions. Today, you are an adult, and I am giving you the gift of freedom of your life. It is a very valuable gift. Now that it is in your hands it is up to you to care for it, as I no longer can do that for you."

As he gave me a big hug that brought us both to tears, he said, "Have a great life."

Many times in my life, I have recalled my father's words when I had a choice to make. Consequences have always been in my mind. Yes, there have been lots of mistakes as well as quite a number of choices I knew my father wouldn't approve of, yet, they worked for me and I went forward with them.

The freedom my father gave me that day: Self-responsibility for creating my life in my way. It was the greatest gift a parent could ever give a child.

**But what if *"all my parents knew"* wasn't much? How, then, do I take responsibility for my life?**

You're right, life isn't fair. Some people get great childhoods with lots of support and nurturing. Others do not and find themselves entering their adulthood unsure of many pieces of their Life Puzzle.

There's a section in Geneen Roth's book, *When Food is Love,* where she's recounting growing up in an alcoholic home. Her mother was unable to provide the emotional support she needed to help her get through childhood. As an adult, Geneen's life was greatly affected by compulsive eating and dieting. One day she found herself yelling at her mother, "You should have known better!" Finally, a lightbulb goes off in Geneen's mind: "And now I should know better…and if I don't, I'd better learn how to know better."

And that's the bottom line. There are no perfect childhoods. A good portion of your adulthood will be spent in either undoing the wounds of your childhood or finding answers to questions that were never addressed. Doing this work is how you take responsibility for your Life Puzzle.

Only you can decide to "learn how to know better." Will you?

# *"What the heck, it's easier to stay a victim!"*

That's what my client said one day as we were discussing Life Puzzle-making. She said it somewhat facetiously, but there is definitely a hint of truth in it.

When you look over your Life Puzzle, it's obvious that it will take a lot of work throughout your lifetime to create a well-balanced Life Puzzle. In the short run, it's actually easier to not take responsibility for your Life Puzzle. And it's easy to do because there are lots of other people who will be more than happy to make most of your life decisions.

You don't have to choose healthy foods when the fast food industry has no problem taking your dollars in exchange for low quality foods. Sitting on your butt is easier than exercising even if it does result in a bigger and bigger butt every year (oh, and maybe heart disease in your 40's). It is easier to let people walk all over you, hurting your feelings, intimidating you, than to actually stand up for yourself and own your own feelings and thoughts. It is easier to keep quiet when people are communicating with you rather than to challenge them with your own ideas and needs. Why rock the boat in your marriage and create outward friction when it's so much easier to suffer in silence?

And yes, your sexual relationship with your partner is a bore, but it's too awkward to actually communicate this and then work together to improve it. And hey, it's easier to keep charging more stuff on the credit card than to sit down and make a budget for the family so there will be enough for the college funds in 16 years.

You get my point, I'm sure. We have so many excuses available for why we don't get involved in our lives. It is hard to confront ourselves and challenge the victim roles we've become habitually comfortable in playing. Blaming others is acceptable in our society, and we get lots of reinforcement from others to keep doing this. Breaking out of the group that is all caught up in playing the victim game (about 90% of our society!) is difficult. But it can be done, and only you can make the choice to do so.

I was working with another woman and had given her the book *The Power of Positive Thinking* by Norman Vincent Peale. It is a terrific book (more about it in Chapter 6) and most people like it. I asked her if she had read the book and she sort of shrugged her shoulders and said, "Well, I got through a chapter or two, but it didn't seem quite right for me." I was surprised because her life was a jumbled mess at the time. And we both knew that most of that mess was created through lots of reactive decisions that had pinned her down. Three children, no child support (she didn't ask for it), emotionally abused by her mother to whom she would not stand up, even though she knew her mother was abusing her. And because she was stuck on welfare, she was financially strapped. She was a very intelligent woman and she knew that she repeatedly avoided making decisions in her life until she found herself up against a wall and forced to react at the last minute.

As we talked a little more, I challenged her with why I thought she didn't like Peale's book. I asked her, "Is it possible you don't like that book because at the end of each chapter you're confronted with ideas that will require you to change your behavior? As much as you dislike your situation, it's still easier to complain than it is to actually take responsibility for your life and make proactive instead of reactive decisions. Could that be why Peale's book makes you uncomfortable?"

We didn't come to any agreement on this, but I suspect I'm correct. And she's not unlike so many people in this world. I can agree with her that her childhood was tough and no, she didn't have many of the advantages that some have. But she does have a good brain and she could break out of this victim cycle. No, in the short run it will not be easy. It will require lots of effort. But in the long run it will create a much healthier and happier life.

Alas, few people can see the long term benefits in contrast to the immediate pain that breaking the victim cycle requires. Accepting responsibility for one's life is the first step. This is an act of consciousness, and the more you become involved in making the daily effort to assume

responsibility for your life the easier it gets.

One other reason for focusing on the long term through self responsibility instead of short term victimhood: *your children.* Victims create more victims. Inevitably, playing the victim game overflows to your children. They see you doing it and they will respond in one of two ways. They will either follow in your footsteps and become victims, or they will resist you and your victim game, forcing them to divide from the family in order to survive and become self-responsible. Whatever they choose, you lose.

Over and over again, I see families playing out this scenario. Families where everyone is entangled in each others lives, using each other to keep from taking responsibility and growing their own lives. That's what's happening with my book reader friend. Her mother is a bitter victim and works hard at keeping her children (now all adults) under her control.

My friend is a passive victim, letting everyone run all over her. Her mother and her children control her life. And her children? Already her 12 year-old is a passive victim. Like his mother, he quickly gives up when confronted with a challenge. However, this appears to be changing with the onset of puberty. He is becoming verbally and physically abusive to her, and this may be an attempt to resist the victim role model.

Other clients come into counseling to work on breaking the cycle of victimhood they learned from their parents. A common outcome is a complete break from the parents as the only way to establish their new, healthy, self-responsible self. Sometimes these relationships will resume at a later date but often the victim parent is much too insistent that the adult child get back into the victim process and there is no way to mend the relationship.

Everyone loses under the blame game. It is time to break the cycle.

As you read this book, over and over again you will confront the issue of self-responsibility. And there will be a part of you that might prefer to take the short term, victim route. But each time ask yourself this:

"It may be okay if I choose to play the victim game, but what message does this teach my children?"

In a world that is going crazy, where people are sitting back and blaming everyone else but refusing to get involved for change, the continuation of the victim model is having dire consequences for our society and our children. Each of us plays a part in this. Pick up any newspaper and you see the victim blame game in so many ways. Murder, theft, white collar crime, child abuse. It seems to be out of control, and it certainly gives those who like playing the blame game lots of ammunition to convince themselves they're normal. "Hey everybody else is doing it."

You may not be able to change all the others, but you can certainly change yourself. And it must start with self-responsibility, owning your Life Puzzle and directing your life, and modeling a conscious, proactive lifestyle for your children. If each of us did this, what a wonderful world we could each create.

## Well, what if I do it but nobody else does? GOOD FOR YOU.

Taking responsibility for your Life Puzzle requires effort. You will discover as you start breaking away from the victim model that it can be a lot of work. You will also find that you receive very little reinforcement from those around you. As you make proactive choices in your life, it may create conflict with old friendships, it may push on the edges of your marriage, it may upset your co-workers. Those who are fully invested in playing the victim model get uncomfortable around those who choose not to continue to play the game.

That's the bad news: it's work and it upsets the apple cart of the victim game. Here's the good news: it's well worth it. You will discover new friends, you will become a better model for your children and you will be a change agent for our world.

Life Puzzle making is not the norm in our society, but it could be. However the society at large is not going to change. It will be you, the individual that will change the society. Despite great odds and against the normal victim system around you, you can do it. As more and more do it we will begin to see a transformation.

As you begin taking more responsibility for your Life Puzzle it won't be long before you begin to run into those people who are also doing the same. They are out there, and you will be pleasantly surprised at how often what seems to be chance encounters with a stranger suddenly turns into an entirely new support system for you and your family. Despite the bleakness of the world, there is a glimmer of hope from people like you.

## Suggested reading list

| | |
|---|---|
| Covey, Stephen R. | *7 Habits of Highly Effective People* |
| Quinn, Daniel | *Ishmael* |
| Weil, Andrew, M.D | *Natural Health, Natural Healing* |

# ACTION PLAN

Review the pieces of your Life Puzzle. As you look over these pieces determine which ones you are currently taking responsibility for on a daily, proactive level. After you finish this, place the remaining ones on the other side of the list.

## Pieces of Your Life Puzzle

These are the Pieces I
am taking responsibility for:

_____

_____

_____

_____

_____

_____

_____

_____

_____

These are the Pieces I
am *not actively* taking responsibility for:

_____

_____

_____

_____

_____

_____

_____

_____

_____

Now, look at the list on the right. Choose one of these and ask yourself the following question. Write your responses in your journal:

1. What is it about this Piece that I don't like?
2. What is it about this Piece that makes me uncomfortable?
3. What did I learn while growing up about this Piece?
4. How is this early learning affecting me now in relation to this Piece?
5. What one small step could I make to take more responsibility for this piece?

If you choose to, repeat this process with all the other pieces on this side of the list.

# Exercise!

## *Caring for your physical body*

# *Exercise*

Caring for your physical body is a dynamic part of Life Puzzle making and yet few people in America have a regular fitness program. Even though Reebok and Nike sell a gazillion sneakers, and you see everyone from 2 year-olds to 92 year-olds in jogging outfits, apparently the only place we're wearing these is to the restaurants!

The fitness craze has only affected 15-25% of Americans. Studies show that only a small portion of us are regularly exercising 2-3 times a week, year in and year out. What an unfortunate situation. That means the great majority of Americans are missing out on one of the easiest and most rewarding processes in Life Puzzle making. Exercise!

## Healthy bodies don't just happen, they are a result of effort and care.

Most of us take care of our cars and houses better than we take care of our own bodies. We seem to have no trouble imagining what would happen if we never changed the oil in the car or cleaned the house once in a while....we'd expect it to fall apart.

But we ignore our physical bodies year in and year out. Then we end up with a heart attack or we discover we can't take a long walk without huffing and puffing, and we're surprised! How could this have happened?

Many of us like to relinquish, or give up, responsibility for our bodies and use time and genetics as an excuse for why we've gotten out of shape and are not able to function well. Let's stop doing that now. The human body was designed to function—if taken care of properly with good nutrition and exercise—in good form right up to the 80s and 90s.

IT IS A MYTH THAT OLDER BODIES CAN'T BE IN GOOD SHAPE! If you eat well and exercise regularly, your body at age 55 or 75 can have excellent muscle tone, function in good form and keep you actively involved in the world around you.

## It's simple to get started.

Exercise doesn't have to be fancy or expensive to be good. Something as simple as walking can produce dramatic benefits for your body and mind.

The goal of exercising is to increase your heart rate. That's because the heart is the #1 muscle in your body. If your heart isn't healthy, the rest of your body will have a difficult time doing its job. So you can quickly see why you need to exercise this muscle and keep it in excellent health.

The heart muscle's job is to pump blood through the body. It does this by squeezing itself hard enough to force the blood that is inside the heart cavity out and into the rest of the body. If the heart is weak, and it squeezes weakly, the blood is pushed out weakly as well. Before long your body gets weaker and weaker too.

The body is very dependent on this blood, so if your heart is weak the rest of your body is greatly affected.

The great news? You can get started today on an exercise program and see the benefits within just a few weeks of regular exercise. (If you haven't exercised in a long time or are experiencing health problems, consult with your doctor before choosing the best exercise for your current health status.)

## Use it or lose it!

Bodies that do not exercise end up with flabby muscles, inside and outside. This NEVER has to happen to you.

If you've been telling yourself, "Hey, I'm getting older, it's okay if I have a little extra around the middle," or "I've had two kids, what do they expect" or perhaps, "Well, I'm 52 and menopause has set in, so I can't control my body," then it's time to start talking to yourself in a new way.

None of the above comments have any basis in reality when it comes to having a healthy, firmly toned body. No matter what your age, you can get your body in good shape and keep it there.

New studies show that if we exercise regularly there is only a slight loss of muscle tone as we get older. Part of the reason that skin gets so loose on us as we get older is because of poor muscle tone. Skin is attached to muscle and if the muscle tone is weak, then the skin has little to hold onto and the result is loose, hanging skin. Firm the muscle and you will improve the look of your entire body.

## It's not just about your body, it's also about your mind.

A regular exercise program improves your physical health but also greatly improves your mental and emotional health.

In the process of exercising and moving your body, a series of chemical reactions take place. One of these reactions produces hormones and chemicals in the body that actually stimulate your mind. As a result, you can think better, mild depression or lethargy is removed, and you end up being much more productive overall.

If you feel tired all the time, find yourself with lots of "blue moods", are short tempered and irritable, *start exercising*. All of these problems can be eliminated with a good, regular exercise program. Exercise is the cheapest and easiest way to manage stress.

### What can you do?

FIRST: Commit yourself to your own Life Puzzle.

SECOND: List all the reasons why you haven't exercised regularly.

THIRD: Look at the list and challenge it! Most of our reasons for not exercising are excuses. The #1 reason: time. Where do you find time? Turn off the TV! Kids? Take them with you. Don't let these excuses control your life!

FOURTH: Stop making excuses, start making choices. What exercise program is most appropriate for your current health status and your lifestyle? Choose something you enjoy because you're more likely to keep doing it.

FIFTH: Get started!

SIXTH: Commit to *stick with it* for six months and do it, no ifs, ands or Butts!

# Some exercise choices

• • • • • • • • • • • • • • • • • •

## The 324 rule:
## 3 times a week
## 20 minutes each
## 4 life!

• • • • • • • • • • • • • • • • • •

IF I KEEP THIS MUSCLE STRONG ALL MY MUSCLES CAN STAY STRONG

## Walking

A 15-45 minute daily walk is a great exercise choice. Keep a brisk pace to create aerobic benefits. If you're walking with a friend and you can talk easily...you're not walking fast enough!

## Swimming

Whether swimming laps or taking a water aerobics class, the pool provides options for those with physical limitations as well as adding variety to your other choices.

## Yoga

Yoga is a series of stretching exercises that when performed correctly are actually aerobic as well! For people who haven't exercised in a long time, an introductory yoga class can be a great way to get started. Many people are surprised at how stimulating a yoga routine can be.

## Jogging

Be sure to invest in good shoes and do lots of stretching before you start running. Start with a mile or less and don't overdo it in the beginning.

## Biking

If you've got one, terrific! Be sure to maintain a good pace. Gentle riding doesn't really count for aerobic value.

## Jumping rope

Remember this when you were young? Jumping rope is fun and aerobic. Go for it!

## Exercise tapes

There are tons of these to pick from. Try renting a few from the video store and see what type you enjoy the most. Then you might consider purchasing one for your home. You can usually buy these for between $10 and $20.

## A fitness club membership

This can be an excellent option, but move cautiously before joining a club. Visit several and look at membership fees and plans. Do not purchase on impulse! Though clubs can give you a wide variety of exercise programs, including cardiovascular workout with bikes, and treadmills, strength training equipment and lots of aerobic classes, they can be expensive, especially if you don't use them consistently. I've been a member of clubs for 17 years and enjoy them very much, but then I use them! Be sure you'll use it before you buy it!

**These are just some of the choices you can make.**
**Try several and enjoy them all!**

## I'd love to exercise...but I have children.

Over and over again I hear people, especially women, tell me that they would love to exercise but they just don't have time—they have children.

If you've committed to making your Life Puzzle, using your children as a reactive reason why you don't exercise doesn't work. Exercise is so necessary for your mental and physical health that it cannot be ignored. It is also necessary if you're going to have the energy needed to be able to parent effectively!

Besides that, your children need exercise too. So instead of complaining that you can't exercise because of them, exercise *with* them.

Ride bikes, take a walk, push that carriage at an aerobic pace or have your children join you with an exercise videotape.

If you aren't an example of Life Puzzle-making, who will be? Taking the time to exercise is showing your children how important taking care of one's physical body is. They will respect you for this.

Say you don't have time in between taking them to all their activities. What message does that send? That they have value, and you don't? Drop them off at soccer practice, then take a jog or walk around the field while you're waiting.

Life Puzzle-making means you will create a way to put this into your life. Turn off the TV and exercise instead by slipping an exercise video in for this same half hour!

● ● ● ● ● ● ● ● ● ● ● ● ● ● ● ● ● ● ● ● ● ● ● ● ● ● ● ● ● ● ● ● ● ● ● ● ● ● ● ● ● ● ● ● ● ● ● ●

## Relax! Relaxation is a choice we make to care for our physical bodies.

**Breathing:** Breath is the source of our physical life. Stop breathing for just a few minutes and you'll die. Deep breathing is a way of bringing more "life energy" into your body. To breath correctly: Release your abdomen first, then breath deep into the belly, then follow with filling your lungs. This gives you maximum air intake, energizing your body as well as helping it to relax. Release air in lungs first, belly second.

**Stretching:** A great stress buster, the simple act of stretching rejuvenates your body. Try Yoga!

**Deep relaxation:** This is the process of tightening and then releasing the muscles of your body. Start with your feet, then slowly move up the body; calves, thighs, buttocks, pelvis, abdomen, upper chest, shoulders, facial muscles, arms, fingers. Remember to deep breathe during this process and be aware of your body. Where are you feeling tension? It is important to listen to your body.

**Meditation:** Quiet the mind, still the body. Meditation is simply a process of shutting off all the noises of the world around us and turning within. Find a quiet space, sit in a comfortable position, breathe slowly and deeply. You may repeat a simple word, as this helps your mind to keep from straying off into conscious thinking. When you do find yourself thinking, remind yourself to return to quiet. Amazingly, meditation rejuvenates the physical body as well as the mind.

**Sleep:** Sleep is vital for a healthy Life Puzzle...ask any mother with a newborn and she will tell you, sleep deprivation is an ugly thing! It seems so simple, but so many of us have created such rushed lives that we aren't taking enough time to sleep. Please do! It is a great way to take care of your body, mind and spirit...8 hours each night, please!

## What's happening to our children? They need exercise too.
### YOUR FAMILY LIFE PUZZLE

Do you remember your childhood? If you're over the age of 30 you probably recall a childhood filled with lots of outdoor playing. Bike riding, kick ball, softball or generally playing with neighborhood kids was the usual thing.

Neighborhoods were safe places. After school and on weekends, children were outdoors running, playing and being active. That's not true any longer. While our parents may have known all the other families in a neighborhood, today you might not even know your next door neighbor. Before, other parents kept an eye on all the children in the neighborhood, disciplining if necessary, or at least calling the parents. Today, other children in the neighborhood are off limits, as adults fear touching or disciplining a child which isn't their own.

The biggest difference, though is that the children just aren't outside much at all. There are lots of reasons for this and we don't need to discuss them in this book. What's most important to recognize is the consequence of this change: the current generation of children are in the worst physical condition of any in the 20th century. Between lack of exercise, too much television, and snack foods that are loaded with fat and calories (chips, cookies, crackers, cheese, pizza), our children are turning into blobs! Forty percent of our children are obese.

The President's Fitness test —recall how easy that seemed in the 1970's? In the 1990's our children can't pass it.

Yes, the world is different from the one we grew up in. But that does not prevent us from finding solutions that will allow our children to get the exercise they need to build a healthy body and mind. It just becomes imperative that we structure our family life with exercise as a major commitment.

Exercise is a central need for all family members. If it's important for your Life Puzzle, it is just as important for your children's Life Puzzles. They are dependent on you to teach them this. The best way is to incorporate it into your family lifestyle. If you have young children, start today—take a walk with them, ride bikes together or let them participate while you do an exercise video.

If your children are in the 8-12 year-old range, sit down with them and discuss ideas for bringing exercise into the family. What group activity could you all do? Join the recreation center and swim, play basketball or take a karate class together. Maybe you prefer hiking and choose to walk daily to keep in shape for the big hike. If they like inline skating, ask them to teach you how to do it and get outside with them. Whatever it is, work together as a group to find a way to bring exercise into your home on a very regular basis.

If your children are in their teenage years there are several issues to look at. First, what is their physical condition? Have they already learned to be couch potatoes? Start an open dialogue and bring this issue up. Share with them why you are concerned about your and their exercise level. Then discuss the need for change and work together to make a commitment towards this change.

On the other hand, if your teenagers are involved with sports it will be much easier to bring exercise into the family. Or, are they seasonal exercisers, working hard to get ready for football season but doing very little after the season? It's important to stress to these children the need for LIFELONG exercise designed to keep their bodies healthy as compared to "outcome" exercise that is focused on winning games. (How many of us competed in a sport, took dance lessons or some other exercise in our childhood but stopped it....*and every other form of exercise* when we grew up and became an adult?)

There is another wonderful benefit for getting your children involved in regular exercise with the family. It builds and strengthens your family. If you do it together, it gives you quality time with your children. You can plan vacations around exercise—hiking, camping, horse back riding, swimming or other activities children enjoy, and it is good for the family too.

So tonight, turn off the television. Have a family meeting and discuss the need for all of you to exercise. Then pull out the calendar and find the places you can put this into all of your lives. You will be doing your children a giant favor as you get involved with your life...and theirs...through exercise.

● ● ● ● ● ● ● ● ● ● ● ● ● ● ● ● ● ● ● ● ● ● ● ● ● ● ● ● ● ● ● ● ● ● ● ● ● ● ● ● ● ● ● ● ● ● ●

## Breathe!

We all know that exercise helps tone our muscles, inside ones like the heart and outside ones like the hamstring or calf. But one other key value of exercising is breathing. Exercise increases the amount of oxygen we bring into our bodies. This air is vital as the primary source of energy to our bodies and mind. Take away air and you'll be "energyless" (dead) in a very short amount of time. On a less extreme level though, we tend to slowly die during the day when we breathe short, shallow breaths.

Regular exercise helps to compensate for the short breathing process that is so common. However, we don't have to go jogging to increase our breathing.

Deep breathing can be used as a relaxation technique and done anywhere at any time. The other terrific way to bring more air into your system is YOGA.

Many think that yoga is just contortionist stretching but it's not. Done correctly, yoga is centered in the breathing. At the end of a yoga session you have actually had an aerobic workout without any panting or heavy duty sweating.

If you haven't exercised in ages, try yoga. It gives you tremendous benefits without the strain that many think is necessary in order to call it real exercise. You'll be amazed at the terrific workout you'll receive.

# *Health care crisis: Solution found here!*

If I haven't convinced you yet of the necessity of exercise for building your Life Puzzle, then there's one more argument I can make: If you aren't a regular exerciser, you are the cause of our health care crisis.

I know that's rather bold, but it's quite true. We know that people who do not exercise will spend more time at the doctor's office, will cost more to treat than people who do exercise, and in the long run will end up with many more illnesses.

Over the last 30 years we have watched the cost of health care go up and up. And we have seen a change in the types of illnesses that send us to the doctors. Today, most of the illnesses are directly related to one's lifestyle practices. Exercise is a lifestyle practice, and when it's missing in an individual's life, they're much more likely to become ill with heart disease, cancer, Type II diabetes and general infections.

Study after study shows that exercise (coupled with nutrition, which we cover in the next chapter!) will help reduce heart disease, cholesterol levels, Type II diabetes and its complications, and colds and flus. And in the case of cancer we know that exercise improves the immune system, which is the system that protects us from cancer.

Unfortunately there is no exercise pill. You can't get the same benefits you receive from exercise from any doctor you visit. Exercise requires you to take responsibility for your physical body. Nobody else can do that for you.

But it's not just you. It's the rest of the 75-85% of Americans who are not exercising regularly who are contributing to the increased cost of health care. It is this simple! Yet we don't like to admit it, do we? We know that poor nutrition and no exercise result in 40-70% of our illnesses, yet we continue to eat poorly and sit on our butts. Then we run to the doctor and scream, "Fix me!!!!!"

## Fix yourself. Start exercising now.

**3.** We need to exercise regularly: three times a week at least.

**20.** A minimum of twenty minutes at one time. Hey, twenty minutes of brisk vacuuming counts! Walking twenty minutes through the downtown district where you work counts. Combine two breaks and go for it.

**4.** —**Life!** This seems to be the hardest part of exercise. We're all very good at getting started. Most of us have started exercising once a year every year of our adult life. But we don't stick with it. Exercising should be as much a part of your lifestyle as brushing your teeth or eating. We don't brush our teeth for three months and then forget about it until January when we make a new resolution to start brushing again. It's the same with exercise.

If we would all start exercising we would solve the health care crisis.

## Suggested reading list

| Arnot, Bob, M.D. | *Dr. Bob Arnot's Guide to Turning Back the Clock* |
| Vedral, Joyce, L. | *12 Minute Total Body Workout* |
| Vedral, Joyce, L. | *Top Shape* |
| Lidell, Lucinda | *The Book of Massage* |

# ACTION PLAN

## Begin at the beginning, start small and grow for a lifetime!

### Exercise 1.

List all the reasons you don't regularly exercise. Of these reasons, what's the number #1 issue? Time? Boredom? Laziness?

1. Now write down what you would tell someone if you were explaining why you can't exercise.

2. Now go back and read it with a critical eye. Where are you on the Choosing Continuum? Where do you want to be?

### Exercise 2.

Can you commit to exercising? Below, write down a very simple exercise commitment that you are willing to make. Do not overdo it. Keep it very simple. For example: walking. I commit to walking for 15 minutes, twice a week.

1. Exercise commitment:

2. How long: I commit to maintaining this exercise regime for _____months. At that time, I will review this commitment and make a decision on whether to change this exercise regime.

# Get started today!

*When you are finished reading this chapter, go take a walk!*

*The building blocks
of your Life Puzzle
begin with*

# Good Nutrition

# There is no more powerful place to start taking responsibility for your Life Puzzle than in the area of nutrition.

*There are two reasons for this:*

## #1

Every food you eat impacts your mental and physical health, either positively or negatively. Thus, the importance of your food selection becomes obvious.

## #2

If you eat high quality foods on a regular basis you will have the energy and stamina available so you will be able to make other conscious decisions about your life.

On the other hand, eating a poor quality diet will leave you tired. This leaves you less able to make other conscious decisions about your life.

*Start with taking responsibility in the area of nutrition and the rest of your Life Puzzle-making will be much easier.*

## It may seem too simplistic, but it is true!

# *The Power of the Pyramid: Good Nutrition!*

**T**his is the healthy way of eating and yet few of us eat like this. Americans have become accustomed to eating large amounts of meat and dairy but small amounts of fruits, vegetables and grains. This has resulted in a high fat diet that is leading us to many health problems such as heart disease and cancer. One definite step you can take in creating your healthiest self is to shift to eating based on the *Pyramid of Good Nutrition.*

## Picture This!

In 1992, the Pyramid of Nutrition was introduced. As you can see, grains lead the list. This is a big shift in the way that most of us picture the way we should be eating.

Centering our diet around grains means becoming confident to let go of the meat first mentality. Many of us don't realize how indoctrinated we are with having meat be the center of every meal. Yet, by the picture presented here, it is obvious that meat is really at the bottom of the pyramid not the top. In addition, the portion size of meat servings needs to be considerably smaller than what most of us typically eat.

## ramid of Good Nutrition

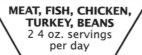

**GRAINS**
Rice, Wheat, Millet, Pasta, Whole Grain Breads, Cereals, Barley
6 1/2 c. servings per day

**VEGETABLES**
Cabbage, Carrots, Squash, Potatoes, etc.
3-5 1/2 c. servings per day

**FRUITS**
Apples, Oranges, Bananas, Grapes
Fresh is best! 2 servings per day

**DAIRY**
Low fat or Skim Milk products
Low fat cheese
2 4 oz. servings per day

**MEAT, FISH, CHICKEN, TURKEY, BEANS**
2 4 oz. servings per day

**SWEETS**
Fast Foods
Oils
LIMIT

There's one thing I would change on this Pyramid. I'd move beans up next to grains. Here's why: Beans, when mixed with grains, make a complete protein. This is how vegetarians receive most of their protein. Also, beans are high in fiber— something most of us need more of in our diets.

## The "Four Food Groups" is OUT!

Actually, the four food groups weren't so bad. What happened was people forgot to notice the fine print. As a result, we ended up with diets that are loaded with meat and dairy, and reduced in fruits, vegetables and grain! And as you saw on the previous page, the Pyramid of Health is based in grains, vegetables and fruits.

How many times have you said to yourself: "Okay, I've got a piece of meat, some rice or pasta, a veggie and if I add a glass of milk, I'll have a balanced meal. We've all said it because that's what we learned in home-ec or wherever. But it's too much protein, too little carbohydrates and if the meat is beef...too much fat.

There are physical and mental benefits to shifting our diets from high fat and protein to high complex carbohdyrates. Complex carbohydrates provide your body and mind with energy to help you get through the day. These are your high energy foods and you'll find if you increase these in your diet, while at the same time decreasing the amount of fat, you will feel more energized.

• • • • • • • • • • • • • • • • • • • • • • • • • • • • • • • • • • • • • •

## YOUR BODY AND MIND NEED THESE FOODS:
## 1. Simple Carbohydrates vs. Complex Carbohydrates

SIMPLE= Quick sugar burst in the body

*White sugar, white flour products (bread, cakes, pastries, cookies, crackers), fruit juice, sodas, candy, ice cream, most desserts, corn syrup, maple syrup, glucose, fructose, honey, dextrose, sucrose, etc.*

Simple carbohydrates require almost no digestion by the body, they are used almost immediately. This flood of sugar creates a reaction in your body which then rushes to get the flood under control. So, soon after eating these foods you feel energized but within 45 more minutes you'll feel sluggish again. This "riding the blood sugar rapids" has a negative effect overall on your energy level.

COMPLEX= Slow sugar drip in the body

*Whole grains: rice, barley, millet, cereals, grits, bread, rye, quinoa, etc. Whole grain breads, pastas, crackers. Vegetables—fresh & frozen are best. Fruits—fresh & frozen are best. Beans—pinto, black, kidney, etc.*

The above foods are true energy foods. Because they require quite a bit of digestion before the sugar is released into your system you end up with a very steady energy flow. Complex carbohydrates allow your body to manage the sugar that comes from these foods in a controlled fashion. ***Pick most from this list!***

### Try this experiment on yourself:
One morning for breakfast, eat a bagel—the typical kind made from white flour. The next day, eat a whole grain bagel (you'll probably have to go to the health food store for this kind). Pay attention each day to when you feel your energy "dip". Most people are amazed to find how much longer their energy stays up with the whole grain bagel. How about you?

Carbohydrates should make up 60-70% of your daily diet. 90% of this total should be complex carbohydrate

## 2. Protein

What do protein foods do for your body?

Protein foods are used to make up your physical body. Touch your hair and skin, flex a muscle and you are touching protein. In addition, proteins are used inside your cells to make a variety of substances such as hormones.

Fifteen percent isn't very much…don't we need more than that?

No. Think about it, if you sat down and ate 10 steaks, 40 eggs, 15 glasses of milk all in one day, would you wake up tomorrow with hair down to your waist, and muscles as big as the Hulk? No, of course not. That's because your body can only use so much protein each day. It can't convert a lot of protein at once, thus eating huge quantities is just a waste of food. Fifteen percent of your daily diet from protein is plenty!

_____

otein should
ovide only 15% of
ur daily diet.

_____

## 3. Fat

Fat is necessary in the diet to make hormones and a wide variety of different chemicals used throughout the system. In addition, fat creates an insulation around the body to help us stay warm and cool. Still, it must be limited in the diet, as excess fat clogs arteries and veins, leading to heart disease.

_____

maximum of 25-30% of your daily diet
an come from fat. New studies are
eginning to suggest that 20% might be
etter.

_____

### Protein foods:

Meat—beef, lamb, pork
Poultry—chicken, turkey, duck, eggs
Fish—tuna, shrimp, clams etc.
Dairy—milk, cheese, yogurt etc.
Beans—pinto, black, navy etc.

### Fat Foods:

Meat*—beef, lamb, pork
Poultry*—chicken, turkey, duck, eggs
Dairy*—milk, cheese, butter, margarine, ice cream, sour cream, cottage cheese, etc.
Oils—all oils are 100% fat
Processed foods—foods cooked in oil or that have oils or butter added to them, such as cakes, cookies, pies, donuts, etc.
Candy—chocolate bars, yogurt covered raisins, etc.

*You'll notice that these foods are also in the protein food list. So keep in mind, while eating beef, whole dairy foods and the skin on the chicken, that you are actually eating fat as well as eating protein. In fact, in the case of beef, many of the most popular cuts we enjoy are more than 50% fat!

### From junk food junkie to now: The difference is amazing.

"If you ate better, you'd feel better," declared Patti as I bit into my burger.

"What I eat has nothing to do with my body," I replied smugly. "But if it will make you happy, I promise not to eat meat when we're together." So, to humor a friend I began eating better.

At the time, I was a major junk food junkie, eating at my favorite fast food joints as much as five times per week. Vegetables were the shredded lettuce and anemic tomato topping my burger, along with the ever popular vegetable—french fries.

I was 21 and believed that "if you're thin you must be healthy" and I was thin! Five foot six and 100 lbs., what could be healthier? Me. Despite my thinness, I was sick all the time, had constant headaches, intestinal problems and depressions that would send me to bed for three days. I truly believed, even though I had a college degree and was well educated, that the food I ate had nothing to do with my body.

### The educated fool!

When I started eating better I was amazed. My friend taught me good nutrition and within a year my health improved tremendously. The problems I mentioned above were gone. Now, 20 years later, I eat great foods, feel terrific, and know that everything I eat has something to do with my body and mind. And I'm just as thin, only now I'm healthy! When people ask me what I eat to stay so thin I say, "Anything I want." They say it isn't possible but I say it is: the key is in what you want. When you're committed to building a healthy Life Puzzle, you want great foods, not junk!

### I tried eating healthy and didn't see any results. Give me back my ice cream and pizza.

That seems to be the cry of the day. Food is seen as a source of instant gratification. In a world filled with so many pressures, many of us use food to give us a quick fix pick me up. Bad day? Eat a box of chocolates, indulge in a juicy steak dinner with all the extras.

The recent push in the medical world to encourage people to eat healthier diets has rebounded to the opposite extreme. Expecting to see dramatic results after cutting out the fat, it was easy to abandon this health kick when no obvious results were seen at all. Too bad, because these earlier attempts to change one's diet were a start towards becoming more self-responsible and building a healthy Life Puzzle. But now we're retrenching and heading right back into the 0-5 side of the Choosing Continuum: do enough to get by, eat what I want, when I want it, and without regard to my body, mind or spirit needs.

Healthy eating is a lifestyle that doesn't produce sensational or quick fix results. What it does produce is individuals who are energized, vibrant and more capable of running their lives proactively than those who are still in the poor eating habit. But it happens little by little over the years. It prevents you from being sluggish during your middle to late years of life. It's a part of your Life Puzzle and only you can decide to make the commitment.

# The great nutrition mystery! (There really isn't one.)

**M**y experience in the past 20 years has taught me that most people have a complete misunderstanding of good nutrition. On top of this, there is a misconception that in order to understand good nutrition, one needs lots of education and training in order to feel competent in designing a healthy diet. Nothing could be further from the truth.

## Good nutrition is simple and it always will be.

We may have only begun studying nutrition as a science in the last 100 years, but today we've come to realize that the basics of good nutrition haven't changed in a million years. The foods we would have eaten in the year 708 BCE, are the same types of foods we will be eating in the year 2021.

So what you really need to get under your belt is the nutrition basics. Once you understand these—and they aren't hard to understand—then you can walk into any grocery store or restaurant and make selections based on what your body needs.

## Eat with your body in mind.

Why do you eat? One reason, of course, is to keep your body alive. In fact, that's the only real reason you need to eat. But if that was the only reason there

probably wouldn't be so much confusion about what, and what not, to eat.

You also eat for emotional reasons. Different foods tend to pick you up emotionally. Foods such as chocolate, coffee and sweets generally make you feel good. Other times you use food for a stress release. When we get nervous or upset...we eat. A tremendous amount of our eating is not from hunger but because our emotions tell us to. This is reactive eating and usually we choose foods that do very little to improve our bodies.

When it comes right down to it, the only real reason you need to eat is to keep your body and mind healthy and alive. Now I'm not suggesting this means you have to give up all the foods you love but aren't all that nutritious. That's just not going to happen. But what needs to happen, if you're going to build your healthy Life Puzzle, is for you to make a shift from the reactive side of the Choosing Continuum to the pro-active side.

Instead of the reactive "I want to eat what I want to eat," move instead to the pro-active, "I want to eat with respect for my body and mind, first...emotions second." And that means waking up each day and asking yourself: "What do I need to provide my body today?"

## No mystery here.

If you focus each day on meeting your body's needs, you'll discover that good nutrition is very, very simple. The basic needs don't change and aren't going to any time soon. Learn and use the basics and you'll discover a new, reenergized body and mind that finds itself more and more capable of building a healthy Life Puzzle.

## Your children are depending on you.

It's true that you have probably been raised without the information you need to create a truly healthy, nutritious lifestyle. Which is kind of incredible when you consider how important the foods you eat are to your body, mind...and life. I remember when I was beginning to learn about nutrition, I thought to myself...why wasn't I taught this? I have to live in this body for 80+ years if all goes well. Why didn't my parents and school teachers think it was important to teach me good nutrition?

*Two reasons:*

#1. Until the late '70's we did not have enough information about the value of good nutrition to realize how vital it is to the human body and mind. Thus, no one really knew what to teach me.

#2. Without the information no one thought it necessary to teach nutrition. It was completely taken for granted that short of starving to death, as long as you were eating food, it didn't really matter what you ate.

## We know better now. Will we put this knowledge to use?

Yes, things have changed dramatically. Today we know that the quality and quantity of food we eat dramatically impacts our minds and bodies. We must teach this to our children. They depend on us to bring them the information they need to create their healthy Life Puzzle.

We teach best by example, so it is important for you to learn good nutrition basics: first for yourself, second for your children. Then live it every day.

## Fresh and whole: keep it simple.

Food processing has become a multi-billion dollar industry. In the last 30 years, more and more of our foods have been processed, enriched, preserved and altered. Some of this has been beneficial. With longer shelf life, a wide variety of foods have become available that would not have been possible without this.

The downside of all this processing is that the quality has been lessened in much of our food. We've become accustomed to boxed and packaged foods with lots of preservatives, food colorings, and chemical additives. Through processing, we've stripped whole foods of their vitamin, mineral and fiber content. This results in much lower quality of foods and this impacts our bodies and mind.

For example: bread. A food as simple as bread used to provide a good portion of a day's nutrition needs. Made from whole grains, breads were heavy and solid but packed with vitamins, minerals, complex carbohydrates for energy, a small amount of protein and fat. It was an ideal food. However, in the '40's and '50's large bakeries took over and instead of whole grain breads, processed white flour breads that were light and fluffy were introduced. Being ignorant of good nutrition, we didn't realize then the difference in nutritional value from one to the other. Mothers stopped baking bread at home (an all day affair before the advent of the automatic bread makers we have now!) and we became addicted to white bread. However, white bread has had the fiber and much of the vitamin and mineral content removed. This is now a low energy food because most of the nutrition is missing!

We need to return to fresh, whole foods again. That will be a part of your Life Puzzle building—fresh, whole, simple foods.

## No need to go cold turkey!

If you're getting a little nervous that in order to have a healthy Life Puzzle you're going to have to give up 99% of your current diet, let me calm your fears right now. That will not be necessary, and in fact, I would highly recommend against it.

Taking charge of your nutritional lifestyle is a life-long process. The hardest part, like any new project we undertake, is to just get started. You aren't trying to perfect your diet change overnight.

## Lots of small changes add up to a lifestyle change.

There's really no need to go cold turkey and cut out everything you like and substitute these with foods you're not so sure about. My experience has shown that you will be more successful by making one or two changes, incorporating them for a month or two and then adding another change.

## Twenty one days makes a habit: That's three weeks!

It takes three weeks of consistently doing one behavior before it will become a natural part of you. Whether remembering to buckle your seat belt or remembering to have a piece of fruit for your mid-morning snack, you'll need to concentrate on it for at least three weeks before it becomes a normal thought and behavior process.

So don't give up quickly and don't take on too much, too soon. Choose just one or two things in each three week phase and you're more likely to win. This will reinforce itself over and over again.

## There is no right way to do this, there is only your way.

I will make many suggestions in the next few pages. And all of them will be good for making your Life Puzzle. But you choose what works for you now and go at your own pace. After a while this becomes a way of life more than a way of change.

I can remember when I first started making my transition. I told my girlfriend, "If you think I'm giving up my steak, you are crazy!" She said that was fine, I didn't need to give up meat, just eat it a little less so I could add a few other foods instead. Little by little, over the course of two years, I added more and more of these foods. I didn't really notice what I was giving up because it happened so casually.

The biggest thing I noticed after my

first year of eating transition was that eating became a much more conscious act of choice instead of the old unconscious reaction or habit…"Yeah, uh, I'll have a double cheeseburger, fries and cola."

## It will work for you too. Go slow.

If you've tried before to make a radical diet change, or this is your first attempt at it, the key is to not rush it. All foods are allowable! And they always will be. Today I eat anything I want but I am truly conscious of what I want. I don't want french fries 99.9% of the time. But on that .1% moment I eat it and enjoy it. Same for you!

## The Nutrition Basics: Six Building Blocks

| Protein 15% | Carbohydrates 60-70% | Fat 20-30% |
|---|---|---|
| **Water** One-half your body weight in ounces. | **Fiber** 30 grams | **Vitamins and Minerals** |

## Use the Nutrition Pyramid:

This will give you the foods necessary for the Nutrition Building Blocks.

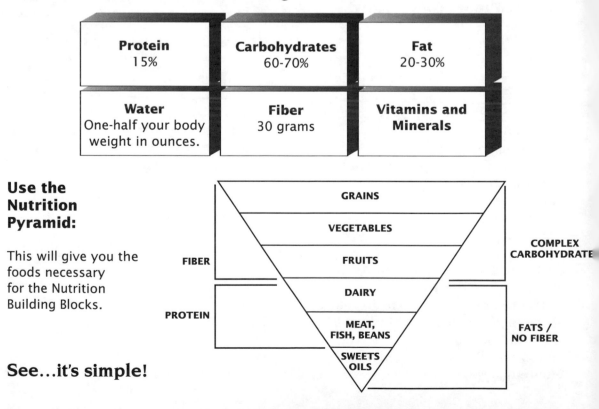

FIBER

PROTEIN

GRAINS

VEGETABLES

FRUITS

DAIRY

MEAT, FISH, BEANS

SWEETS OILS

COMPLEX CARBOHYDRATE

FATS / NO FIBER

## See…it's simple!

# Fiber, what's the big deal?

Fiber, fiber, everywhere! You see it on commercials, and all sorts of health newsletters shout the virtues of a high fiber diet. How come? Colon health.

Fiber is the outer layer of fruits, vegetables, grains and beans. It's the skin of an apple, the brown part of brown rice, the outer covering of beans. This fiber is indigestible by the body and can't be absorbed. Thus, it ends up in the large intestine where it creates bulk to the stool.

As the fiber mixes with the other undigested matter, it helps to firm it up. This firm stool provides resistance in the colon and strengthens the colon muscle. A strong colon muscle pushes the stool through and uh, um…out the other end.

No fiber in your diet? This leads to a weak colon, constipation and other colon problems. If you eat lots of processed foods you'll have a weak colon. We know that many Americans have weak colons because the #2 nonprescription drug purchased in this country is laxative products.

Eating a diet that's high in fiber means it's filled with fresh fruit, vegetables, whole grains, beans and fresh water. That will create a healthy colon and a healthy you!

## What's the best source of fiber: Whole, natural, fresh foods.

As man has evolved over the centuries, his body has become accustomed and dependent on eating natural foods: fresh fruits, vegetables, whole grains and beans from the fields. Most of our time on earth has been spent eating these foods and our colon needs them.

What man hasn't been used to eating is large quantities of meat, processed flour products, packaged and boxed foods that are made in the laboratory. These foods have no fiber in them and lead to poor health.

### It's all about energy!

Calories, what are they? Food provides you with protein, fat or carbohydrates which are used by your body. The way we measure the value of these foods is through calories. Calories are the amount of energy a food provides:

#### CALORIES = ENERGY

So, how much energy does 1 gram of fat, carbohydrate or protein give the body? That's the 9:4:4 rule:

1 gram of FAT = 9 calories
CARBOHYDRATES = 4 calories
PROTEIN = 4 calories.

As you can see, 1 gram of FAT, has twice as many calories as a gram of carbohydrate or protein. This is why fat grams add up so quickly in the amount of calories:

10 grams of protein = 40 calories
10 grams of fat = 90 calories

*It takes twice as long to use the energy found in fat grams than it does to use the energy found in carbohydrates or protein. That's what makes fat so darn fattening!*

## Vitamins and Minerals: how important are they?

Well, let's put it this way: without vitamins and minerals your body and mind could not function. Vitamins and minerals aren't food; what they do is make the food you eat work correctly in your body. They create chain reaction processes—if they're not available at the right time and in the right quantities, then your body doesn't act right.

For example: Vitamin D and Calcium. We know that Vitamin D is necessary for bone formation. A child who doesn't receive enough Vitamin D during the bone growing stage will end up with weak, soft bones. That's because calcium needs the Vitamin D so it can work correctly. If there's not enough Vitamin D, the calcium leaves the body instead of staying in the bone. All of this could have been prevented with proper nutrition. Milk, cheese, broccoli, brussels sprouts, carrots, and yogurt all contain Vitamin D and the mineral calcium.

So you can see the value of vitamins and minerals. When they're missing, your body is greatly affected, sometimes, as in the case stated above, in dramatic, life changing ways. But lack of vitamins and minerals can also have less dramatic effects. B-complex vitamins are used by the nerves in a lot of ways. When we are low on B's, daily stress can overwhelm us, creating anxiety and tension that leaves you short tempered and irritable. It is these many subtle influences that vitamins and minerals have on the body and mind that are just as important.

## Should you supplement?

For as many experts who say you shouldn't, I can find you an equal number who say you should. That means you have to make up your own mind. And the best way to do this is to look at your diet. The natural source for vitamins and minerals is this: food. God in his/her infinite wisdom decided to put the catalyst that is needed by the food…in the food! Pretty amazing, wouldn't you say? I agree.

So how is your diet? Are you eating good quantities of fresh fruit (2 each day), vegetables (2-3 cups), whole grains, brown rice, whole grain bread (six 1/2 c. servings per day), beans (1 c. per day), skim milk dairy products, and low fat cheese (2 servings), and a limited quantity of meat, poultry and fish (no more than two, 4 oz. servings). If you are eating like this, it's likely that you are getting a sufficient daily minimum quantity of vitamins and minerals.

Or is this your diet: a white flour biscuit, toast, donut, cinnamon bun and coffee for breakfast; a sandwich and soda for lunch; and a big meat centered dinner? Do you eat regularly at fast food restaurants with burgers and fries, fried chicken, or tacos as a norm? Do you eat out five or more times per week? Do fruits and vegetables rot in the refrigerator because you never quite get around to eating them? If you're eating the "American" way—mile a minute, on the go—then you probably need two things: First to change your diet, second, vitamin and mineral supplementation.

A good multivitamin/mineral supplement (from a health food store, not the drug store) is a good bet for almost all of us. For those who eat well, it's a support, for those who eat poorly, it's a necessity.

# Nutrition Quiz

Get the basics under your belt. Quick, cover the right side of this page, so you don't peek at the answers. This quiz is really a learning tool, so don't fret over guessing the answer. Realize that the goal is to learn the answers on the right so they become part of your daily living knowledge about healthy nutrition.

1. What foods should make up most of your daily diet?

   1. *Carbohydrates should make up 60-70% of your daily diet.*

2. Simple or complex carbohydrates: which is most important for your diet?

   2. *Complex carbohydrates are the most important foods for my diet.*

3. Name four different sources of complex carbohydrates.

   3. *Grains, beans, fruits, and vegetables.*

4. What do carbohydrates do for your body? What do they turn into?

   4. *Carbohydrate foods provide energy for my body. They turn into sugar which is burned as fuel.*

5. Name four different grains.

   5. *Whole wheat, brown rice, barley, millet.*

6. Name several foods that are made from grains.

   6. *Pasta, cereals, breads*

7. Why does too much sugar, honey, and processed white flour foods hurt the body?

   7. *These are simple carbohydrates. They produce a blood sugar rush with an energy high followed by an energy low. This energy roller coaster hurts the body.*

8. What do protein foods do for your body?

   8. *Protein makes up hair, skin, and muscles. It also makes hormones.*

9. True or False: We need lots of protein every day.

   9. *False: we only need about 15% of our daily diet from protein. Eating excess is a waste.*

10. Name five sources for protein foods.

    10. *Meat, fish, poultry, dairy, beans.*

11. Rank these five protein sources, from those that have the least amount of fat content to those with the highest amount of fat content.

    11. *Beans, most fish, skim milk products, poultry, whole milk products, meat.*

12. True or false: Your body is mostly water.

    12. *True; you are mostly water. If we squeezed out the water, there would be very little of you left!*

*—continued on next page.*

13. How much water should you drink each day?

13. *One-half your body weight in ounces. For example, 100 lbs. = 50 oz., 200 lbs. = 100 oz.*

14. Name several sources for water. Which is the very best source?

14. *Juice, soda, coffee, tea, fresh fruit and vegetables. Best source: plain water.*

15. Why does your body need fat?

15. *Insulates the body for temperature control. Helps in hormone production.*

16. Name five sources of fat.

16. *Beef, whole dairy products (cheese and milk), oils, lard, chips, fried foods, ice cream.*

17. True or false: One gram of fat has twice as many calories as a gram of protein or carbohydrates?

17. *True.*

18. What problems are caused by eating excess fat?

18. *Obesity, clogged arteries and veins, heart disease, Type II Diabetes.*

19. What does your body need most from food: energy, skin and muscle production or insulation?

19. *Energy from food = complex carbohydrates: grains, beans, fruits and vegetables.*

20. What does fiber do for your body?

20. *Fiber is roughage that helps to keep your colon functioning properly.*

21. Name four sources for fiber foods.

21. *Whole grains (brown rice, whole wheat, millet, etc.), beans, fruit (with skin on), vegetables.*

22. True or false: When a food is processed at the factory, most of the fiber remains intact.

22. *False; most of the fiber is removed.*

23. True or False: Vitamins and minerals are foods for my body.

23. *False; vitamins and minerals act as catalysts to make the food you eat work right.*

24. What is a good way to determine the quality of a food that I am about to eat?

24. *Is the food in its most natural form? Example: fruit—fresh or canned? Fresh is best.*

25. Name a breakfast, lunch and dinner that would provide you with a quality diet for one day.

25. *Whole grain cereal with skim milk, pasta with sauteed vegetables and bean chili, with salad and low fat dressing, whole grain rolls.*

# *Another piece of the puzzle: Here's what's going on inside.*

**D**o you ever wonder what happens to food after you swallow it? Or is it out of sight, out of mind? It's important to understand what your body does with the food you eat so you can fully appreciate how to feed your body in a way that benefits it...and doesn't harm it.

Digestion starts right in your mouth. As you chew food you break it into small pieces. The smaller you make the pieces, the easier it will be for your stomach. The other part of digestion going on in the mouth is chemical. The addition of saliva starts the chemical breakdown of food. The more saliva and the smaller the pieces, the better your total digestion will be.

After swallowing, food goes to the stomach. The stomach does two types of digestion. *#1. Squeezing & Crushing:* Your stomach is a muscle that squeezes tightly around the food you eat. In this way it takes the carrots, pasta and hamburger you ate and crushes it into a very soft ball of food (called chyme). *#2. Chemical:* At the same time your stomach is filled with acids. These acids act mainly on protein foods to chemically alter them. Proteins are known as amino acids and they come in chains. When mixed with stomach acids these chains break down. This is important because later on the body will take these amino acids and reform them into different chains to make skin, hair, muscles and hormones for your body.

*Transit time:* this is the amount of time food stays in a particular digestive organ. Transit time for the stomach is 3-4 hours. During this time, food will slowly make its way from the stomach to the small intestine.

The small intestine is a long, narrow tube, about 1-2 inches wide and as long as 25 feet. Like a Slinky, the small intestine folds in on itself, so you can pack a lot of small intestine into a compact area. All the digestion in the small intestine is chemical. With the help of the pancreas and liver, fats are chemically altered. The pancreas also helps with carbohydrate digestion and the final stage of protein digestion. Food travels through the small intestine and chemicals attack it along the way, breaking it down into smaller and smaller pieces. When they're small enough, the food is absorbed through the wall of the small intestine into the blood stream. Once in the blood stream, it will be carried throughout the body and be used as necessary. For example, that apple you just ate will break down into sugar. Once this sugar is in the blood stream, it will pass by the brain. In order to think, your brain needs sugar, so this sugar will be used to create the energy to think!

Transit time in the small intestine is 3-5 hours. What happens if it doesn't break down small enough to get through the wall of the small intestine? It's shipped off to the large intestine. The large intestine is your body's waste disposal center! Anything that wasn't digested, along with dead cells that have been removed throughout the body (cells are dying constantly in the body, while new ones are being made), ends up here. The large intestine is a muscle whose job is to push fecal matter (stool) through this tube until it reaches the anus and is removed when you go to the toilet. I know this isn't very genteel, but it is very important for you to understand. Because when the large intestine isn't working well, all sorts of problems result.

## If it's good at the top, it will be good at the bottom.

As mentioned earlier, fiber is very necessary to keep the large intestine muscle strong. When we eat a high fiber diet the large intestine will have the strength to push out the fecal matter. When we eat a low fiber diet the muscle gets weaker and weaker. Over time it is too weak. That's when we see problems like constipation, spastic colon, and recurring diarrhea. And beyond colon problems, when the body is not eliminating fecal matter daily, problems such as arthritis, psoriasis, headaches and bloated intestinal tract can occur.

You can prevent all of these problems through good nutrition. The stomach, small intestine and large intestine are all quite familiar with fresh fruits, vegetables, whole grains and beans. It's been eating them for hundreds of thousands of years.

On the other hand, your body isn't accustomed to eating jelly donuts, saltines, cookies, lots of red meat (most of our history we ate very little meat because it was very difficult to catch before the advent of guns), processed cheese food, fruit roll-ups, fried chicken, white bread, cinnamon buns, iceberg lettuce (invented in the 1950's), pepperoni pizza, etc. As we've learned how to manufacture foods, we've removed the fiber, vitamins and minerals and left a wholly unnatural product. Our mouths may swallow them but our stomach, small intestine and large intestine are scratching themselves wondering what the heck to do with it!

## It's your body. You choose how to feed it.

Your body will tolerate extremely poor nutrition for a long time. It is actually quite amazing that it does, considering some of the absolutely terrible stuff that we feed it. Maybe it's too bad we don't fall apart after a month of eating poor quality foods, then we'd all become much more aware of our daily nutrition.

As you read through this section, I hope you've come to the conclusion that quality nutrition greatly impacts your Life Puzzle. Not dramatically, or overnight, but over the course of your life. The better you eat throughout your life, the more dynamic, well-balanced and healthy a Life Puzzle you will create. But it's up to you to choose to feed your body with love and care.

# *Menus & Recipes*

There are 30 menus on the next few pages. The meals were designed around the "Pyramid of Nutrition," so you will notice that many of the meals use a variety of different grains and accent the use of lots of vegetables. This is the foundation for healthy eating.

## High density nutrition.

We can only eat so many calories per day, but it isn't the number but the quality of those calories that is most important. For example, six Snickers bars would provide 1500 calories but most of us realize that we're not going to get the nutrition our bodies need if all we eat each day is six Snickers bars.

The recipes found here are designed to give you a low fat, high fiber diet which packs the maximum nutrition into the calories eaten. This is known as high density nutrition: Maximum nutrition in the least amount of calories.

## Looks can be deceiving.

We've become accustomed to seeing a big chunk of meat on our plates, with either rice or potatoes on the side and a vegetable or perhaps a salad as a typical meal. This visual picture provides a comfort zone and tricks us into thinking that we now have a balanced meal. But we don't.

Change the look, change your diet. Everything you read about nutrition will tell you to lower the fat content and increase your fiber. The only way to do that is to shift the look of your dinner plate. You will find that the recipes in this book do just that.

## The new look.

Many of the menus in this book will seem a little different because they look different. But you can feel confident that all of them are based on sound nutrition principles and will help you and your family begin to transition to healthier eating.

I can remember when I first started this transition away from the typical meat and potato eating…there was a little voice back there saying, "You're going to starve to death, you're not eating enough protein." Fortunately, I told those voices to shut up and kept on telling myself, "Yes, this is a healthier way to eat, give it a chance." And I'm glad I did. I discovered after about a year of this transition that I felt better, had more energy and actually found that eating the old way left me tired and sluggish. So be patient, give it a chance and you'll feel better too.

**Cooking note:**
The way the menus are arranged, begin making each meal with the first item at the top of the page, then continue on to the next item. This way you'll get the most time consuming item on its way. Usually, this will be a grain such as rice or millet which require time to steam but doesn't require you to do much else with it.

These menus were put together so you can make them in 10-30 minutes. However, feel free to mix and match different recipes to make a meal that works for you.

# The Pantry List

*You don't have to have all of these all of the time, but the more of them you routinely have the more options you'll have when you walk through the door and say, "Gosh, what shall I make for dinner?"*

## Frozen Foods:
VEGETABLES
*Keep a variety of your favorite frozen veggies.*
Corn
Peas
Broccoli
Spinach
Cauliflower
*(Always keep at least 3 on hand.)*

MEAT/FISH/POULTRY
Fresh ground turkey
Boned turkey breast
Chicken breasts: skinned
  & boned
Beef strips
Fish: flounder, sole, orange roughy, salmon, a favorite white fish of your choice.

DAIRY
Shredded low fat cheese:
Monterey Jack,
Cheddar, Mozzarella, Feta
Eggbeaters

PASTA
Tortellini: cheese, spinach, etc.
*(This is usually found in the refrigerated section near the eggs or milk. It freezes easily in its own package.)*

## Great Grains:
Brown Rice
Millet
Cous Cous
Basmati Rice
Barley (quick cooking)
Bulgur wheat

## Canned Beans:
Pinto
Kidney
Garbanzo
Black eyed peas
Lentils
Black bean

## Canned or Packaged Foods:
Mushroom soup (low fat)
Cooking wine, white & red
Corn Flake Crumbs
Bread crumbs
Butter Buds/Molly McButter
Mandarin orange slices
Pineapple chunks
Honey
Sesame tahini
Red wine vinegar
Rice wine vinegar
Water chestnuts
Bamboo shoots
Artichoke hearts (in water)
Soy sauce-lite
Sesame oil, hot & plain
Black olives
Vegetarian refried beans
Vegetarian chili
Parmesan cheese
Cooking spray
(Butter flavored & plain)
Tomatoes:
   Paste, puree, whole,
   stewed and sauce
Prepared spaghetti sauce
Salsa/Taco sauce
Pesto Sauce
Salad Dressings
Non-Fat Ranch
Non-Fat Italian
Lite Caesar
Non-Fat Thousand Island

*Garlic and Ginger can be bought in a jar, already chopped or crushed. This saves lots of time as it allows you to open the 'frig, grab the jar, twist off the top and— presto!—take a half teaspoon and you're on your way!*

**Bread:**
*Whenever possible, use whole grain bread products. Avoid "refined" or "enriched".*
Pita bread
Whole wheat bread
Whole grain rolls
Whole grain "burger" buns
Whole wheat tortillas
Bagels
Seasoned stuffing mix
Corn muffins
*(Keep at least one pita bread, burger buns and whole wheat tortillas in the freezer at all times.)*

**Refrigerated:**
Eggs
Non-fat plain yogurt
Skim milk
Lemon juice

**Dried Pasta:**
*Keep a wide variety of pasta shapes on hand...from angel hair to ziti! Also, whenever you're making pasta....make the whole box. Leftover pasta is a wonderful snack.*

*Good pasta can be purchased at health food stores. Unfortunately, many of the pastas we purchase at regular grocery stores are made from refined flours. Look for those that say whole grain or 100% Semolina or Durum flour.*

**Spices:**
*Keep a wide variety of spices in your rack. Add one new spice per week and before you know it, a full spice rack!*

NECESSITIES
Garlic, ginger, basil, chili powder, cumin, oregano, parsley, black pepper, sesame oil (plain & hot), mustard, Old Bay Seasoning

SPICE COMBINATIONS
*At all times, keep at least two of these that you like on hand:*
Mrs. Dash, Spice Island, Spike, etc. (there are lots of different ones to pick from)

NEXT IN LINE
bay leaves, curry, dill, paprika, sesame seeds, thyme.

**Fresh Produce:**
Potatoes for baking
Onions
Acorn Squash*
Butternut Squash*
Vegetables for either veggie sticks
or salads
Green peppers
Carrots
Lettuce
Red or green cabbage
Cucumbers
Radishes
Avocado**

*These store very well, so keep plenty on hand.

**There are a couple of recipes that ask for avocado...you can keep it frozen or buy it when you need it for these recipes.

There is a shopping list at the end of the chapter that you can make copies of to take with you to the grocery store. It includes all the foods in this pantry list.

Fresh is great, but don't panic if you open up the 'frig and discover the carrots have gone limp, the peppers are squishy soft and the cukes are shriveled up. It happens to all of us. That's why you keep the frozen veggies in stock too. So, if you're making one of the menus and it calls for fresh veggie sticks and the one's you have look more like noodles, substitute with a frozen selection. There, problem solved!

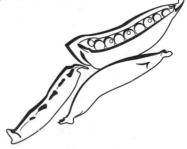

# Tortellini Twist

*This is a "twist" on the typical stir-fry or typical pasta dinner…
it just depends which way you look at the twist!*

1 pkg. fresh Tortellini (you can find these in the refrigerated section of most stores.)
1 c. sweet red pepper, chopped
1 small onion, chopped
2 carrots, cut into thin strips
1 pt. cherry tomatoes, halved
1 can artichoke hearts, drained and quartered
1 tsp. dried basil
1 tsp. dried oregano
1/4 c. Fat free Italian salad dressing

*You can use different vegetables. Use what you've got such as peppers, cauliflower, broccoli, or zucchini. If you don't have fresh, use frozen beans, broccoli, cauliflower, lima beans, etc.*

Cook tortellini according to package directions, omitting salt and oil. While tortellini cooks, place 2 Tbls. Italian dressing in saute pan and over medium heat, add vegetables and cook lightly. Add basil and oregano while cooking. When vegetables are almost done, add cooked tortellini that's been rinsed and drained and the remaining salad dressing. Cover and saute 2 more minutes.

*Variations:* Take a skinned and boned chicken breast cut into small pieces and saute 5 minutes or until cooked, then add the Italian dressing and vegetables. One breast is sufficient for two people.

*Serving ideas:* This meal is quite complete with the pasta and vegetables as is. However, if you want, add some good sourdough bread or other whole grain wheat rolls to increase your complex carbohydrate servings. Avoid serving them with butter, which just adds extra fat grams that will end up on your hips or clogging your arteries. Who needs it!?

Serves 3-4.
*(If you have four big adults, this recipe may only feed three of them, but in general, this should serve four.)*

# Quick Stack Bean Burritos
# with Tex-Mex Rice

### Tex-Mex Rice

1 c. brown rice
1-1/2 c. water
1 small onion, chopped

1 8 oz. can whole tomatoes, chopped up,
   retain liquid
1 tsp. cumin
1/8 tsp. cayenne pepper

Bring water to a boil. Add rice, onions, tomatoes, retained tomato liquid and seasonings. Cover, cook on low heat approximately 25 minutes or until all water has been absorbed.

### Quick Stack Bean Burritos

8 Whole wheat tortillas
1 16 oz. can Vegetarian Refried Beans,
   lightly warmed
8 oz. non-fat plain yogurt
1/3 c. red pepper, chopped
1/3 c. sliced green onion

1 c. low fat or non-fat cheddar cheese,
   shredded
1/4 c. sliced black olives
2 avocados, mashed
2 c. red leaf lettuce, shredded

On platter, lay one tortilla, spread with 1/2 mashed avocado. On second tortilla, spread 1/2 the beans, place on top of first avocado tortilla. Lay third tortilla on top of beans, sprinkle 1/2 the lettuce on top. On fourth tortilla, spread 1/2 the yogurt with 1/2 of the pepper, green onion and cheddar cheese, lay on top of third tortilla. On fifth tortilla, spread remaining avocado, place on previous tortilla. On sixth tortilla, spread remaining beans. On seventh tortilla, sprinkle with remaining lettuce and finish eighth tortilla topped with remaining yogurt, pepper, onions, cheese and olives. Cut into 4 quarters.

Serves 4.

*Brown rice rules!*
   *You will notice the recipes in this book often use brown rice. That's because brown rice is much more nutritious than white rice. The brown portion contains fiber and many B-complex vitamins which are good for you.*
   *If you are "white rice addicted", transition yourself! Start with 1/2 white, 1/2 brown and little by little increase the brown, decrease white.*

---

**Check your
fresh pantry!**
Must haves:
Avocado
Red leaf lettuce
Red pepper

# Chicken in Mushroom Sauce with Cous Cous and Steamed Green Beans

## Chicken

4  4 oz. chicken breasts, boned and skinned
1 can low-fat, mushroom soup
2 Tbls. water

*Make sure you use a low-fat mushroom soup. Campbell's Healthy Request is good. Regular mushroom soup can have as many as 22 grams of fat in it!*

Place chicken breasts in microwave safe dish.  Top with mushroom soup and 2 Tbls. water. Cook on high for 6 minutes, turning the dish halfway, at three minutes.  Let sit 3 minutes after cooking, before serving.

## Cous Cous

1-1/2 c. water
1 c. Cous Cous

2 tsp. Seasoning: this can be any type of seasoning  combination you like such as a Mrs. Dash, Spike, VegIt, etc.

Add seasoning to water. Bring to a boil, add Cous Cous, cover and remove from stove. Let sit 5 minutes.

## Green Beans

1 lb. fresh green beans
  or, 1 pkg. frozen beans: If fresh, clean and cut into reasonable size.

*Stove-top:*  Place water and steamer in pan, fill with  beans.  Over medium high heat, bring to a boil and let steam until they reach desired doneness depending on how crisp your family likes their vegetables approx 3-8 minutes.  If frozen, follow directions on package.

Serves 4.

*Cous Cous:*

*This is Mediterranean pasta.  It's quite good and extremely simple to make. Also, you can create a million different tastes, depending on the particular spice you add to it.  Go with curry, chili powder, ginger and garlic, soy sauce…unlimited potential depending on what mood you're in! You can also buy cous cous with different flavored spice packets included.*

*Hold the Butter, Please!*

*We put butter or margarine on a lot of our vegetables but this is a very fattening habit. One tablespoon of butter has 12 grams of fat in it! Unnecessary fat grams do nothing for your health but add tons to your waistline and your arteries over a lifetime!*

*Try Molly McButter or Butter Buds instead, or try using different spices such as dill, onions, or a Mrs. Dash combination for a lower fat taste.*

# Stir-Fry:
# The Ultimate One Pan Meal

Here's the basic recipe. From here add and change whatever vegetables you like, substitute chicken, beef, pork, shrimp, tofu, or scallops. Stir-fry seasonings can run the whole line from ginger and garlic to Italian pesto to Mexican hot to Indian curry. See what I'm getting at? Do not limit yourself. When you get in the kitchen to make a stir-fry, gather the vegetables and meat and cook them with whatever flavor you're in the mood for that night!

4 oz. chicken breast, boned and skinned
   chopped into bite size pieces
1 Tbls. crushed ginger
1 Tbls. crushed garlic
1/4 tsp. sesame oil (you can use hot
   sesame oil for a snappy twist!)

1 c. red and green pepper, sliced
1 medium red onion, chopped
1 c. carrots, sliced
1 c. mushrooms, sliced
1 c. broccoli florets

Coat skillet with cooking spray. Add the ginger, garlic and chicken breast. Cook over medium heat, until chicken is cooked through (3-5 minutes). Then add vegetables and cook until vegetables reach desired firmness. To speed cooking times, cover and let the vegetables steam. It take about 10-12 minutes to cook. Sprinkle sesame oil over cooked vegetables.

## Add a grain or beans for increased fiber

Rice, millet or barley are all great with stir-fry. Steam some while making the stir-fry!
- 2 c. water, plus 1 c. rice or millet, or
- 3 c. water, plus 1 c. quick cooking barley

   Boil water, add grain, simmer over very low heat, until all water is absorbed. Millet and barley take about 15-20 minutes, brown rice about 25 minutes.

   Stir-Fry is a great, low fat, high fiber meal. To increase the fiber value, throw in some beans, such as garbanzo or black eyed peas.

*Stir-Fry Myth #1.*
*You need a special pan—a wok—in order to do a stir-fry. Not true! You can make stir-fry in any saute pan or skillet that you want.*

*Stir-Fry Myth #2.*
*There is one way to make stir-fry. Not true! Stir-fry can be made lots of different ways. Change the vegetables, change the meat to shrimp, change the seasonings from Oriental to Tex-Mex. It's a great dish to experiment with in the kitchen.*

# Pesto Pasta with Black Eyed Peas
# Low Fat Garlic Bread
# Sliced Vegetable Sticks

1 lb. pasta—whatever shape you like
1 can black eyed peas*, rinsed and drained
Pesto sauce, you can buy packaged or make your own from the recipe below
Whole grain bread, Sourdough or French Bread
Butter flavored cooking spray
Garlic, crushed or powdered

Cook pasta according to directions (omit oil and salt). Drain and set aside. Place black-eyed peas in small dish, cook in microwave oven, HIGH, 1 minute, just before ready to serve.

*Note: if you don't like black-eyed peas…use a bean you do like! Any one will do…garbanzo, pinto, etc.

## Fresh Pesto

2 c. firmly packed fresh basil leaves
1/4 c. pine nuts
1 tsp. garlic, crushed
1/2 c. Parmesan cheese, grated

2 Tbls. Romano cheese
1/2 c. olive oil
1/2 c. water

In food processor, blend basil, pine nuts and garlic. Add cheese, blend again. While blender is on, slowly pour oil into the rest of the mixture. Finish with water. (Note: if you're going to freeze this for later use, omit the water and add it when you actually use it) This is enough for 1 lb. of pasta.

If using packaged pesto, make according to directions (reduce the oil and increase the water called for). Pour over pasta, add beans, toss.

## Bread

Cut whole grain bread in half, spray with buttered flavored cooking spray. Sprinkle with garlic powder or spread with crushed garlic. Wrap in foil and bake at 275 degrees for ten minutes.

## Sliced vegetable sticks round out the meal!

Cut up a carrot or cuke…whatever you like and serve with this nutritious dinner.

Serves 4.

# Steamed Salmon with Mustard Hollandaise
# Barley, Peas and Onion Salad
# Tomato Slices

## Barley, Peas and Onion Salad

This can be served hot or cold, depending on when you cook the barley. The barley can be cooked ahead of time or be leftover from another meal, giving you the option of making this a cold salad. If you're making the barley as you prepare the rest of dinner, it'll be warm.

3 c. water
1 c. quick cooking barley
1-1/2 c. frozen peas, thawed
   (Just place peas in a bowl of water,
   change water several times and
  they'll unthaw quite nicely in about 5 minutes)

1 very small red onion, sliced small
   (about 1/2 c. onion will do)
1/2 Tbls. dried basil
1/2 c. Lite Caesar Salad dressing

Boil water, add barley, cover, then turn heat to low. Cook until all water is absorbed, about 10 minutes. When barley is finished, mix together all remaining ingredients. (If you have time, you can refrigerate this.)

## Steamed Salmon with Mustard Hollandaise

4, 4 oz. Salmon filets
1/2 c. Non-fat plain yogurt
2 Tbls. Mustard (this can be plain yellow, Dijon… whatever kind you have)
1 Tbls. Honey

In microwave safe baking dish, place salmon in 1/4 c. of water or white wine. Cover. Cook on HIGH, 4 minutes for each 1/2 inch thickness of salmon filets, turning dish half-way during cooking time. (For example, if the filets are 1 inch thick, cook 8 minutes). Let fish sit 2 minutes, then check the center of the filet to be sure it is cooked through. Cook an additional minute or two if necessary. While fish cooks; mix together yogurt, mustard and honey.
Remove fish from baking dish, top each portion with a quarter of sauce.

## Tomato slices

Slice 2 tomatoes and place two slices on each plate.

Serves 4.

### Variations
*Don't have salmon? You can use many different fish, especially flounder or orange roughy. For the mustard hollandaise, play around with different mustards as you can get a very tangy mustard to add more pizzazz!*

# Steamed Veggie Plate
# with Rice and Beans

Okay, I admit it, this is a total veggie kind of meal. But it's filling as well as being tasty and healthy. Plus, it takes just a minimum of effort to make while providing your body with lots of vitamins, minerals, fiber and complex carbohydrates.

2 oz. Monterey Jack cheese, shredded or
  one that you like (Use low-fat ones)
2 c. water
1 c. brown rice
1 can Pinto beans…or black eyed peas…
  whichever one you like best,
  rinsed and drained

1 carrot, scrubbed and sliced lengthwise,
  make them fairly thin
1 zucchini, sliced lengthwise,
  make them fairly thin
1 c. broccoli tops
*(You can really use whatever vegetables
you like here.)*

Boil water, add brown rice, lower heat, cook 25 minutes. While rice cooks, prepare veggies. Place veggies in microwave safe bowl, mix together. Add 1/4 c. water, cover and cook HIGH, 3 minutes.

When rice has absorbed just about all the water, remove from stove. Divide into four servings by placing each in a microwave safe bowl (you'll be eating from this bowl, so use something attractive!)

On top of rice, add 3 Tbls. beans, then top with veggies. Place, one bowl at a time in microwave, cover with a paper towel, cook on HIGH, 1 minute. Sprinkle with 1/2 oz. shredded cheese, return to microwave, cook 15 seconds to melt cheese on top. (The other option for melting cheese: wait until all four bowls are set, then place on cookie sheet and run under the broiler for about 30 seconds. Of course, be sure the dishes are broiler safe.)

Serve with Lite soy sauce.

Serves 4.

*That's my whole dinner?*
*Yup…think about it…it really has everything you need in it, whole grain, vegetables, beans, cheese. Mixed together it has a protein in it, because whenever you mix a grain with a bean you create a protein. There's also a sizeable amount of fiber from the brown rice, beans and vegetables. And it's relatively low in fat…about 5-9 grams total for the whole meal.*

# Teriyaki Beef Strips with Onion
# Acorn Squash, "Veggie Stuffed Stuffing"

## Acorn Squash

1 medium acorn squash
1/2 c. water
Butterbuds

> Cut squash in quarters, remove seeds. Place in microwave safe dish, add water, cover tightly. Cook HIGH, 8 minutes, let sit 3 minutes. Serve topped with ButterBuds or Molly McButter.

## Teriyaki Beef Strips

1 lb. beef strips
1 medium red onion*
1 green pepper, sliced
1 tsp. garlic, crushed

1 tsp. ginger, crushed
1/4 c. Lite Soy Sauce
1/4 c. red cooking wine
Cooking spray

> Spray skillet with cooking spray. Over medium heat, add garlic and ginger, saute 30 seconds, then add onion, beef and green pepper. Cook about 7 minutes until beef is almost thoroughly cooked through. Add soy sauce and wine and cook an additional 5 minutes. *(P.S. This meal would be lower in fat if you use chicken instead!)*

## Veggie Stuffed Stuffing

4 c. Stuffing mix (cubed or crumbs, your choice!)
1-1/2 c. water
1 chicken bouillon cube
   (use low sodium)

1 small onion, chopped*
1 green pepper, chopped
1 c. mushrooms, sliced (optional)
1 Tbls. Italian seasoning
Cooking spray

> *Note: chop veggies for teriyaki beef & stuffing at the same time.

> Spray skillet with cooking spray. Over medium heat, add onion, pepper and mushrooms. Sprinkle with seasoning. Saute about 5 minutes or until veggies are softened nicely.

> Place stuffing mix in bowl. Boil water, add bouillon cube, let dissolve. When veggies are cooked through, add to stuffing mix. Then pour water over stuffing mix. Mix thoroughly so all stuffing is moistened. (Add water slowly, adding just enough to moisten without soaking the stuffing and making it soggy.)

> Serves 4.

*It may seem impossible to make all this in about 20 minutes but it's not! The acorn squash takes less than a minute to prep, then cooks itself. You'll chop all the veggies for the beef teriyaki and stuffing at the same time, then have two skillets going which makes it easy to watch both. You'll dump the stuffing veggies into a bowl with the bread, add water, stir and you're done. About this time, the beef is cooked through and dinner is ready to be served.*

# "Chili Hot Potatoes" with Sliced Vegetables Strips or Mini-Salad

*This meal is more filling than you might think at first glance. Because of the fiber in the potato, chili beans and salad you'll feel quite full and satisfied.*

## Chili Hot Potatoes

4 baking potatoes
1 can Vegetarian chili (preferably *with* beans!)
ButterBuds
2 oz. Low-fat cheddar cheese, shredded.

Scrub potatoes. Wrap each, individually in a paper towel. Place all 4 potatoes in microwave oven, cook on HIGH for 15 minutes. Let sit 5 minutes. While these are cooking, warm chili in a pan on the stove. Cut open potatoes, sprinkle with ButterBuds, then top with chili. Sprinkle each with 1/2 oz. cheese, each. Place back in microwave, cook 30 seconds or until cheese melts over chili.

## Salad fixings

Look in the 'fridge. What do you see? Make a salad from it! Serve with a non-fat salad dressing.

**Or,** not in the mood to chop up everything? Then take 4 carrots, 4 radishes, 4 celery stalks and make vegetable sticks. Use non-fat salad dressing for a dip.

**Or,** if everything in the 'fridge looks likes it's been there since the dawn of time, go to the freezer and pull out a selection from there. Spinach, corn, green beans, etc. I like to mix corn and green peas as a nice combination for a side vegetable dish.

Serves 4.

*Why do you let potatoes sit for 5 minutes after the microwave is done cooking?*
*Microwaves work like sunrays. Food absorbs the rays from the outside towards the inside. Just like we continue to tan after we've gone inside, food that has been microwaved continues to cook as the heat moves toward the center. With potatoes, that extra 5 minutes makes sure the center is as soft as the outside.*

# Pita Pizza
# Black Eyed Pea Salad

## Black Eyed Pea Salad

1 can black-eyed peas, rinsed and drained
1 medium red onion, chopped fine
1 c. green peas, thawed and drained
1 green pepper, chopped small

1 tsp. basil
1/2 c. lite Caesar Salad dressing
   (Fat-free Italian also works)

Mix all ingredients together! If you have time, you can chill until ready to serve.

## Pita Pizza

1 package, whole wheat pita bread
1 jar prepared spaghetti sauce
   (use your favorite, low-fat sauce)
4 oz. lite Mozzarella cheese, shredded

Veggies: mushrooms, green pepper ...
   your choice of pizza toppings
   (skip pepperoni and sausage—too
fattening)

*Take one whole pita, spread with*
1/2 c. (or more if you like) spaghetti sauce. Sprinkle with 1 oz. cheese and any choice of veggie topping you like. Place under broiler until cheese melts (about 2 minutes)

**Or,** place in microwave, cook HIGH for 45 seconds for one, 90 seconds for two at a time. (Note: If you put them in a microwave they will be a little moist as compared to under the broiler. That's because the moisture in the pizza sauce will soak into the pita bread. )

*Children usually like Pita Pizza because it looks like a "personal" pizza and it is easy to pick up.*

Serves 4.

*Minimize the amount of cheese you use and instead focus on the veggies.*
*Every ounce of low-fat cheese still has 5 grams of fat in it! Fat in the diet leads to heart disease and cancer, so try to limit fat gram intake to 25-40 grams per day. Cheese adds up fast...2 oz. ...18 grams! Most cheeses are made from whole milk, not skim. So a cheese and cracker snack is loaded with FAT!*

# Chicken Nuggets with Baked Potato Slices
# Spinach Salad

## Baked Potato Slices

2 medium-sized baking potatoes, scrubbed
  and sliced into thin rounds
Butter flavored cooking spray

Seasoning: Mrs. Dash, Spike...or just
  black pepper....your choice!

Pre-heat oven to 450°. Spray cookie sheet with cooking spray. Place potato slices on sheet, then spray again with cooking spray. Sprinkle lightly with seasoning. Place in oven for 10 minutes. Remove from oven, turn slices over, re-spray with cooking spray and light seasoning. Return to oven for 5-7 minutes. Test with fork for desired doneness.

## Spinach Salad

1 lb. fresh spinach
10 cherry tomatoes, halved
1 small cuke, sliced round
1 red onion, thinly sliced, round

1/2 c. crumbled feta cheese
  (or if you don't have it substitute
  lite mozzarella, shredded)
2/3 c. lite red wine vinegar dressing

Clean fresh spinach. Combine with all other ingredients.

## Chicken Nuggets

1 lb. chicken breast, boned and skinned,
  cut into small, bite-size pieces
2 c. corn flake crumbs

1 c. skim milk
1 Tbls. seasoning; your choice

Dip chicken pieces into milk, then corn flake crumbs until well-coated. Place in microwave safe dish and cover, leaving vent. Cook HIGH, 1 minute. Let sit one minute. (Check for doneness. If still pink, cook for additional time in 1/2 minute increments.)

Serves 4.

*If you have a child 7 years or older, this is an ideal meal for them to help you make.*
*Let them pull the spinach into bite size pieces. Give them a small knife and let them cut the tomatoes and cuke...you do the onion. They can also dip the chicken in milk and cornflakes. Children love to help in the kitchen. If you start them on simple dishes like this that they can handle and be successful at, you will help them build self-esteem as they become valuable, helpful members of the family,*

**Pantry must
haves:**
fresh spinach,
feta cheese

# Sloppy Pita Pockets
# Quick Lentil Pilaf

## Quick Lentil Pilaf

1/2 c. lentils, rinsed and drained
2 c. water
1 small onion, chopped
1 c. frozen corn
1 c. frozen peas
1 Tbls. seasoning, your choice

Bring water to a boil. Add remaining ingredients. Cover, turn heat to low, cook 20-25 minutes, until water is absorbed and lentils are soft.

## Sloppy Pita Pockets

4 whole wheat pita
1 lb. fresh ground turkey
1 c. red kidney beans, rinsed and drained
1 medium onion, chopped small
1 carrot, shredded fine
1 tsp. chili powder (use less if you don't
   like foods too hot!)
1/2 tsp. cumin
1/4 tsp. oregano
1/8 tsp. black pepper
Salsa

Place ground turkey in microwave safe dish. Cover tightly, cook HIGH, 5 minutes. Remove from microwave, place in colander and drain any fat that has collected. Return to microwave dish. Add onion, carrot, kidney beans and spices. Mix well. Cover and cook HIGH, 3 minutes. Let sit 2 minutes.

Cut pita bread in half, and gently open for stuffing. Spoon 2 large spoonfuls into each pita half, top with some salsa.

Serves 4.

# Hearty Vegetable Bean Soup
# Whole Grain Rolls

## Vegetable Bean Soup

1 c. lentils & 2-1/2 c. water
1 tsp. garlic, crushed
2 stalks celery, chopped
1 medium onion, chopped
1 c. carrots, chopped
2 potatoes, chopped
5 c. water

2 c. tomato juice
1 tsp. thyme
1/3 c. brown rice
1 c. frozen corn
1 can kidney beans, rinsed and drained
Cooking spray

In saucepan, bring 2-1/2 c. water to boil. Add lentils, cover and lower heat. Simmer lentils 15 minutes.

Spray large pot with cooking spray. Saute garlic, celery and onion for 1 minute. Add all remaining ingredients. Cover, bring to a boil, then reduce heat and simmer. Add lentils to this pan at the 15 minute mark, continue to cook 10 more minutes. (If you have more time, let it cook longer. All soups taste better, the longer they cook.)

Serve this hearty vegetable bean soup with some whole grain rolls, or sourdough bread. Avoid using butter or margarine. Let the bread's taste stand out on its own. Remember, 1 tablespoon of butter equals 12 grams of fat, yuk!

Serves 4.

*Want an even heartier soup?*
*While soup is cooking, make some pasta. Use whatever you have, although a Rotini would be attractive for the soup. Cook according to directions, omitting salt and oil. Rinse and drain. When ready to serve soup, add the amount of pasta you desire to the individual serving bowl, add soup and mix together. Doing it this way keeps the big pan of soup from thickening too much from the pasta.*

# Pasta and Traditional Sauce
# Garlic Bagels, Steamed Corn and Carrots

## Pasta

1 lb. pasta,
1 large jar, prepared spaghetti sauce (choose a low-fat sauce)
Parmesan cheese
*Optional:* Add a can of garbanzo or white kidney beans to sauce while it cooks to increase nutrition value.

> It doesn't get easier than this! Cook pasta according to directions, omit salt and oil. Warm up the spaghetti sauce and pour over the pasta. Sprinkle with Parmesan cheese, as desired.

## Steamed Corn and Carrots

3 carrots, sliced
2 c. frozen corn, thawed and drained
1 tsp. dried dill
Butter flavored cooking spray.

> Place carrots in microwave safe dish, cover tightly. Cook HIGH, 1-1/2 minutes. Add corn, cook HIGH, 1 minute. Let sit 1 minute. Then check carrots, if crispier than you like, cook for one more minute. Just before serving, spray with butter flavored cooking spray, sprinkle with dried dill, mix lightly. (If you don't like dill…use a seasoning you do like!)

## Garlic Bagels

4 whole grain bagels, halved
Butter flavor cooking spray
garlic powder

> Pre-heat oven broiler. Put bagels on cookie sheet. Spray each bagel lightly with butter flavored cooking spray. Sprinkle liberally with garlic powder. Place bagels under broiler, toast to desired level…some like them quite crunchy, others just lightly warmed.

> Serves 4.

*Pasta: Twice is Nice!*
*Make more pasta than you need for one meal and keep it in the refrigerator. Pasta makes a great snack or quick leftover meal with Parmesan cheese or spaghetti sauce on top.*

# Soft Bean Taco Stuffed with Barley
# Steamed Broccoli

## Soft Bean Tacos Stuffed with Barley

1 pkg. whole wheat tortillas
2 cans non-fat refried beans
1 c. quick-cooking barley

2 c. water
salsa
4 oz. low-fat cheddar cheese, shredded

Boil water, add barley. Cover, lower heat and cook until all water is absorbed (about 10 minutes). While barley cooks, warm refried beans either on stove or in microwave. When barley is finished lay one tortilla on microwave safe dish. Spoon 2-3 Tbls. of beans on tortilla, spreading around the center area. Take 2 Tbls. barley and lay down center line of tortilla. Add 1 Tbls. salsa. Roll tortilla up, laying edges on bottom of plate to secure. Sprinkle with 1/2 oz. cheddar cheese. Make 7 more tacos. When finished, place entire plate in microwave with 8 rolled tacos, cook HIGH 1 minute, until cheese melts.

If you have leftover rice this meal takes 10 minutes to prepare! Warm up leftover rice, warm beans, spread on a tortilla…done!

## Steamed Broccoli

1 lb. broccoli, chopped
or frozen broccoli, thawed and drained

Seasoning: Mrs. Dash, Spike, etc.
ButterBuds

While barley cooks, prepare broccoli. Place in steamer over medium heat, cook until suitably tender, about 5 minutes. Sprinkle lightly with Butterbuds and seasoning.

Serves 4.

*Nutrition tip:*

*Whenever you mix together a grain with a bean, you make a protein food out of the combination of two complex carbohydrates. That's how vegetarians get their protein.*

*Keep this in mind when making meals. Can you add some beans into a recipe to increase the nutritional value? Beans are also a great source of fiber which is something most people need more of on a daily basis.*

# Millet Pilaf, Orange Roughy (fish) in Wine Lemon-Dill Brussels Sprouts

## Millet Pilaf

1 c. millet
2 c. water
1 small onion, chopped

1 c. frozen corn
1 chicken bouillon cube (use low sodium)
1 Tbls. seasoning

Boil water, add all remaining ingredients. Cover, cook on low heat until all water is absorbed, about 15 minutes.

*Millet is a high protein grain. You can buy it at the health food store. It is inexpensive and tasty!*

## Lemon-Dill Brussel Sprouts

1 lb. Brussels sprouts
1/2 Tbls. lemon juice

1 tsp. dried dill
Butter flavored cooking spray

To prepare Brussels sprouts: Cut off tough bottom end, then peel back one layer, more if the next layer has brown spots or dried edges and they don't look pretty. Place steamer in pot, add 2 c. water. Add Brussels sprouts, bring to a boil and let steam until tender, about 8 minutes. Remove from pan, place in serving dish, sprinkle with lemon juice, cooking spray and dill. Mix thoroughly, serve.

*If you don't have Brussels sprouts, try using carrots, asparagus or peas.*

## Orange Roughy in Wine

1 lb. Orange Roughy, or other suitable white fish that you like
1/2 c. White wine
1 tbls. Italian seasoning

In microwave safe dish, lay Orange Roughy. Pour white wine and sprinkle Italian seasoning over fish. Cover tightly. Cook in microwave, HIGH about 4 minutes. Let sit, 1 minute before serving. (Remember the guideline for microwaving fish: for every half inch thickness, cook 4 minutes.)

*Orange Roughy comes from Australia and New Zealand. It is a very pleasant, light tasting white fish.*

Serves 4.

# Pasta Salad
*(a meal in a bowl!)*

Salads don't take long to make at all...they average only 7-14 minutes! Another benefit...salads don't make a lot of dishes for clean up either.

Americans should eat more salads! High in fiber, they also provide lots of vitamins, minerals and complex carbohydrates.

There isn't any one way to make a salad...so use the following lists, add the ingredients you like to make a healthy, hearty bowl full of good nutrition.

## Pasta

Start the pasta first, then begin preparing the veggies. It'll be done about the time you're done cutting. Cook pasta according to directions, omit salt and oil. Rinse and drain with cool water to completely cool down the pasta before adding to the salad. (P.S. Make extra pasta to keep in the 'fridge for a quick snack!)

*Start with choices from this list to be the base or bulk of your salad:*

Lettuce—Boston or Red Leaf
Red Cabbage
Carrots
Cucumbers
Radishes

Broccoli
Cauliflower
Green cabbage
Peppers—green, yellow or red

*Then add choices from this list:*

Water chestnuts
Beets—fresh or canned
Bamboo shoots
Beans—rinse and drain your favorite...
   red kidney, pinto, etc.
Corn—thawed and drained
Green Peas—thawed and drained
Jicama
Zucchini
Olives—black or green

Leftover meat chopped up
Tuna packed in water, flaked
Mandarin orange slices
Fruit slices
Raisins, dates
Hot peppers
Pimientos
Nuts—almond slices, pecans, etc.
Croutons
USE YOUR IMAGINATION

## Salad Dressing

Use your favorite low-fat or non-fat dressing right from the bottle. (Remember, regular salad dressing can add as much as 14 grams of fat per tablespoon to your healthy salad! Try the new non-fat dressings instead. They have about 1 gram of fat per tablespoon—it's actually .9, that's how come they get to say, "no" fat)

# Oriental Salad with Chicken and "Crunchies" Steamed Basmati Rice

## Steamed Basmati Rice

1 c. Basmati Rice
2 c. water

Boil water, add rice. Cover tightly, cook on low heat, about 17 minutes.

### Basmati Rice

*Basmati rice is a rice that was originally grown in India. It has a unique, nutty flavor that is wonderful. Now it is grown in Texas and California as well but these are brown rices. Some of the American Basmati has been polished, so always check the box to make sure you are getting the whole grain, not refined!*

## Oriental Salad

1 lb. angel hair pasta
2 c. chicken breast, skinned and boned, cut into cubes
1 c. broccoli florets
1 c. sliced red pepper
2 c. carrots, shredded or chopped small
1/2 c. red onion, chopped
1 can sliced water chestnuts, rinsed and drained
1 c. grapes, halved (optional)

Cook pasta according to directions, omit salt and oil. Rinse and drain. Set aside. Take chicken cubes, place in microwave, cook HIGH 1-1/2 minutes. Let sit 1 minute. Allow to cool. In serving bowl, mix pasta, chicken and remaining ingredients together. Pour dressing over the salad and mix thoroughly.

*Want it warm?* You could steam the vegetables lightly and serve this dish warm instead of a cool salad. Your option!

## Dressing

1/4 c. rice vinegar
1/4 c. lite soy sauce
1/2 tsp. fresh ginger, crushed
1 Tbls. sesame oil
1/4 c. white wine
1/2 tsp. garlic, crushed
1/4 tsp. crushed hot peppers (optional)

Combine all the ingredients and mix well.

Serves 4.

### A note on rice:

*If your rice is coming out too chewy you're cooking it too fast by having the heat up too high. When the heat is up, the water gets evaporated too fast, which doesn't allow the rice time to absorb it. Rice softens with the process of absorbing water over the cooking time.*

# Steamed Shrimp, Butternut Squash Millet and Brown Rice Pilaf

## Millet and Brown Rice Pilaf

2 c. water
1/2 c. millet
1/2 c. brown rice
1/2 c. frozen corn
1/2 c. frozen peas
1/2 Tbls. seasoning, like
 Mrs. Dash or Spice Island

Boil water. Add millet and brown rice, corn, peas and seasoning. Cover and cook over low heat until all water is absorbed, about 25 minutes.

## Butternut Squash

Cut butternut squash in quarters, remove all seeds. Place quarters in microwave safe dish, add 1/2 c. water. Cover tightly and put in microwave. Cook HIGH for 8 minutes, then let sit for 3 minutes before serving. Top with ButterBuds instead of butter! Ground black pepper also is nice.

*Note: the outer layer or shell can't be eaten, but the shell quickly separates from the edible pulp once it is cooked.*

## Steamed Shrimp

1 lb. shrimp, rinsed
1 Tbls. Old Bay seasoning
1 c. water
1 Tbls. vinegar
Red Cocktail sauce

Bring water, vinegar and seasoning to a boil. Add shrimp, stir lightly, then let steam until shrimp have all turned pink, about 3 minutes. Do not over cook the shrimp, as this makes them tough.

Rinse and drain. Serve with cocktail sauce instead of butter, as cocktail sauce has no fat in it. You can peel the shrimp at the table!

Serves 4.

# Fettucini Primavera
# Turkey Breast Saute

## Fettucini Primavera

1 lb. fettuccini
2 c. broccoli florets
1/4 c. water
1 c. carrots, thinly sliced
1 small red onion, sliced in rings

1 c. mushrooms, sliced
1 tsp. garlic
1/2 c. non-fat, Italian dressing
Cooking spray
Parmesan cheese

Cook pasta according to directions, omit salt and oil. Rinse and drain, set aside.

Spray skillet with cooking spray, add garlic, saute 30 seconds. Add broccoli, carrots, onion, water and let steam about 3 minutes while covered. Uncover, add mushrooms and continue to cook about 5 more minutes, until vegetables are tender. Add Italian dressing, mix thoroughly. Cook 1 more minute. Pour pasta in serving bowl and add cooked vegetables. Toss together. Top with Parmesan cheese.

## Turkey Breast Saute

1 lb. turkey breast, like a Louis Rich® or Perdue®—
   pre-cooked, sliced into 1/2 inch thick slices.

Spray skillet with cooking spray. Add turkey slices and cook on medium heat, turning occasionally until warmed through…about 5 minutes.

*If you like a smoked flavoring, Wright's Hickory seasoning can be used:* Add 1/2 tsp. mix to 1/4 c. water, pour into skillet and add turkey breasts, cook until all water has been cooked off.

Serves 4.

*We eat too much!*

*Our lifestyles have changed so much in the last 100 years. When we were actively farming and doing heavy manual labor we required lots of food to provide our bodies with the necessary energy to do this work. But now, we sit still to do our jobs. This requires much less energy, yet many of us continue to eat like farmers! Cutting back on the amount of food you eat, will keep you from being sluggish. Excess calories turn to fat and burden the body which has to carry all this extra weight.*

# Marcia's Chicken Oriental
# Basmati Rice, Sesame Bagels

## Basmati Rice

1 c. rice
2 c. water

Bring water to boil, add rice, cover tightly and steam over low heat until all water is absorbed (about 17 minutes).

## Marcia's Chicken Oriental

1 lb. chicken breast, skinned and boned, cut into 4 filets
1 tsp. ginger, crushed
2 tsp. garlic, crushed
1 can pineapple chunks, drained but retain this juice
1/4 c. low sodium soy sauce
1 pepper, cut into chunks
1 red onion, chopped into big pieces
2 stalk celery, chopped into big pieces
2 carrots, chopped into big pieces

Place chicken breasts in microwave safe dish. Mix together ginger, garlic, pineapple juice, water, soy sauce. Pour over chicken. Top with vegetable chunks and pineapple. Cover tightly, cook HIGH, 7 minutes, turning at 3 minutes. Let sit 1 minute after cooking.

*To serve:* Place 1 c. cooked rice on plate, cover with 1 chicken breast and 1/4 vegetable mixture.

## Sesame Bagels

4 whole grain bagels
Sesame Tahini
Sesame seeds

Toast bagels, drip lightly with sesame tahini, sprinkle with sesame seeds.

Serves 4.

# Chicken Jambalaya
# with Low-Fat Ranch Coleslaw

## Chicken Jambalaya

1 green pepper, chopped
1/2 c. celery, chopped
1 onion chopped
1 Tsp. garlic
1 (14 oz.) can no-salt stewed tomatoes,
   undrained
2 c. low sodium chicken broth
   (or use 2 bouillon cubes in water)

2/3 c. Basmati rice
1 bay leaf
1/2 tsp. thyme
1/2 tsp. chili powder
1 chicken breast, boned and skinned

Place chicken breast in microwave dish with 1 Tbls. water, cover and cook HIGH, 3 minutes or until cooked through and no pink is showing. While chicken cooks, cut vegetables. When chicken is finished, cut into bite-size pieces. Then take a large skillet with a cover. Spray with cooking spray, then over medium heat, saute pepper, onion, celery, and garlic, about one minute. Stir in chicken broth and remaining ingredients, bring to boil, cover and simmer about 15 minutes. Uncover and let remaining liquid steam away, stir occasionally.

## Coleslaw

Green cabbage
Red cabbage
Carrots
Low-fat Ranch dressing

Shred or chop in a food processor, add dressing!

To save time, purchase pre-cut coleslaw veggies. To this add desired amount of low-fat Ranch dressing (some people like their coleslaw "wet", others prefer it with just a little bit of dressing—do it as you like.)

*Options:* Instead of Ranch dressing, try a French or Thousand Island on top of the coleslaw mixture. Each time you use a different dressing you change the flavor of the meal! Just be sure to use low-fat or non-fat dressings.

Serves 4.

# Snappy Chicken Nuggets
# Cucumber Nugget Salad with Corn
# Baked Potatoes Topped with
# Low-Fat, Ranch Dressing

### Baked Potatoes with Low-Fat Ranch Dressing

4 baked potatoes, scrubbed and pricked with fork
Ranch dressing (FAT FREE is preferable!)

Wrap each potato in microwave safe paper towel. Place in microwave and cook HIGH, 15 minutes. Let sit 5 minutes before cutting open. Top with 3 Tbls. Ranch dressing.

### Cucumber Nugget Salad with Corn

1 cucumber, chopped into small bits
1 c. frozen corn, thawed
1/4 c. white vinegar (rice vinegar is good too, if you have it)
1/4 c. water
1 Tbls. sugar

Mix all ingredients together and let sit until ready to serve. (You can chill it if you want.)

### Snappy Chicken Nuggets

2 chicken breasts, skinned and boned and cut into small pieces
corn flake crumbs
skim milk
1 Tbls. hot pepper seasoning combo (it might also be a Tex-Mex seasoning…just look for something that has "hot" flavor to it)

In separate bowls, pour corn flake crumbs and milk (start with about a cup of each, adding more if necessary as you go along). Add hot pepper seasoning to corn flake crumbs. Drop chicken piece in milk, then into corn flake crumbs, coating thoroughly. Place in microwave safe dish, cover, leave a vent and cook HIGH, about 1 to 1-1/2 minutes. Remove and cut one piece open…if still slightly pink, cook another 1/2 minute.

Serves 4.

# Creamy Low-Fat Potato & Corn Chowder
# Three Bean Salad, Corn Muffins

## Creamy Low Fat Potato & Corn Chowder

cooking spray
1 c. chopped onion
1 c. red pepper, chopped
1 1/2 tsp. flour
1/2 tsp. cumin
2 c. water
2 c. red potato, cubed

1 tsp. chicken bouillon
2 c. whole frozen corn, thawed
1 c. evaporated skim milk
1 c. garbanzo beans, canned and drained
1/4 tsp. black pepper
1/8 tsp. cayenne pepper

Spray large saucepan with cooking spray, add onions and pepper. Saute over medium heat about 2 minutes. Place flour and cumin in measuring cup. Add a small amount of water and stir with fork, making sure the flour mixture is smooth, not lumpy. Add remaining water, stir lightly, pour into pan. Add potato and bouillon. Bring to a boil and cover, then let simmer 10 minutes over medium high heat until potatoes are softened.

Add corn, milk, garbanzo beans, cayenne and black peppers. Cook an additional 5 minutes until heated through.

## Three Bean Salad

1 can red kidney beans, rinsed and drained
1 pkg. green beans, rinsed and thawed
1 can black-eyed peas, rinsed and drained
3/4 c. chopped green onions
1/2 c. ripe olive slices
1/2 c. red wine vinegar
1/2 Tbls. olive oil

2 Tbls. water
1 tsp. sugar
1 tsp. dry mustard
1 Tbls. cilantro (optional)
1/2 tsp. white pepper
1/2 tsp. garlic, mashed

Combine the 3 beans, onions and olives in a bowl, set aside. Mix vinegar, oil, water, sugar, mustard, cilantro, pepper and garlic. Pour over beans. (You can chill this if you have time.)

## Corn Muffins

Use prepared muffins from freezer. If you don't have any, substitute with a roll or pita bread.

Serves 4.

# Cuban Black Beans & Rice
# Whole Wheat Bagels, Lively Corn Salad

## Cuban Black Beans & Rice

1 c. brown rice
2 c. water
cooking spray
1 onion, chopped
1 green pepper, chopped
2 c. tomato juice (no salt added)
1 tsp. oregano
2 cans (15 oz.) black beans, rinsed
   and drained

1 large can tomatoes, quartered,
   retain liquid
1 (8 oz.) can tomato sauce (no salt added)
1 tsp. cumin
1 tsp. black pepper
1 tsp. garlic powder

Boil water, add rice, cover tightly, simmer on low heat until all liquid absorbed (about 25 minutes).

*While rice cooks:* Spray sauce pan with cooking spray, add onion and green pepper. Saute over medium heat about 5 minutes. Then add all remaining ingredients. Cover and cook on medium heat.

*When rice is done:* Spoon 1/2 c. rice into individual serving bowl. Top with 1 cup black bean mixture.

## Lively Corn Salad

2 c. frozen corn, thawed
1 red pepper, chopped fine
1 small red onion, chopped fine
1/2 c. salsa
2 tbls. rice wine vinegar

Mix together all ingredients!

If you don't have red pepper then use green pepper. Another substitution, use pimento from a jar! Third choice, use frozen peas!

## Whole Wheat Bagels

2 bagels, sliced in half

Toast and spread with just a light touch of margarine (remember, 1 Tbls. of butter or margarine = 12 grams of fat!) Each person gets 1/2 bagel.

Serves 4.

# Tofu Scramble Stuffed in Pita Bread
# Low-Fat Hash Browns
# Mandarin Orange Yogurt Cup

*Some days, instead of dinner, do you really feel like breakfast?*
*This meal meets that need! A nice light meal that will fill you up, but not stuff you.*

## Low-Fat Hash Browns

4 potatoes, chopped into small squares
butter flavored cooking spray
Seasoning, like Spike or Mrs. Dash

Preheat oven, 400. Spray cookie sheet with cooking spray, spread potatoes over sheet. Spray again with cooking spray, sprinkle with seasoning of your choice. Place in oven, cook for 10 minutes. Remove sheet from oven, "turn" potatoes, return to oven, cook 10 more minutes, or until fork easily presses through potatoes.

## Tofu Scramble

1 package, soft tofu mashed
1 onion, chopped
1 green pepper, chopped

1 pkg. whole wheat pita bread
1 Tbls. seasoning, like Spike or Mrs. Dash
cooking spray

Spray skillet with cooking spray. Add onions and green peppers, saute over low heat about 5 minutes. Add tofu and seasoning and continue to cook, uncovered, for 10 minutes, letting the moisture from the tofu evaporate.

When finished sauteing, cut pita bread in half, open each half and stuff with tofu mixture.

## Mandarin Orange Yogurt Cup

16 oz. Non-fat plain yogurt
1 can mandarin oranges, drained, retain liquid

Place yogurt in a bowl and pour in liquid from mandarin orange can. Mix together. In individual serving bowls, place 4 oz. yogurt, then top each with 1/4 of the mandarin orange slices. (Make a pretty arrangement of these… even better, let your children make this!)

Serves 4.

# Not the Same Ol' Burger
# Barley & Beans Pilaf, Steamed Carrots

## Not the Same Ol' Burger

1 lb. fresh ground turkey
1/2 c. red onion, chopped fine
2 Tbls. seasoning (Mrs. Dash, Spike etc.)
1/2 c. corn flake crumbs
Whole Wheat Burger Buns

Mix ingredients together and make into 4 patties. Broil, about 2 inches from flame, turning after 4-6 minutes. Burgers will take about 10 minutes total under a broiler flame. Remove from oven. Place small amount of Special sauce on bottom of each bun, top with burger.

## Special Sauce

1/2 c. Non-fat Thousand Island Dressing
1/2 Tbls. Prepared Mustard

Combine ingredients.

## Barley & Bean Pilaf

2/3 c. quick-cooking barley
2 c. water
1 c. canned black-eyed peas, red kidney or pinto beans (your choice),
    rinsed and drained
1 Tbls. seasoning like Mrs. Dash.

Bring water to boil. Add barley and seasoning, cover and cook over low heat about 10 minutes or until all water is absorbed. Add beans, mix well, and cook another 2 minutes until beans are heated through.

## Steamed Dill Carrots

3 medium carrots, sliced
1/4 c. water
1 tsp. dried dill weed
Butter Buds

Place carrots in microwave safe dish, add water. Cook HIGH 2 minutes in microwave oven. Remove from microwave, drain excess water, sprinkle with Butter Buds and dill. (If you like your carrots a little softer, cook an additional minute.)

Serves 4.

# Sesame Noodles with
# Red Pepper and Garbanzo Beans
# Szechuan Green Beans, Baked Pita Slices

*This meal is great to serve when you have guests coming over for dinner. So easy to make, but it is unique enough to wow the guests while getting you out of the kitchen quickly!*

## Sesame Noodles

1 lb. pasta—you choose shape!
1 Tbls. ginger
1 Tbls. sesame seeds
1/2 c. water
1/3 c. low-sodium soy sauce
1/3 c. sesame Tahini

1/4 c. dry sherry
   (it's okay if you don't have this)
2 tsp. sugar
1 Tbls. garlic, crushed
1 red pepper, sliced
1 can garbanzo beans

Cook pasta according to directions, omit oil and salt. Rinse and drain when finished. Keep warm.

In food processor, mix together ginger, sesame seeds, water, soy sauce, Tahini, sherry, sugar and garlic. Process until smooth…1 minute or so.

Place red pepper and garbanzo beans in microwave safe dish. Add 1 Tbls. water. Cook on HIGH 1 minute.

Pour pasta into serving bowl top with red pepper and garbanzo beans, then pour sesame sauce over pasta. Mix well, coating all the pasta.

## Szechuan Green Beans

1 pkg. frozen beans, thawed *OR*
1 lb. fresh beans, trimmed, washed and "snapped" into small pieces.
1/4 tsp. hot sesame oil

Place fresh beans and 1/4 c. water in microwave safe dish, cook HIGH, 2 minutes. If using frozen beans, cook according to directions. Drain excess water, then sprinkle hot sesame oil over beans and mix well. (1/4 tsp. may not seem like a lot but this is very concentrated!)

## Baked Pita Pieces

4 slices, whole wheat pita bread, cut into quarters.

Place pita pieces on cookie sheet, bake in oven, about 300° for 10 minutes.

Serves 4.

# Stuffed Acorn Squash
# Chicken Breasts with Stewed Tomatoes

## Stuffed Acorn Squash

2 acorn squash
2/3 c. quick-cooking barley
2 c. water
green onions
3 c. vegetables: I suggest *broccoli, cauliflower* or *carrots,* but use whatever you've got, either fresh or frozen. If frozen, thaw and be sure pieces are small, since you're going to stuff this into the acorn squash. A monstrous piece of cauliflower is hard to work with! If fresh, cut into small pieces using however much you want of each to make about 3 cups.
1 c. non-fat Italian dressing
2 tsp. dried basil
2 oz. low-sodium Swiss cheese, shredded (you can use any cheese you have available)

Bring water to boil in sauce pan. Add barley, cover and cook over low heat until all water is absorbed. (about 10 minutes).

Cut acorn squash in half, remove seeds. Place in microwave safe dish with 1/2 c. water. Cover tightly and cook 12 minutes. Remove from microwave, then let sit for 5 more minutes. Start chicken now, see below.

While barley and squash cook, spray saute pan with cooking spray. Add green onions and saute lightly, about 1 minute. Then add broccoli, cauliflower, carrots, Italian dressing and basil. Cover and simmer over medium-low heat until vegetables are tender, about 5 minutes.

When veggies and barley are finished, mix together. Then take acorn squash half, stuff with barley vegetable combo, sprinkle with 1/4 of the shredded cheese, place in microwave and cook HIGH 15 seconds to melt cheese.

## Chicken Breasts with Stewed Tomatoes

1 lb. chicken breasts, skinned and boned, cut into 4 oz. filets
1 15 oz. can stewed tomatoes (if you don't have this, take a can of whole tomatoes, chop up into small pieces and sprinkle with 1 tbls. Italian seasoning)

Place chicken breasts in microwave safe dish. Top with stewed tomatoes, cover and cook HIGH 6 minutes, turning at 3 minutes. Let sit 2 minutes before serving. (Obviously, cook these after you've cooked the squash.)

Serves 4.

# Healthy Turkey Nachos
# & Green Pepper Pieces

*This meal is great for an informal dinner where you might be sitting down
to catch a baseball game or favorite movie on TV.*

## Healthy Nachos

1 bag corn tortillas (or FAT Free Tortilla chips instead of making your own)
salt
Butter flavored cooking spray

> *To make your own non-fat tortilla chips:* Pre-heat oven to 400. Cut corn tortillas
> into quarters. Spray cookie sheet with cooking spray, lay down tortillas, spray
> with cooking spray again. Place in oven, cook about 10 minutes. Remove, salt
> very lightly (remember, too much salt is not good for you!)

## Nacho topping

1 c. basmati rice
2 c. water
1/2 lb. fresh ground turkey
1 (15 oz) can pinto beans
1 can, no-salt tomatoes, undrained,
   chopped small

1 red onion, chopped small
3 Tbls. tomato paste
1/2 Tbls. chili powder (more if you like it hot!)
1 tsp. cumin
1/2 c. low fat cheddar cheese, shredded

> Boil water, add basmati rice, cover and cook until all water is absorbed, about
> 17 minutes.

> *While this cooks:* Place turkey in microwave safe dish, cover tightly, cook HIGH 3
> minutes. Remove, stir, return and cook HIGH 2 minutes. Remove, drain into a
> colander to release fat that has collected. Return to dish, add beans and next
> five ingredients. Stir well. Cover, cook HIGH 4 minutes. Spoon rice onto
> serving platter. Top rice with turkey mixture, sprinkle with cheese and onions.
> Circle with tortillas chips.

## Green Pepper Pieces

2 green peppers, sliced
Non-fat salad dressing, for dipping

> Slice green peppers, place on dish. Put 1/2 c. of non-fat salad dressing in
> dipping bowl.

> Serves 4.

# Shopping List

**Produce:**
Potatoes
Onions
Acorn Squash or Butternut
Veggies for salads
    Green peppers
    Carrots
    Lettuce
    Red & green cabbage
    Cucumbers
    Radishes
    Avocados*

**Bakery:**
Pita bread
Whole wheat rolls
Whole wheat burger buns
Whole wheat tortillas
Corn muffins
Bagels

**Dairy:**
Skim milk
Shredded low-fat cheeses:
    cheddar, mozzarella
    feta cheese
Eggs
Non-fat plain yogurt
Lemon juice

**Meat:**
Fresh ground turkey
Boned turkey breast
Chicken breast-skinned
    & boned
Beef strips

**Fish:**
Flounder, sole or
    orange roughy
    (choose one you like)
Salmon

**Pasta:**
Variety of shapes from
    angel hair to ziti!
Tortellini
    cheese or spinach

**Grains:**
Brown rice
Cous Cous
Basmati rice
Quick-cooking barley
Millet

**Canned Beans:**
Pinto
Red kidney
Garbanzo
Lentils
Black
Black-eyed peas

**Frozen:**
Veggies: at least 3
    Corn
    Peas
    Spinach
    Broccoli
    etc.

**Packaged:**
Tomatoes
    Paste, puree, whole,
    stewed & sauce
Spaghetti sauce
Taco sauce
Salsa
Vegetarian refried beans
Vegetarian chili
Pesto sauce
Low-sodium soy sauce
Sesame oil-hot & regular
Parmesan cheese
Mushroom soup-low fat
Red and White
    cooking wine
Mandarin oranges
Pineapple chunks
Cornflake crumbs
Stuffing mix
Bread crumbs
Water chestnuts
Bamboo shoots
Artichoke hearts
    (in water)
Black olives
Sesame Tahini
Honey

**Salad dressings:**
Non-fat Ranch, Italian,
Thousand Island
Lite Caesar
Red wine vinegar
Rice wine vinegar

**Spices:**
Garlic-powdered & crushed
Ginger-fresh in jar
Basil
Chili powder
Cumin
Oregano
Parsley
Black pepper
Prepared mustard
Dill
Old Bay seasoning
Combinations:
    Mrs. Dash
    Spike
    Spice Island types

Butter Buds or
    Molly McButter
Cooking spray

*Avocado is used in just a
few recipes, you can buy
fresh as needed or frozen.*

# A Word on Water

**Y**our body is made up of mostly water. If we could squeeze out the water that is in every cell of your body there would be a big puddle on the floor. Water is such a vital component of your daily nutrition needs that I cannot stress enough the importance of getting in the habit of drinking sufficient quantities of fresh water each day.

The recommended amount: Drink one-half your body weight in ounces. For example, 100 lbs. - 50 oz. of water, 200 lbs. = 100 oz. This can be water from many sources: fruit juice, coffee, tea, soda, fruit, vegetables, etc. BUT THE VERY BEST SOURCE OF WATER FOR YOUR BODY IS JUST PLAIN WATER!

I know, I can hear you right now… "Well, yeah, but I hate the taste of water. I need some taste, like soda or coffee."

Well, I'll let you in on a secret. Water has a wonderful taste which you will discover after you start drinking more of it. When we are accustomed to drinking sugary water from fruit juice and soda, we become conditioned to needing this artificial flavor. But when you wean away from these and begin drinking fresh water again, you will become aware of the different tastes of waters and how refreshing and rejuve-nating a cool glass of water can be—better than anything else!

But you'll have to decide to wean yourself and try this experiment. For three weeks drink at least five glasses of water per day. This will replace soda, juice, tea, etc. After three weeks try introducing these again. You'll discover how sickeningly sweet these liquids are and how unnecessary they are for your good health.

Because there's water in every cell, your body depends on you to give it a fresh supply. Unless fresh water comes into the body, the water that's already in you can't get replaced. Considering that water acts as a method of getting waste out of the cells so it can be removed from the body, it becomes obvious that when you don't have enough new water coming in each day, the old water and the "waste" stays inside you. Not the best way to care for yourself!

Water maintains balance for your body and is used in so many different ways. To improve your overall health, be sure water is a part of your good nutrition lifestyle!

## Suggested reading list

There are numerous books on good nutrition available. I'm listing just a few of the top writers. In a bookstore section, look for nutrition books that center on lifestyle and balance. Avoid any that focus on dieting or the "only way to do it" types that reduce quality nutrition to a formula.

Brody, Jane                    *Jane Brody's Nutrition Book*

I like Jane's books because they are based in sound nutrition principles and good science. She is also one of the few who stands up against products that she thinks research shows to be a potential cancer-causing agent or could pose serious health risks to the body and mind, even if they're very popular.

Duffy, Williams               *Sugar Blues*

Crook, Williams G., M.D.      *Yeast Connection*

Smith, Lendon, M.D.           *Feed Your Kids Right*

Lansky, Vicky                 *Feed Me, I'm Yours*

Dunne, editor                 *Nutrition Almanac*

Tracy, Lisa                   *The Gradual Vegetarian*

# ACTION PLAN
## The gradual great eater: YOU

A diet is not something you go on so you can eventually go off. A diet is something you live...every day. If you feel your living diet needs improvement, it doesn't have to be done overnight. You will be much more successful starting small and building up over the next two years.

**Exercise #1:**
**Begin at the beginning: review your current diet lifestyle.**
Does it fit within the Pyramid? Are you eating with this balance? Answer yes or no to the following categories...a yes if you're eating the recommended amounts, no, if you're not.

YES      NO

\_\_\_\_   \_\_\_\_   GRAINS: six to eleven 1/2 c. servings per day
Examples: cereal, whole grains breads, pasta, Brown rice, millet, quinoa, amaranth, bulgur wheat

\_\_\_\_   \_\_\_\_   FRUITS: two pieces of fresh fruit per day

\_\_\_\_   \_\_\_\_   VEGETABLES: five 1/2 c. servings each day

\_\_\_\_   \_\_\_\_   DAIRY: two 4 oz. servings per day
Skim milk products: fresh milk, cottage cheese, yogurt
Whole cheese: not to exceed 2 oz. servings (limit this due to high fat content)

\_\_\_\_   \_\_\_\_   MEAT, FISH, POULTRY, BEANS: Two 4 oz. servings per day
Limit beef & pork; Mostly fish, poultry with skin removed
Beans: daily for fiber content and protein value (mixed with grains)

\_\_\_\_   \_\_\_\_   JUNK: candy, crackers, cookies, chips, sweets, fried foods, oils or lard, ice cream, soda (no more than 1 per day).

\_\_\_\_   \_\_\_\_   WATER: preferably in natural form instead of coffee, tea, soda, juice.
Good daily average = 1/2 your body weight in ounces.

Look over this list: What's missing? What food groups do you eat more than you need to, which one's are too little?
Are you ready to change this and take responsibility for this piece of your Life Puzzle?

**Exercise #2. Twenty-one days makes a habit.**

It's best to concentrate on what you're going to add to your diet, not take away. It's much more effective to build your healthy diet instead of attacking and destroying your previous, less healthy diet.

So what shall you add to your diet? Look at the list below and choose one from each group to add to your diet for the next 21 days. DON'T OVERDO IT. If, (depending on your current life circumstances,) one from each group is too much don't do it. Choose just one from any of the groups. It is better to start small and be successful than to take on too much and find yourself unable to maintain your commitment. Remember: there are 17 three-week periods during a year. This gives you lots of time to build your nutrition lifestyle over the next year.

## NUTRITION LIFESTYLE ADDITIONS:

1. **Grains:** For three weeks add a 1/2 c. serving per week from the following list of whole grains. Brown rice, cous cous, quinoa, high quality pasta, bulgur wheat, millet, Basmati rice, wild rice, barley, orzo, veggie burgers, whole grain breads. These can be in the form of the grain, a cereal, bread, or a pasta.

2. **Veggies:** For three weeks add one extra fresh or frozen vegetable serving to your diet each day.

3. **Fresh fruit:** For three weeks add one per day.

4. **Beans:** For three weeks, add two 1/2 c. servings per week. Black beans, garbanzo, black-eyed peas, navy, kidney, lentil, etc.
   You can either buy them canned or prepare them fresh. (Contrary to popular belief, beans do not have to be soaked overnight. You can rinse them and put them straight into a pot, cover with water, bring to a boil, then reduce heat to a simmer and cook until they are soft—watch the water level while cooking, don't let beans soak up all the water and then burn the pot!)

5. **Proteins:** Change from high saturated fat protein (beef, pork, lamb) to lower fat selections: For three weeks use these selections instead of beef, pork or lamb.
   A. Fish: Broiled or baked, not fried.
   B. Skinless chicken servings
   C. Try vegetarian protein sources: grains + beans, or tofu = protein
   D. Skim milk dairy sources instead of whole milk.

6. **Fats:** add nothing in this category.

7. **Water:** For three weeks increase water consumption by one extra glass each day. If you currently drink no fresh water, add one glass per day. If you drink three glasses a day, increase to four, etc.

# Think!

*Consciously choose pro-active thinking to build your Life Puzzle.*

# *Think! ...about it.*

**T**hinking is your responsibility. Responsibility? Yeah…what you are thinking about right this second…who else could be responsible for it? I can't think for you…your mother can't think for you…your employer can't do it for you, your kids, your partner… nobody else can do it for you.

---

I think, therefore I am...

I AM, *WHAT*?

---

So are you thinking about it? Thinking is a skill, and one that you can always get better at if you just take the time to think about thinking!

Are you consciously aware of your thinking? Or have you stopped thinking and use a set pattern of reactions depending on the situation? Many of us get very good at reactive pattern thinking. Don't think unless you have to? Just do enough thinking to get you through the day?

If you're going to create a dynamic Life Puzzle, then you need to get pro-active in your thinking. There are six levels of thinking skills*. Which do you use most?

**1) Knowledge.** This is just basic fact or word gathering. We do fact gathering all our lives but especially when we are young. The simple fact of cat, dog, rabbit has to be learned. We're pretty factless when we get here!

**2) Understanding.** Facts don't mean much unless you understand what they mean. For instance if someone said to you "le chat", unless you understand it is the "fact" of the cat in the French language, then you have a fact, but no understanding. So, first we must learn the fact, then what it means.

**3) Applying or using it.** The third level of thinking is knowing when to use the facts that you understand. This takes practice, trial and error, throughout our lives.

For example, you might understand the fact of "a cat" but when do you apply this knowledge? Young children understand the word cat, but they don't always apply it correctly, calling every furry animal, "Cat!"

**4) Analyze.** This is pushing into high-level thinking. It requires good skills of knowledge, understanding and the risk of actually applying knowledge.

Many people quit thinking at this level because analyzing requires deep thinking or an extra effort to think at this level. It means making choices,

---

*based on Bloom's Taxonomy, Bloom, B. Englehart M., E. Furst, W. Hill and D. Krathwohl. (1956) Taxonomy of educational objectives. Handbook 1, Cognitive domain. New York: David McKay.

comparing one choice to another based on the facts, and the realization that more than one choice is possible. In many cases, more than one might be good. This confusion of what choice to make often shuts down the thinking process as people throw up their hands and give up. But if you're going to build your best Life Puzzle you need to think on this level...every day!

**5) Creativity.** New thinking! Creativity requires you to take old facts that you've understood and come up with a whole new way of using them that has not been thought of before. For example, in writing this book I'm doing creative thinking because I'm using common words but putting them down in a totally original way!

**6) Evaluating.** The toughest level of all. In this level of thinking, one has to place value or judgement on an object or idea. In some cases there is a standard to base the value or judgement on. In other cases one has to reject the current standard and create one's own before judging and thinking about the new idea. Probably as you are reading this book you are busy evaluating whether or not building a Life Puzzle is right for you and your lifestyle. You are judging against the norm of the old model you are familiar with!

### News flash:

*Most of the education you received in school centered around the first three levels of thinking!*\*

Studies show that the majority of learning that takes place in school is based around the first three levels of thinking skills: gathering facts, understanding them and using facts. But very little is done in the areas of analyzing, creativity and evaluation. Why?

High-level thinking requires a lot of effort! Think about it! It's easier to give a classroom of children a book on Egypt that gives them history facts and then ask them to regurgitate these facts on a test than it is to develop a unit on Egypt that digs into analyzing the political system, or focuses on creating a hieroglyphics alphabet and language used to send messages from one group to another.

It isn't because of any conspiracy by the teachers. It's just a simple matter of time in some cases. Or too many children in one class who are all functioning at different levels making the implementation of a high-level thinking class very difficult. And unfortunately for some, the teachers in your children's classrooms also were taught primarily on low-level thinking skills and that's where they feel most comfortable.

The sad fact is, very few of us are as good at thinking as we could be. The good news? You can teach yourself to be a better thinker!

### If you changed your thinking would you change your world? Yes. Emphatically yes.

The human brain is incredible in its ability to take in information, but what it does with this information is a unique mixture that results from thinking. If you are thinking at one level about an

---

\* read *A Place Called School,* by John Goodlad, McGraw-Hill Publisher, 1984

issue and someone else is thinking at a different level, will you end up with the same results, even though the information was the same? Obviously not.

So you can see why two people with the exact same information can end up with totally different results because they think, or process information, very differently.

Following along then, if you take the current information you have and change the way you are thinking about it, could you come out with a different result? Yes.

The reality about thinking? Reality only exists based on the thinking level you apply to it. Change your thinking level, change your world.

### It doesn't get more real than an ice cube or a hot coal, does it?

The power of the human mind to create reality based on the information that is fed to the brain results in your current reality. In an interesting case, inductees at a college fraternity hazing, were blindfolded and set down in front of a roaring fire. The frat brothers told the inductees that one of the tests was to withstand a hot coal being placed on the back of their necks. The frat brothers intensified the scene by screaming and acting as if they were being burned. Finally, the time came and the "coals" were placed on the inductees necks. Some necks showed burns. Yet when the blindfolds were removed, it wasn't hot coals that had been placed on their necks, but ice cubes! How did that happen? The power of the mind...believing makes it real, even when the "facts" prove otherwise. So it isn't the facts, it is the decision we make on how to use those facts that is the key.

## IDEAS FOR IMPROVING YOUR THINKING

• • • • • • • • • • • • • • • • • • • • • • •

### Imagination— believing is seeing!

Our society values logical thinking over fantasy thinking, leaving our imaginations, in many cases, to die! But it is in imagination and the freedom to dream that allows us to adventure into new areas.

To improve your thinking, honor yourself and open yourself up to imagine! A good starting point? Imagine a safe, wonderful place where you can go to find peace and tranquility. It may be in the mountains or near the ocean (mine's in Barbados!) but wherever it is, imagine it in the finest detail. Use your senses: What does it look like? What do you hear or smell? Are there any tastes (Pina Colada!)? What are you touching?

Imagine it until it is so real, simply by closing your eyes and imagining it, it becomes a real space for you where you can be rested and safe. Use it during times of stress or in the midst of chaos. Discover the power that imaginative thinking gives you in designing your Life Puzzle.

Imagination is a high-level thinking skill. It requires creativity, analyzing and in some cases evaluation if what you are imagining is also to have a practical application later on. Imagination opens up possibilities into new realms that need exploring in your life and the world around you.

## Brainstorming

We tend to solve problems in our Life Puzzle building by thinking linearly or in one dimension; we respond with the first thought that comes into our brains and then stick on it. This "one solution thinking" rarely produces the best results, whether it is an issue at work or more personal, such as what career to choose. Brainstorming is a method of expanding the possible number of solutions for any problem or dilemma that comes into your life.

In the first stage of brainstorming, the problem is presented and then all possible thoughts on the issue are written down. They don't have to be workable ideas, just list anything that comes into your head. No judgement allowed. The goal is to come up with as many ideas as possible within a short amount of time.

Next, let the ideas smolder for a while. Later, come back to the ideas and start sorting them out and making a decision on which one or ones are best for the problem being addressed. After you've weighed the pros and cons of each idea, choose what best fits the situation.

Brainstorming solutions to a problem produces amazing results. It can be used for almost any problem or issue that comes into your life. Brainstorming can be used in all sorts of ways:

1. With your family at the dinner table: Come up with ideas for keeping the house cleaner that you can all work together on.

2. Bored at work? Take time to brainstorm ideas to change how and what you do at work, ideas that are more stimulating for you and better for the business.

## Positive thinker or negative thinker? Which do you choose to be?

Why would anyone choose to be a negative thinker? Especially when you consider the alternative…being a positive thinker! Well, for many of us being a negative thinker, again, comes out of our childhood experiences. We got in the habit of thinking something wouldn't work out for us; that we weren't good enough; that if we tried, we'd fail. It doesn't take too many times of raising your hand with an answer, getting it wrong and hearing kids laugh at you before you interpret the world from a negative slant. This misinterpretation of the world around us as being scary, hard, awful, a dragon to be conquered, leads us to a negative thinking pattern. It helps protect us from all the hurts we felt as children.

The thinking habits we pick up as children are usually what we keep using as adults. If the world was scary and overwhelming to us, if we thought we were very different from others around us, we carry this into adulthood and continue to think these things…unless we decide to think differently.

Want to switch your thinking? The best recommendation I can give you is to read Norman Vincent Peale's *The Power of Positive Thinking*. In this book you will find yourself…both the old, negative thinker, and the potential for the new positive thinker. This book, written decades ago, is still a best seller because it works. It may not be the only book you read on thinking positively, but it is by far the best book to start with.

### "Another book report. Oh, no."

At one point in my career I taught psychology at the local community college. Each semester I assigned a book report, allowing only one person to sign up for each book. This offered variety when the oral reports were done.

Peale's, *The Power of Positive Thinking* was on the suggested booklist and invariably someone read it. And every semester I watched a life be transformed!

The most dramatic incident was a young boy, probably 19 years old. When he started the semester he sat in the back of the room, never adding anything to the usually vocal discussions that occurred in my classes. His eyes stayed looking down all the time. He was an attractive boy, but withdrawn.

However, halfway through the class, I started to notice a difference. One day he actually answered a question! Then he started adding ideas to the on-going discussion. He looked up, began to smile and had light in his eyes. What happened?

When I received his written book report, and he gave his oral, it was one of the most moving experiences I ever had in teaching. This boy got up and gave a very personal account of what this book had done for him. He shared how he had lived in borderline poverty his whole life, had never thought he was good enough and had started drinking and doing drugs. But when he read this book,

he learned that he could change his life, simply by confronting the way he thought about himself. He challenged his old negative thinking and was now actively finding ways to approach his world from the positive. He encouraged everyone to read it. I know many others did and changed their thinking too!

### Open your mind: expand your vision, let go of the old way of seeing an issue.

There was a time in my life when, in response to another person's actions, I became completely caught up in a negative thinking process. Every day, my mind dwelled on these events, "How could another person do this? This person is hurting my life. These actions must be dealt with through punishment. I must spend all my time making sure it doesn't happen again, being ready to be angry if it does happen again."

This consumed most of my daily thinking time. Even at work, as soon as I could switch my brain from thinking about some work that had to be done, I was back on this negative thinking process.

Then one day, as a result of moving away from this scene, it suddenly occurred to me that I was no longer having these thoughts, which of course had taken up practically every waking moment of the past year.

I was absolutely floored! It suddenly dawned on me that I was now thinking about all sorts of other things. I noticed I was much happier. I kept myself busy putting together a new household, making new friends and being quite productive. And in that moment I came to realize one very important lesson about thinking: We choose where and on what we decide to focus our thinking. I know now that I never had to waste all my time thinking about all those issues mentioned above. That was my choice and I could have spent that whole year thinking about a million things other than this person. So now, whenever I find myself getting caught in a thinking rut, I challenge myself to open my mind and expand the vision of things I am currently thinking about. Most important of all, I ask myself; Is there a totally different way of looking at this issue than the one I have come up with? More often than not the answer is yes.

## Creative thinking: a high level thinking skill we all have within us.

Creative thinking is the ability to make something new out of old ideas. It may be writing a poem that is new—the old idea is the typical words, the new is the way we arrange them to make a poem.

Anyone is capable of being creative.

What limits our creativity is often fear that what we create, whether it be a piece of art, a book, a crazy cartoon, a new dish in the kitchen, etc., won't be "right". This thinking rut leaves many of us to be dull thinkers missing out on our creative self.

Our creative thinking skills got muffled in the early school years. Studies show that by the time a child is 11 years old, most have stopped making attempts at artistic creativity, usually because early attempts have been ridiculed or didn't measure up.

To become a creative thinker again means taking the step to be vulnerable and open. You might take an unrestricted art class, write to yourself in a journal or perhaps join a class to learn floral design or pottery. Find a program that encourages you to be creative that isn't heavily judgemental.

What you'll find is with just a little effort, it is possible to become a creative thinker again! It is an exhilarating feeling to be back in touch with this part of your Life Puzzle. And the more you do it? The more you enjoy it!

# Distorted thinking: Getting caught in the rut. It's time to get out of it!

For most of us, the way we think becomes a habit. A bad habit. For example, the phone rings and it is your mother-in-law. Your thinking reaction is immediate, "Uh, oh, this is going to be trouble. Every time she calls, she upsets everyone." We're so busy setting our thinking pattern up we don't even listen to the other person. Like a bad tape that keeps going over and over in our minds, these thinking ruts control our response to the world around us.

## Thinking ruts make life stressful!

Change your thinking, and life becomes much less stressful.

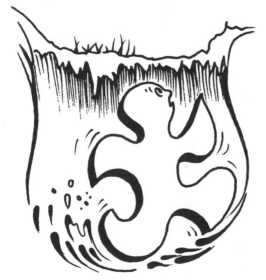

As an intelligent thinking human being you can change the way you think. Anyone can get caught in a thinking rut, but you can also get out of them! Positive self-talk or affirmations are a good starting point. It is helpful to write them down and say them to yourself every day. For example, if "oughtism" is your rut, write down all your "shoulds". "I should be rich and successful by the age of 35. I ought to be driving an expensive car. I should know how to do all jobs that my company has available." Now counter them. Why should you be rich and successful at 35? Is it true that only good people are rich and successful at age 35? Why are you tying your self-worth to this rich and successful "oughtism"?

Fight negative thinking ruts by replacing them with positives. Accept, for instance, that all sorts of terrific people never become rich or successful and they're still okay. So are you.

Every day work on countering your thinking ruts. One day you'll wake up to discover that you've countered them so well they no longer control your life.

If you find it very difficult to counter your negative thinking ruts, seek short-term counseling with this specific goal in mind as you work with the counselor.

# Which thinking rut are you in?

### All or Nothing Thinking:
It's all black or white, right or wrong, perfect or total failure—no middle ground allowed. (One typo on a report, the whole report was bad.)

### Overgeneralization
When we overgeneralize we take one event that turned out poorly and attach it to every similar event. Then we know all events will turn out this way. (I blew it once, I'll always blow it.)

### Avoid the Positive
Stop and ask yourself, what are the most positive things about yourself? Can't come up with any? You are in a thinking rut because everyone has good points. If you can find all negatives but not any positives, it's time for a change!

### Concentrate on the Negative
Here you interpret everything that's going on in your world from the negative side. You jump to immediate conclusions that all will turn out poorly, that others are reacting negatively to you. (Walking down the street, two people are talking. They start to laugh as you pass. Your thinking rut assumes they are laughing at you.)

### "Oughtism"
"I should" be this, think this, do this, have this, be treated a certain way. When you constantly find yourself thinking the world "should" be a certain way, you limit your life. Because your shoulds don't often happen exactly like they "should," leaving you always feeling defeated.

### Labeling/Mislabeling
This is extreme overgeneralization, where you tag every event with an emotional label. "I'm such a jerk, I'm awful, stupid." This thinking rut is a tape inside your mind that is playing on high. Turn it off!

### I'm responsible for the whole world
In this rut you assume responsibility for everyone's moods, feelings or life. You cause all bad things to happen (even though facts prove otherwise). This rut results in a lot of self-torture and guilt. Spending your life trying to make everyone else happy or making up for your last supposed mistake or hurt of another is exhausting. It takes up your whole life!

# What thinking rut are you in? Let's work on getting out.

Shushhhhhhhh…can you hear it? What's "she/he" saying? You say you don't hear it? It's there, you've just become so accustomed to the noise that you're not even aware it's there anymore. But it's very important that you learn to hear it again because it plays a big part in the way you decide to add the pieces to your Life Puzzle.

Do you know who I'm talking about? It's the inner voice that's directing your life. I liken it to a little guy or gal that sits on your shoulder and is constantly yelling at you. We all have it, but many of us are either completely unaware of it or have become so bombarded by the voice that we are like zombies…going through the motion of life but with the feeling that somebody else is directing us.

Some people call that little guy or gal the conscience and in some cases they're right. Like ol' Jimminy Cricket, that inner voice can help us stay on a moral track of treating ourselves and our fellow human beings appropriately. But for more of us, that little guy or gal is not the conscience but a distorted voice that keeps repeating negative thinking habits: thinking ruts. When your inner voice is controlled by thinking ruts it is impossible to design a Life Puzzle that is based in self-responsibility. When that little guy or gal is warping your view of the world around you with a negative slant, you spend most of your time living up to the distortion instead of focusing on pro-active choice making.

How do you get the guy or gal off your shoulder? Stop for a moment and acknowledge him or her. Is this inner voice your friend? Does this inner voice that sits on your shoulder directing your day keep you focused on the positive? Or the negative? Does it constantly leave you in a state of anxiety or fear? Has that negative inner voice become so loud that it colors everything in your world? If so, it's time for a change.

## You can't get the little guy or gal off your shoulder, but you can make it your friend!

You need your inner voice. Once you decide to make it your friend and refuse to let it keep you stuck in the (thinking) rut of negativism, you'll discover that the little guy or gal can actually be your best friend. But first you'll need to confront the thinking ruts he or she constantly slips you into when the world comes knocking at your door.

Let's examine again the thinking ruts. It's important for you to truly acknowledge which one(s) you use in your life. These are controlling your life. They get you through the day but prevent you from fully experiencing it with the joy and enthusiasm that can be yours when the little guy or gal is working as your friend.

## All or nothing thinking:

Do you see everything in black or white…all good or all bad? This is a high-anxiety way of living. We often get into this thinking rut as children because we have so little perspective on the world around us. As a child, a simple way of ordering our world is: bad or good…right or wrong. A 4 year-old will look at his or her drawing (scribble) and decide if it's good (goes on the refrigerator) or bad (in the trash). Then he or she goes on to the next task. But for some children, this ordering system overflows into everything they do so that at 16, they're either all pretty or all ugly, they're smart or stupid…but no in-between. And then we enter adulthood and we're still doing it: good mom, bad mom…good employee, bad employee…good person, bad person.

YES ___ NO ___        *My inner voice uses this thinking rut to order my life.*

## Overgeneralization:

Is this your thinking rut? When we overgeneralize we tend to take one event that ends up as a negative experience and assume that any similar event will end up the same. For example, if as a teenager you had a love relationship that you trusted, only to find out that the other person was cheating on you, do you now approach all relationships expecting that it's impossible to trust again? Does this now affect all your relationships?

When we overgeneralize negative events in our lives our thinking becomes consumed to such a degree that it clouds all of our life. We see the world through this overgeneralized haze that falls over all similar events. We become wary of the world around us and quite fearful of it— it becomes an expectation that life works out for other people….but not for me.

YES ___ NO ___        *Does your inner voice use this thinking rut as a cloud over your life?*

## Avoid the Positive:

Quick, ask your inner voice what are your five best qualities? What did it say? What, you don't have five good qualities? Yes you do...we all have at least five things that are good about ourselves. If you aren't able to come up with any positive statements about yourself then you are probably in the "Avoid the positive" thinking rut. It may not mean that you concentrate on the negative (a different thinking rut) but instead you fail to notice the positive in a given situation. As a result you'll give up more quickly because you can't see enough positive in order to continue.

YES ___ NO ___     *Is this a thinking rut that keeps you from your full potential?*

## Concentrate on the negative:

What's that dark cloud hanging over your head? Oh, the little guy or gal on your shoulder is covering you with a negative thinking rut. When this thinking rut has control of your life, every moment of your life becomes shadowed by the negative. You expect things to go wrong, that others are talking behind your back, that disaster lies just around the corner, that nothing is going to go right in your life. With this thinking rut, life becomes a stress-filled drudgery. It is next to impossible to create a healthy, well-balanced self when this thinking rut is in control of your life.

YES ___ NO ___     *Are you a negative thinking rut specialist? Can you instantly find the negative in any situation resulting in your doing very little in your life?*

## Oughtism:

I ought to be this, I ought to have this, I ought to do this, I ought, I ought, I ought...that's "oughtism". This thinking rut is one in which the little guy or gal who sits on your shoulder loves to whisper in your ear, " You should...be richer, smarter, thinner, farther up on the corporate line, have a bigger house, have more cars, be a better mother, be a better wife, be a taller man...etc." These "shoulds" become overwhelming and drive people crazy! Oughtism is a thinking rut that so completely runs one's life that literally you become wrapped up in fulfilling the "shoulds". And when we don't live up to that "should", which of course we can't because as soon as we reach one level—the thinking rut convinces us that we should be even better, it creates a lose/lose situation.

YES ___ NO ___     *Are you "oughtistic"? Is this thinking rut running your life?*

## Labeling/Mislabeling:

Caution: loud noise sitting on your shoulder. In the thinking rut of labeling/mislabeling, the little guy or gal has learned to tag everything you do with a label. And unfortunately the label is usually quite emotional and negative: "I'm hopeless, I'm a jerk, I'm no good, I'm *soooo* ugly, I'm the worst mother, all men are awful, all women can't be trusted"…on and on you go labeling the world. The problem with these labels is that once you attach them you act as if they're stuck there forever. This means your negative labeling has now become part of an extreme overgeneralization process. To stop this thinking rut you'll need to learn to listen to the inner voice and catch it before it labels your whole life into a negative process.

YES ___ NO ___    *Name five labels you've attached to yourself: Are they positive or negative? Name five labels you attached to one of the following groups: Blacks, Chinese, Gay Women, Men…are they positive or negative?*

## I'm responsible for the whole world:

Do you find yourself pulled in a million different directions while trying to please everyone you know: family, church, fellow workers, neighborhood groups, etc.? When you can't please everyone do you find yourself filled with guilt and anxiety? This thinking rut is a self-destructive process based on one gigantic, mistaken idea…that you have the ability to make everyone happy. Remember the Choosing Continuum? The pro-active, 5-10 side is based in self responsibility…not "self and the whole rest of the world responsibility!" When you run your life under this thinking rut two things happen: You go crazy as you carry the weight of the world on your shoulders, and secondly, you prevent others from taking responsibility for themselves because you're always rushing in ahead.

YES ___ NO ___    *Take a load off your shoulders! This thinking rut is unnecessary for your Life Puzzle. Teach others to take on their own responsibilities and work in partnership so that everyone wins.*

## Guiltism: negative thinking gone wild

Earlier in the book we discussed the issue of guilt. Guilt, if looked at correctly, is a breach of moral conduct. It is an offense that violates another person and for which the violator must accept moral guilt and its consequences.

However, for many people guilt is not just a breach of moral conduct (like the Ten Commandments). Guilt is tied to almost any offense, real or imagined, that happens in one's life. Guilt is also the word used when we feel inadequate, for example some people feel guilty when they try to do their best but it still doesn't quite measure up.

When we mix up true guilt with exaggerated and misplaced guilt life can go crazy. At this point, our lives become consumed with guilt as it controls our every move. When this happens, guilt has lots its true value to our lives: conscience.

When guilt becomes all-consuming it moves beyond the voice of conscience and becomes a self-destructive force in our lives. When overwhelmed with the guilt feeling, one's life becomes limited and you begin to feel a victim to the world around you. Everywhere you look everything you do leaves you feeling guilty. This is exhausting! When guilt is running your life you are in a reactive pattern to the events of your day. Guiltism defines your reaction, "I am guilty about everything."

YES ___ NO ___ *Enough already. Remind yourself daily of the true definition of guilt! Breach of moral conduct…are you really as guilty as you tell yourself? NO!*

---

## What's your (mis)perception?

One's perception is one's view of the world. This world view is known as one's personal truth of the world as they see it. Thus, everyone's perception is unique and individual. Though you and I might agree on many aspects of the world we perceive, if we talk long enough it won't be long before we find some issue on which we differ.

There are many reasons why each of us perceives the world differently. If I'm a woman and you're a man, we're very likely to have different perceptions on issues. Take boxing, for example. I see no value in it, but a man may give me a dozen reasons why it's good. My perception is based on female gender, where I grew up, and experiences I've had with the issue. A man's perception is also based on gender, where he grew up, and experience on the issue—say, for example his dad taught him to box when he was twelve and it was a great bonding time for the two of them. Well this man's perception is probably much more favorable of boxing than mine.

And thus, with the millions of different issues out there, we each have our own perceptions. One of the factors that highly affects our perceptions of the world is our thinking style. If you are a negative thinker, then your perception of the world will be seen through this thinking filter of negativity. If you are an optimistic, positive thinker, then your perception of the world will be seen through this thinking filter of positiveness.

Will these two people be different? You bet they will. One is likely to be reactive, feeling victimized and frustrated by the world around them. They often blame others for their life problems. On the other hand, a positive thinker is much more likely to be pro-active and self-responsible for their lives.

The problem for many of us is that we are completely unaware of the different influences that have merged together to create our world view. And many of us set our world view…in stone…by the time we are 14 or 15 years old. We decide then what's true about the world: It's mean, it's bad, it's out to get me, it hurts. Or we might have come to the conclusion that life is an adventure to be lived like a giant rollercoaster ride…on to the next hill! Once we decide what's true about the world we operate our lives based on this perception.

But what if your perception is really a "mis"perception? A truth arrived at through faulty interpretation of information and experiences? Think about this now…if you are running your life based on misinterpretation of information or life experiences instead of the correct interpretation, how will this affect your life? You'll be acting out life based on a truth that isn't true. Yikes!

For example, I once heard an adolescent describe her mother's abandonment of the family when she was 4 years old. According to this girl the mother left and didn't return for six months. When the mother described the event (backed by other adult family members) she was actually gone for only two days before returning. At that time she proceeded to move in with another man, but maintained daily contact with her daughter. However the trauma of this event had become confused in this girl's mind. While she sat describing the pain of this six month abandonment— which for her was a "real truth"—she cried and spewed anger at her mother. This anger, based on a total (mis)perception of the real events, was controlling her relationship with her mother into the present. She wanted an apology for this.

Now her mother was sitting there with her mouth hanging open. She knew she hadn't left for six months, and others corroborated this information to her 16 year-old daughter. Her mother said, "How do I apologize for something I didn't do? I'm sorry I left your father but I never left you but for two days. And I was in your life every day after that. How did you get it into your head that I was gone for six months?"

We never could figure out how this girl had created this misperception. But confronted with it, she was able to release her anger and resume a healthy relationship with her mother.

## What is your misperception?

The truths so many of us hold aren't really true, although like the girl above we will cry out and insist that our perception of the world can only be the one that we have. However, as many of us examine our lives, especially in the way we think, we will discover the truths we hold so dear are ready to be changed. Get out of old thinking ruts, open up your creative self…even though you perceive (or misperceive?) that you're not creative!

If you are a negative thinker, it's quite possible that it came from a misperception of events earlier in your life. It's helpful to work with a counselor to help you find these misperceptions, put them into a new perspective, and begin again to grow your Life Puzzle.

## Suggested reading list

Gerald Jampolsky                      *Change Your Mind, Change Your Life.*

David Burns                           *The Feeling Good Book*

Martin Seligman                       *Learned Optimism*

John Roger & Peter McWilliams         *Life 101 series*

Manuel Smith                          *When I Say No, I Feel Guilty*

Norman Vincent Peale                  *The Power of Positive Thinking*

---

# ACTION PLAN

### Exercise #1.

*The Power of Positive Thinking*, by Norman Vincent Peale: If you haven't read it, now would be a good time to do so.

### Exercise #2.
### Time for a discussion with the little guy or gal on your shoulder.

Go to your journal and write a letter to your inner voice: talk back to it. Write a letter as if you are writing to a friend. Confront negative thought patterns that are controlling your life. You might give this guy or gal a name and ask it to stop making you think poorly of yourself, or to be more supportive when certain events happen.

Often when writing incidences down on paper we are able to reread them and then— using positive thinking skills, creative thinking and brainstorming—we can rewrite our lives and live them more effectively.

### Exercise #3.
### Review the thinking ruts.

Below, write the one(s) you think you get caught up in on a day to day level.

1. List specific issues/examples/actions that are connected to this thinking rut. What triggers this thinking process? The more specific examples you write down the better.

   *Example:* Overgeneralization—husband is late coming home from work and hasn't called. (Lateness overgeneralizes to "something bad has happened.")

2. After you list the specific trigger event that sets off the thinking rut, then describe the exact thinking process you go through.

   *Example:* You start worrying that there's been a car accident or that he's dead. You are moving to near panic thinking...pacing back and forth. By the time your husband walks through the door you find yourself screaming at him for making you this upset and angry. He stands there in shock, saying..."What did I do now?"

3. Now, undo this thinking rut. What would you do instead? Do you need to overgeneralize this situation?
   A. Why do you overgeneralize his lateness?
   B. Why do you assume the worst imaginable possibility?
   C. What would you say to yourself instead of these overgeneralized thoughts?

   What could you visualize instead? If this happens repeatedly with your husband, could the two of you discuss ways to work out a system so you don't react in overgeneralizing?

   Repeat this process for all your thinking ruts.

# Feelings

## Do we think first then feel?

*As young children, we feel first, think second. Then, after the age of about 10, it becomes a 'crazy 8'. Sometimes our feelings impact our thinking, other times our thinking creates our feelings. Learning to manage our feelings and be fully conscious thinkers is very important!*

# *Feelings*

**H**ow many feelings can you name? I asked this once of a class I was teaching and this is what we came up with:

| | | | |
|---|---|---|---|
| Frustrated | Melancholy | Lonely | Explosive |
| Angry | Blue mood | Hopeful | Exhausted |
| Sad | Depressed | Hopeless | Exhilarated |
| Happy | Lethargic | Useless | Excited |
| Elated | Dull | Stupid | Hatred |
| Ticked off | Glad | Sinister | Love |
| Tense | Isolated | Evil | Indifferent |
| Nervous | Estranged | Bad | Numb |
| Irritable | Giddy Silly | Sick | Wonderful |
| Anxious | Tied in knots | Revengeful | Joyous |
| Afraid | Anticipation | Violent | Dumb |
| Fearful | Overwhelmed | Mean | Peaceful |
| | | | Relaxed |

Do you notice something about the list above? Try categorizing the list under these two subheadings: Positive Feelings and Negative Feelings.

The totals: Of 50 feelings identified, the majority, 32, fall under negative feelings, while only 18 fall into the positive feelings category. For some reason it was much easier to come up with a large number of negative feelings. I've tried this experiment several times and always have the same results. Oh, the numbers fluctuate a little bit, but the basic results keep recurring. We are consumed with lots of negative feelings and very few positive feelings.

Why? I don't know that there is a simple explanation to it but you can trace a lot of it back to our early days.

## Fight or Flight?

At a core level, feelings are a survival skill that helped man get through some of his early history. For early man feelings were a response to a very scary environment: This is known as the fight or flight response. As man evolved, the ones who made it were the ones who could quickly react to any threats, be it other men, animals or the environment. Man's early emotions were fairly limited…and mostly centered around negative fear reactions: attack it or run from it. As man continues to evolve, his environment has become a little less hostile in some ways (no more of those Saber-toothed Tigers) but is more hostile in subtle, non-physically threatening ways.

Our emotional evolvement has improved only slightly. Many people still run their emotional self in reaction to a world they find very threatening. Whether it is your boss yelling at you, overdue bills piling up on your desk, or a decision to change jobs, life still provides many threats to us. We continue to respond to many of these threats with negative, fear-based feelings. It was a successful tactic for most of man's existence, why not now? Well, that's the tricky part about taking responsibility for our feelings. Many of these negative feelings have stopped serving man and his survival and are actually limiting it. It's time for us all to evolve to the next level: pro-active Life Puzzle-making.

## Getting past survival feelings:

Feelings still happen on a rather gut level. In fact, the feeling area of the brain, the limbic system, lies in the "gut" of the brain, deep and dark in there!

As an adult, a lot of our feeling responses are deeply ingrained as a result of our childhood. Young children's feelings are often based in fight or flight as they try to deal with a very scary environment. The fact is, when you're young and small and just about everything you encounter is either bigger, stronger or very strange, survival emotions of fight or flight serve

you quite well. Anger and fear reactions are very common even in newborns as these responses usually get results. A crying baby who is hungry, gets fed…a baby that is giggling and smiling doesn't get a feeding response…so what does the baby learn to do…cry when hungry. Lo and behold, looks what's coming…a bottle! Boy, that works well!

A lot of our early feelings work like this. Another area where we learn what feelings to use and when, is by watching the adults that are taking care of us.

Thus, if we watch our parents or other caretakers fly off the handle in anger at other adults, or they hit us in anger because we accidently spilled the milk, we begin to learn about anger. How we interpret this information about feelings, what they are, and how to use them will play a big part in our adulthood and how we emotionally respond to the world around us.

Many adults never develop their feelings much beyond their early, young childhood level. While they may be adults in age and size, emotionally, they are still children who spend every day, fighting or running from the scary world they were raised in.

## Reinterpreting your feelings: getting beyond survival reactions

If you grew up in a world where abuse occurred, where you watched emotionally unbalanced adults as role models, or if you had alcoholic parents or care-givers, then the likelihood of your growing into your own adulthood with a good understanding of your true feelings about the world around you is at risk.

This is not to say that you should go blame your parents for not being better "feeling role models." Yes, maybe they should've been, but in most cases you will find that your parents did the best they could, because they too grew up in a world where their own feelings got all screwed up.

Taking responsibility for your feelings at this point of your journey is about relearning what your true feelings are instead of continuing to respond from the old patterns you were shown.

One thing many of us did as young children was to misunderstand what was actually happening when our parents were mad, sad or scared. We took it way too personally! Young children think they are the center of the universe and everything that happens is because of them. Thus, when parents are mad, scared or sad, children think it's because of something they did. The connection many children make is that they are bad, awful children. A child's emotional reaction to this confusion may be to withdraw, decide to hate himself or to act out, becoming a rebel.

We don't usually pick a wide variety of feeling labels for ourselves. As children we pick one or two that work for the moment and they often stick with us for life. Thus, if Suzy withdraws as a feeling response and Harold responds as a bully to cover up his feelings, they will likely continue to do this as adults.

Let's get back on track! You can learn to feel, with appropriate feelings for the situation at hand. To do this you need to explore the feelings you have about yourself.

How do you define yourself? Are you really a short-tempered person? Are you an anger-control person allowing yourself to feel nothing because you're afraid that once you let one angry feeling in you'll have an anger that just won't quit?

Only you know exactly what you are feeling inside. If you have blocked this aspect of yourself, or are still living out a child's perceptional feeling, it is time to stop and look within.

Because relearning the true feelings about ourselves can be confusing and at times downright overwhelming, I encourage you to consider working with a counselor. A good counselor can help you to address feelings connected to earlier misinterpretations and help you set them straight.

*"But she makes me so angry, I can't see straight when I talk to her.*
*Last night I got so mad that I punched a hole in the wall!"*

"No Jason, she doesn't make you mad, you make yourself mad," I said as I propped the phone receiver on my shoulder. I knew this was going to be a long conversation.

"No, you're wrong Ann, you don't know her like I know her. She lies, cheats, makes up stories about me. She's done drugs, been an alcoholic for years and every time I see her or talk to her I just want to explode she makes me so angry," was his reply. His voice was getting kind of testy.

"Well Jason, I hear what you're saying and I agree with you. Based on the court records I have in my hands that show me what the two of you have been doing to each other over this custody battle, your ex-wife doesn't have a stellar record. However, at this time she's cleaned up her act, has been drug and alcohol free for two years, is re-employed and wants custody of your daughter who says she wants to live with her."

Jason broke in, "Yes, and all that's a fake. I know her, you guys don't. Just thinking about everything she's done to me I get so angry. She's ruining my life and I am so mad I could kill her. You'd be angry too if you'd gone through what I've gone through with her."

Again, I said, "You don't have to be angry Jason, you could choose to just relax and let it go." This resulted in another round of "No I don't have a choice, I have to be angry at her because if I don't, she'll get me." This conversation went on for 45 minutes, with him insisting he had to be angry, me insisting he could choose something else.

Jason is like many people, they assign one emotion to everything that happens in their world. His emotion was anger to the point of rage. I decided to send Jason some information on anger and how to control it. In a nutshell, it challenged him to re-look at anger and realize that emotions don't choose where to go, we choose what emotional response we assign to a set of circumstances.

A week later Jason's social worker calls and says, "What did you do to Jason?" I tentatively responded, "I didn't do anything."

"Well, you must have done something because a miracle has occurred! For the first time in six years he and his wife sat in the same room and didn't have a fight. In fact, they had a nice peaceful conversation. He's agreed to let her have custody. What did you do?"

"All I did was send him a book that said he could choose to have another feeling about any situation if he would choose to…apparently he chose to!"

Two years later I saw Elizabeth at the park and she introduced me to her father, Jason. He thanked me for changing his life. He and his wife were friends again and his daughter was much happier now that they didn't fight every time they got together.

"I didn't change your life Jason, you did. You received information that could change your life…and you chose to use it. You changed your life by owning your own feelings."

## What am I feeling?

At the core of it all, there are only four feelings: mad, sad, glad or fear. There are subtle variations within each of these four allowing us a wide range of emotions to use in our lives.

The emotions we assign to a particular set of circumstances are learned behaviors that are tied up with our thinking process. In others words, feelings don't just happen. We feel based on previous experience (learned behavior) along with our current thinking patterns.

For example, you're going to a baby shower. What are you feeling? Well, if you have children, like the person the baby shower is for and have time to attend, you'll probably feel glad—happy, excited, relaxed, pleased.

However, if this baby shower is for someone you don't like or this is their fourth child and they have neglected and abused their other children, what are you feeling now? Mad? Sad? Certainly not glad! Will you arrive with a clenched jaw, talk to no one and glare at the expectant mother?

Did she make you feel this anger? NO. You chose the feeling, based on circumstances and your thinking pattern. Could you choose to unclench your jaw? Sure! Smile at the expectant mother and offer her help and support because you understand she grew up in an abusive home and needs help? What are you feeling now?

## Feelings don't just happen!

We choose what feelings we attach to every moment of our day. You can either choose through a conscious act or out of habit. To become more conscious of what you are feeling it is necessary for you to have an inner dialogue with yourself and ask: Is this what I want to feel? What could I feel instead? What action do I need to take to change my feelings?

Many of our feelings are tied to our thinking (mis)perceptions. As you become a more conscious thinker it will allow you to become a more conscious feeler. When our thinking is skewed toward the negative it is likely the feelings we assign to events will also be skewed.

An excellent book to read is *The Feeling Good Book* by David Burns. This book connects feelings and thinking, teaching you how to break out of old patterns and become much more pro-active in both.

## Is it love or is it fear?

In many ways, all feelings fall under these two categories. A simple exercise throughout the day is to repeatedly ask yourself, "What am I feeling at this moment, love or fear?" If it is fear…why am I feeling this? How could I change the way I am approaching this situation so I could have feelings of love instead?

This is a way to become much more conscious of what you are feeling as well as becoming more conscious of your ability to change feelings by pro-actively challenging your feelings. It may seem simplistic, but it will work for you as you attempt to bring your feelings into greater awareness and focus throughout your day. You will find as you get in the habit of doing this that it helps you quickly refocus when the stress of the day is beginning to overwhelm you. When you label your anxiety over the boss's phone call, you can challenge whether or not you must react to it with fear (anxiety) or could choose love (acceptance) instead. Or when yelling angrily at the children, ask yourself…love or fear? Which do I want? This helps you center on choosing emotions that work for you, not against.

## How can a person not know what they are feeling?

As a counselor I hear this question a lot from people who can't understand how individuals can be so out of touch with their own feelings that they can commit a crime, like child sexual abuse or premeditated murder.

Because feelings are learned behaviors often connected to our childhoods, many children enter adulthood with a confusion of what to do with feelings that overwhelmed them as children. If you've been abused or grew up in an alcoholic or drug-abusing family, it is very likely you learned to cut off all feelings. You've learned how to numb yourself as an effective coping skill. It helped you get through a crazy, pain filled childhood but it will hinder your adulthood.

Working with adult child abusers, we often find that they too were abused. They can abuse children because they have become numb to their own feelings. They don't understand the pain they are creating in the children they abuse, because they feel nothing.*

I worked with one such man who literally had to be taught to assign feelings to his day. Every half hour he had to look at a list of index cards that had feelings labeled on them: mad, sad, glad, fear. Each card had a description of what this might feel like by describing behavior attached to these feelings. Then he had to write down his current feeling.

Along with this we taught him how to manage his feelings. Previously he abused his children when he was very frustrated. He only knew how to vent frustration through the physical release of sex and orgasm. We taught him another option: to feel his feelings. To understand he was frustrated and to have appropriate responses: take a walk, talk it out, do positive self-talk, etc.

## Too much or too little: feelings and you.

Most of us can understand how the example of child abuse can create a problem with one's feelings. Yet many of us who have never experienced such a trauma may have grown up in an environment that taught us to mask our feelings from ourselves and others.

Men are notorious for learning to numb all feelings as an efficient way to deal with the confusion they feel as children. But this numbing can have life-long consequences. One gentleman I was talking to made it clear that he was quite proud of his ability to control his feelings so that very little hurt him. One day this ability had a dramatic impact on how extreme the control of one's feelings can become.

He was wearing shorts and I looked at his leg and said, "Do you realize that your left ankle is swollen?" He looked down and agreed it did look a bit swollen. He removed his shoes and socks and it was

---

*Please note: A common perception is that if you've been molested or abused as child that you will grow up to be a molester too. This is not true. The majority of people who have been molested as children do not grow up to repeat this behavior. However, of those few adults who are child molesters it is usually found that they were abused as children. Thus while most abused children do not repeat it as adults, a very small minority do.

apparent his foot was swollen too. I asked him if he experienced any pain and he admitted that only recently had it reached a pain level that he could no longer ignore. So I asked him how long this had been going on and he responded "Oh, three or four months, but I'm so good at ignoring my pain that it hasn't even bothered me." There was a smile on his face that showed pride. It obviously never occurred to him that this skill of blocking his feelings was actually hurting him.

I insisted he head to the doctor for an x-ray. And the report? He had a hairline fracture in this foot. Talk about not listening to your feelings! This is a simple example of how not being consciously aware of your feelings, *choosing to not feel them* can hurt you.

Many others go to the opposite extreme and let one or two strong emotions become their response pattern. Anger, fear and hopelessness can become predominant feelings that influence everything else in one's life. Until these individuals expand their consciousness of the full range of feelings this excess of the one or two feelings will hurt their life.

How about you? Do you know your true feelings?

## The Crazy 8 of feelings and thinking.

When we're young, we feel first and think second. That's because a very young child's logic or thinking portion of his brain is still developing. How often do we shake our heads at a 5 year old and say "what were you thinking?" Of course, that young, they weren't necessarily thinking logically, because they don't have the data/facts to be able to make logical choices.

Around age 10, logic is possible when our life experiences have provided data/facts from which we can make good choices. Sometimes, however, our thinking can get 'skewed' and when this happens our skewed logic results in creating feelings that skew the choices we make. This is the "Crazy 8" of feelings and thinking.

For example, your husband is late arriving home for dinner and your 'logic' says, "Oh my, maybe he's been in a car accident.". As you nurture this 'thought' your emotions begin to rise and fear takes over. You begin to panic, blood pressure goes up and as each minute goes by, you're more convinced your 'logic' is right and your fear is appropriate. You are now in the 'Crazy 8' of feelings and thinking—your skewed thoughts are creating skewed feelings.

Breaking the cycle starts with becoming aware of the intricate dance that your feelings and thinking do together. Then it's time to pay attention and train your SELF to decide where you place your thoughts and whether your SELF manages feelings or feelings manage SELF.

Whenever you get into this type of Crazy 8 cycle, STOP. Gather your SELF, and ask, "Where am I putting my thoughts and is this logical or skewed?, and secondly, Are my feelings in charge of my SELF or my SELF in charge of my feelings. SELF needs to take charge of both thoughts and feelings. If you are overwhelmed by it all, write it down and look at it in black and white!

# *Feelings : a vital part of your Life Puzzle*

**Y**ou may be wondering why feelings have a separate section of the Life Puzzle. Whereas nutrition, exercise or work are obvious parts of your Life Puzzle, why do feelings play such an important part of your quest for balance and wholeness?

Feelings or emotions, along with thinking, are a part of your survival mechanism. For example, feelings such as fear help you respond to loud noises. On a much higher level, feelings help you manage the sensory stimulation from your eyes, ears, skin, nose and mouth. Everything that comes into your life creates some level of feeling response. Feelings are present to help you through life.

At the same time though, when inappropriate emotional responses are connected to outside events, these very same feelings can hurt you...and at the extreme kill you. You can almost scare your self to death. That is why it is important for you to become conscious of your feelings. In doing so you determine which emotions are best suited for the events of the day.

## Emotions from the head affect the body.

Your body hears everything your mind says and reacts accordingly. As such, if your mind is overwhelmed with emotions such as fear, the body will instantly react and change itself. If it is short-range fear, for example someone running after you with a knife, then it's terrific that your body "hears" the fear and runs. But after this threat is over, if your mind continues to replay the event and the anxiety and fear builds up, your body will hear this too and react. Only now, there's nothing to run from so what will your body do? Instead of physically running your body will create havoc inside itself. You might find yourself with an upset stomach, racing heart, continual headaches or panic attacks. Unless you learn to manage your emotions these bodily reactions to this emotional fear will create sickness.

This body-mind connection has become well documented in studies. The stress in one's life and the emotional reaction to it, is a great cause of illness. That's the bad news. The good news is that all of us, by taking conscious responsibility for learning about our feelings, can use our emotions effectively *for* ourselves instead of against.

Norman Cousins' book, *The Biology of Hope,* is an excellent representation of the body-mind connection as it relates to illness. This book documents world wide studies being done on the feeling of hope. In this book it becomes clear that each of us has the ability to direct our emotions in ways that can help or harm. For those who choose to focus their emotions towards a positive balance, even in the midst of high stress, it is possible to improve the state of one's physical health.

This is not to say that we can "feel" ourselves out of all health problems. When one is ill there is certainly more to one's health care than simply throwing positive feelings at the problem. But if you are not aware of the mind-body connection then it is likely that you will not use your emotions as a powerful ally in your health.

That's why it is important to make feelings a separate section of your Life Puzzle. They are vital and need an awareness in your life as great as your daily nutrition, exercise or the work you choose. Your feelings impact your Life Puzzle, yet few of us have been taught to give them the recognition and importance that are necessary. This awareness is a critical step in putting together your healthiest Life Puzzle.

## Where are you on the Choosing Continuum when it comes to your feelings?

You might be thinking that on the left side of the Continuum, feelings would fall in the negative range, on the right side feelings would be positive, but that's not what the Choosing Continuum is asking you about. The real question is this: Are you reactive in your feelings (left side) or are you pro-active and consciously choosing your feelings to the world (right side). Are you aware of them or do you ignore them?

We become so busy in our world that we become numb to our feelings. This numbness doesn't mean that you are feeling negative or positive…it's more like you're not feeling your true feelings at all. So using the Choosing Continuum, the key issue here is are you aware of, conscious of, a full range of feelings in your life? Are you in a conscious process of choosing how you emotionally respond to the world around you? Even in the midst of a depression or blue mood you can still be on the right side of the Continuum if you are allowing yourself to recognize and fully own the feeling.

For example, in the process of moving to a new town my feelings became a hodgepodge filled with highs and lows. One day I was excited as I made new contacts and explored the different possibilities available. Then there were days when I felt blue and wanted to just call an old friend for a cup of coffee but alas, she's 300 miles away! The highs I was pleased to have. Of course, who wouldn't be? But the lows were actually just as important to be aware of and grow through in order to make the transition complete.

By this I mean that to have hidden from the blue mood by keeping myself too busy to feel, or nursing it with alcohol or other drugs or simply to have just refused to feel it, I would have stuffed those feelings deep inside, leaving me numb.

Negative feelings make many of us so uncomfortable that we avoid the lessons of growth that can come out of them. Life isn't supposed to be a bed of roses—it is filled with lumps and bumps along the way. We can use the lumps and bumps to make us stronger. But if we hide ourselves from the full range of feelings we actually become more anxious and afraid of the world around us. Then we don't grow, we stagnate and exist...doing just enough to get by. Stuffed feelings also lead to health problems: irritable bowel, headaches and heart attacks.

With practice, we can instead allow ourselves to recognize and validate any and all feelings that come into our lives and consciously choose what to do with them. I know for myself, now that I've been through a few of these big moves that out of this sadness will emerge a new and stronger self. But I can't find that self unless I'm willing to acknowledge the positive feelings as well as the negatives and choose appropriate responses from which to grow my life.

## Smile or frown?
## Is it reflecting your feelings?

One easy way to become aware of your feelings is to become aware of your face. Close your eyes for a second...if someone was looking at you, what would your face be telling them? What type of look is on it? Are you frowning? Are you smiling? Is your face blank? Do you have any idea what other people see when they are looking at your face?

Most of us are unconscious and totally unaware of our facial expression when resting. Whether walking down the street, sitting at your desk concentrating on a new project or reading the morning newspaper at the breakfast table, what is your face saying? To

yourself and then to others? You may not be aware of it but your facial expression is sending your inner self and those around you lots of messages. The question is, is it a conscious message or a numb one? Do you know what it's saying? Why not?

I'm not suggesting you slap a firm smile on your face and never let it change. I'm encouraging you to become more conscious of your daily presence to yourself and others. Your facial expression is a part of this. If you look at most people around you, you'll notice that most wear a blank look or a frown. Why? Considering the fact that it actually takes less muscles of the face to wear a smile than it does to frown, it would appear more natural for you to smile. So why don't we?

The next time you go outside, start looking at people and their faces. What are their faces telling you? Do you think they have any idea of the messages their faces are sending out to you? Or are their faces on autopilot? Notice how the lines become etched—does the deepness suggest they've been wearing this expression a long time?

Are we really as stressed out, angry or frustrated as our faces seem to say? Or are we just so unaware of ourselves it has never occurred to us to ask this question? Have we taken our numbness so for granted it seems normal?

I attended a weekend retreat with health professionals that really brought the facial issue home to me. At the end of the experiential seminar one of the participants challenged me, saying that he had noticed that my face had a smile on it all weekend and he didn't really find it to be true, because no one smiles that much without it being a mask. I challenged him back, saying it is a crazy world that thinks wearing a frown (which I reminded him he had shared with me the entire weekend!) is a true and natural face but one with a smile is not.

My face is not always in a smile, but I am consciously choosing my "at rest face" to reflect a small smile instead of a frown. It's more relaxing than a frown and will leave me with a few less lines when all is said and done! When you become aware of your Life Puzzle making you will discover that your face can reflect many feelings, by conscious choice.

## Men, Sex and Feelings

Ask almost any woman what she would like her husband or partner to share with her and it won't be money… it would be true, honest feelings. The constant lament from women is that men just do not share their feelings enough (and many men think that women share too much of them!). This dilemma causes many problems in marriages but even more importantly for men, it causes many problems within themselves.

Let me assure you before you think this section is going to be blasting of men and their lack of feelings and expression. It isn't! Men do not share their feelings in this society because we have set it up that: 1) they do not learn to feel a wide range of emotions, 2) We do not allow or even encourage them to express emotions in appropriate forms, 3) We raise them in a world that teaches that sharing your feelings leaves you vulnerable and open to attack from others. In short, our society gets what it deserves when it comes to men knowing, expressing and trusting true feelings because of what we teach them as boys.

Feelings are a learned behavior. Babies quickly learn which emotions get them the quickest response to their needs. As we grow older though, we get much more subtle lessons about our feelings. Young girls are encouraged to feel, and in fact, it is by sharing our feelings with other girls that we are rewarded with friendships and create our supportive community. Little boys on the other hand get a mixed message. A little boy who shares his feelings becomes ostracized or called a sissy. This gets him cast out from male society, though it will welcome him for a time into female society. What is our man learning? Keep feelings inside you, hide your heart.

By the time a boy is 10 years old he has learned this quite well. Walk by a playground and you can see the different way boys and girls act.

Now puberty hits and it's going to get a little more confusing for our young gentleman. Lots of different things are going on inside his body and his mind. Confusion reigns. Where does he go to express this feelings? His friends? His parents? Not likely. There are few outlets available to most boys who grow up in our society. These things just aren't talked about, and so he learns again to stuff the feelings inside. This is building up a lot of pent up energy. How to release it? Ah, the blessing in disguise…he may not be able to share his feelings of confusion, pain, or sorrow verbally, but he can release a lot of energy through an orgasm—a new and powerful outlet that has just become available.

Add on top of this all the messages he receives through media and peers to use sex as an outlet for feelings, and we have set up a lose/lose proposition for everyone! We have provided a society for boys that teaches them to hide their true feelings from everyone because it leaves them vulnerable. Instead we have taught them to connect and release feelings—frustration, anger, fear, sadness, anxiety, and joy,—through sex. Sex equals power and control, albeit, temporarily since orgasm is so fleeting.

A boy grows up and is taught to stuff his feelings inside and then women somehow expect that as adults these very same men will know how to verbally express their true feelings. Sorry ladies, it just doesn't happen! We are as responsible for creating this problem as men because we reinforced it as mothers, sisters and girlfriends.

If a boy has learned to express his emotions through a sexual outlet he will naturally continue to do this as an adult. He is usually completely unaware of this link. Think of the last fight you had with your partner. You're still mad at each other and you go to bed. While you're laying there quite stiffly the husband reaches out and touches you. Instantly you know what he wants: sex. And what does a woman think? "How dare he!" And she rebuffs him mightily. You know what ladies? You just missed his apology. Reaching out to you to make love is his way of saying, "I'm sorry and I'm feeling awful we just fought. *Let's have sex* equals *Let's make up.*

Now gentlemen, you may be chuckling as you read this (or feeling indignant that she didn't understand this— "How dare she!"), but your partner needs to talk and share her feelings. Women find it very difficult to make love when they're mad at their partner, as sex does not release anger for a woman. But it does for a man who uses sex to express feelings of all kinds instead of talking about them directly.

Another example of how men stuff their feelings is directly linked to their hearts, as in heart attacks. Interesting research shows that when men under the age of 50, were asked why they thought they had a heart attack, the reason was always tied to an emotional event, such as a death in the family, divorce or loss of a job. Unable to speak openly about their emotional pain, their heart attack allowed them to receive socially approved nurturing and support without them having to ask.

## How do we break this cycle? You start with yourself and your immediate family members.

If you are female, change your attitude about men and their feelings. They are not deceptively trying to hide their feelings from you anymore than they are aware of hiding them from themselves. Few men have ever learned to experience a full range of emotions, so they'll have a difficult time sharing what they don't know. So add compassion and understanding when approaching men on this level. Then, begin to nurture a trusting environment where all men will be able to share feelings without fear of retaliation. Go to the chapter on communication and review some of the steps you can take to build positive communication.

Ask yourself if you are sending mixed signals to your male family members. Do you laugh at your son when he complains of a hurt leg, telling him to buck up and ignore it? After a hard day at work for the both of you, do you walk away in disgust when your partner tries to engage you in sex instead of appreciating and understanding why some men enjoy a quick sex release? Do you open up a dialogue on this? Can you balance your needs with his?

If you are male: first and foremost you need to go back and look at your childhood. What were the messages you learned about men and their feelings? Was your father loving, able to show physical caring with hugs and kissing, or was he cold and rough and hard-edged, sending you a message that this is what a "real man" feels? Was your mother overindulgent or cold shouldered? Did your family talk about feelings? Was there physical, emotional or sexual abuse in your family? Who did you use as a male role model? What type of feelings did you see him display? Are you following in these footsteps?

If you are aware that you have a difficult time expressing emotions, consider again some counseling for personal growth. Though this will be tough work for you since you've spent a lifetime holding in your feelings, counseling could provide you with the very

environment you need to break this cycle. A good counselor will create a trusting space where you can open up and share with no risk of failure or attack. In this way you can confront old issues and learn to deal with the emotions appropriately.

It is vitally important to understand that emotions such as anger, fear, rage and grief that have been bottled up inside you will eventually find their way out. This can happen in inappropriate ways, including rape, murder, physical assault, suicide, drug and alcohol abuse to name a few of the negative outlets for pent-up emotions. Or, if you choose to take responsibility for your Life Puzzle and go back to learn how to feel, you can learn appropriate ways of letting out stuffed emotions: open dialogue, crying, laughing, happiness, sadness, gladness and joy.

## So many rewards come from learning to feel

When we don't know how to feel, our lives take on a survival instinct filled with fear. Why do we want to continue raising children with such poor learning models for feelings? It only creates another generation of confused and hurting adults.

There are great rewards for changing this now. First the men in our lives will be healthier and happier (and probably have a few less heart attacks!).

Second, they'll be better able to teach the next generation of men to feel. Since boys use men as role models for expressing feelings, if you learn to be better in touch with your feelings you'll be much more aware and a much better teacher to those young boys who are looking up to you!

Third, you'll create a better community. When we are blocked from our feelings it is very easy to believe that others don't feel either. This results in the constant violation of personal boundaries and results in poor community. However, when you are aware of your feelings—you respect, honor, nurture and express them appropriately, then you're able to know and appreciate that others have them too. This creates respect from one to another and brings harmony to the community.

Fourth, it creates a better world. When we operate with integrity that comes from an awareness of our feelings, it impacts the entire world. Considering the chaotic state of the world, learning more about our feelings is imperative.

## Your first feeling of the day: How does your day go?

It's Monday morning. See yourself lying in your bed. There's a smile on your face as you finish your last dream of the night. *Uh, oh...* there goes the alarm. Your hand reaches out and slaps the clock to turn off the intrusive noise.

Now what's going to happen? What are you feeling? Excited? Happy? Pleasure at the thought of starting a new day? Or...are you groaning, feeling tension rise in your body, tightness in your stomach? Are you feeling angry at the world, frustration with your life? Or are you feeling...nothing? Do you just stumble out of bed, into the shower, dressed and out the door with nary a feeling at all?

Looking at the way you start your day is an excellent key to your feeling state. If you crawl out of bed wishing you could crawl back in, your feelings are probably on automatic (reactive) pilot. Is this how you want to feel? Why are you choosing this side of the Continuum? Are you really a victim to the world outside?

Let's move inside...to your feelings. As you wake up, it is possible to greet the day with a joyous feeling, ready to begin another day of making your Life Puzzle. But you will need to do this by looking inside and confronting the reactive habit response of your feelings. It is a process of becoming aware of your feelings, and conscious of the feelings, that you attach to different events. The morning ritual of waking up is such an event. Are you excitedly jumping out of bed or just frustratingly dragging yourself out? If you've never taken the time to ask yourself, now is the time!

How many other events of the day are you letting go through the reactive process? For example, you're driving in the car to work and someone cuts you off—what do you feel? You're yelling and cursing at the other driver, blood pressure rising, and now that he's out of sight you're still steamed. Is that what you choose to feel or is it just your habit response? You can change this, especially considering the person you're hurting the most is yourself...not the other driver.

There are a million events in our day to which we unconsciously assign feelings. Whether it's walking through the door at the end of a long day and, as our children run to us with big smiles, we react with an, "Oh, no...not now" or a "Great to see you" smile. We have to ask ourselves again and again how the choices or reactions of our feelings are defining our Life Puzzle building. The more conscious you are of the feelings you choose, instead of letting them be a quick reaction, the more dynamic and healthy your Life Puzzle will become.

## Lots of little events add up to make our lives: Let's be conscious of each one.

My friend brought this idea home to me one day as we pulled into an underground garage. She drives a car with an automatic sensor in it that turns the headlights on in dark areas. The lights also go out 20 seconds after exiting the car. As we got out of the car and started to walk away, another driver in a car called out to us, "You left your lights on!" My friend turned around and smiled, said thank you, and explained they were on a timer but she did appreciate his concern. As we walked away she looked at me and said, "I've heard that at least a thousand times and it took me until my four hundredth before I realized that I didn't have to snarl at everyone who said it, I could feel appreciative instead of angry. I much prefer my day this way!"

---

## Suggested reading list

There are lots of books that impact your emotions. This is just a starter list!

| | |
|---|---|
| Cortis, Bruno, M.D. | *Heart & Soul* |
| Borysenko, Joan | *Minding the Body, Mending the Mind* |
| Roth, Geneen | *When Food is Love* |
| Viscott, David, M.D. | *The Language of Feelings* |
| Burns, David | *The Feeling Good Book* |
| Jampolsky, Gerald | *Love is Letting Go of Fear* |
| Newberger, Eli, M.D. | *The Men They Will Become: The Nature and Nurture of Male Character* |

# ACTION PLAN
# (Re)-Learning to Feel

## Exercise #1.

Go back to the beginning of the chapter and review the list of feelings. From this list choose three feelings based on the following criteria: Identify feelings that you avoid experiencing, identify feelings that caused problems for you growing up (for example, anger—not being allowed to express it without getting in trouble), and feelings that are currently defining your life, such as helplessness.

In your journal, write down those three feelings and then go into detail about each one and how it is affecting or limiting your life experience today.

## Exercise #2. Food and Feelings

Food is where many of us go to "feel". Food makes us feel warm and happy in an otherwise cold world. But using food as a feeling outlet is an inappropriate way of handling your feelings. You need to recognize your feelings and just feel them.

This exercise is designed to help you see which feelings you connect to food. There are two parts to this exercise.

### PART A.

For the next three days, write down what you are eating and what you are feeling at that exact time. Include in this every food craving you have—even if you don't indulge it. Write down what you are feeling during the craving. For example, you just received a phone call at work asking you to finish your report two days earlier than expected. You find yourself craving potato chips but you ignore it and get right to work (potato chips continue to pop into your mind!). Your feeling: anxiety.

Make your sheet like this example:

| Food eaten | Food craving | Feelings/event that is occurring |
|---|---|---|
| Yogurt cone | | Felt lonely after a hard day at office, treated myself. |
| | M&M peanuts | Had fight with boyfriend, feel sad. |
| Steak dinner | | No feelings, just gulped food down. |

PART B.

Do a one day fast. During this fast you may drink an unlimited supply of fresh juice, water, decaffeinated coffee or tea, and vegetable broth. This will provide your body with plenty of fluids and nutrition for this one day. During the day write down what you are feeling, particularly noting when you want to eat something and what your feeling state is at that moment.

The following day, review what you experienced. What were you feeling? Was it difficult to give up food? Did you find yourself more anxious? When under stress during the day did you find yourself mad that you couldn't eat anything...did you sneak a little food?

[DO NOT DO PART B OF THIS EXERCISE IF YOU ARE
DIABETIC, A HEART PATIENT OR ARE EXPERIENCING ANY
OTHER SIGNIFICANT HEALTH PROBLEM AT THE TIME.]

Now review your responses. Do you use food as a feeling outlet? How is that hurting your life? Now if you recognize a connection, what other steps might you take in your life to break this connection?

# Work

## *...and your Life Puzzle.*

# *Hi, ho, hi, ho...it's off to work I go. Yet, what shall I be when I grow up?*

**W**elcome to the world of work...the ever-changing rollercoaster where we exchange time for money.

Of all the areas of your Life Puzzle, work will probably take up more of your daily time than anything else you do (except maybe sleep). We don't eat eight hours a day, or focus on our family for eight hours a day, but work, that can take up some time!

Consider also that in the world you are now entering you will probably start into the workforce sometime in your teens and still be there into your late 60's. That's why it is very important for you to view this area of your Life Puzzle as needing great care. Most of your life will be spent working, but it is up to you to decide if it will be a pro-active place you spend your life or simply a reactive place that ends up spending you!

This is an exciting time and depressing time to be entering the

work world. There are exciting possibilities as well as tremendous risks to take within the work world. You will have on average, 5 to 10 jobs throughout your career and the newest phenomenon to occur is you will likely have two to three different careers throughout your life.

The days of entering a company and staying until you die arc very, very dead. The businesses that are on top today may be completely out of business in ten years. And businesses that didn't exist ten years ago will be going gangbusters. In 1980, I would have written this book on a typewriter or word processor. In the 90's I write on a computer with a sophisticated software system that allows me to change the size of type and move type all over the page. Just a few years ago I would have sent this book to a typesetter. Now I typeset and write all in the same process. I've eliminated one person's job in doing this.

So how do you prepare for this ever-changing work world? That's a great question and I wish I had a quick answer. The simplest answer I can give is to keep your eyes and ears open.

Learn to embrace with gusto...change! Because there will be plenty of change out there.

If you choose to make your Life Puzzle, you will discover it is the perfect model for preparing you to live peacefully within the roller coaster work world. As noted in the earlier part of this book, the process of making a Life Puzzle is a lifestyle of ever changing awareness, taking on a new growth stage, living at this growth level for a while, and then becoming aware of the next level of growth that is available, doing more learning and growing.

The work world of the 2000's will be just like this. You'll work in a company doing one thing for a while, but as the company grows you'll need to continue your own skills growth. Take on new projects, take more classes, look for new places to market the company's products, re-work your engineering skills to add another dimension to an earlier product. If you expect to go to work and just do the same job you were hired for, in many cases this just won't be possible.

Within your own Life Puzzle, remaining stagnant will leave you frustrated in the long run. To stay stagnant in a job is to remain on the reactive side of the Continuum. It is to place the responsibility of creating quality life work, in someone else's hands, i.e., "they" should have provided me with more work, more interesting things to do. And since "they" didn't, I'm stuck.

It is this stuck feeling that has actually created a lot of boring, useless jobs for the world. When we operate from the position that someone else should provide us a job we end up having to take what's available.

And often what's available is not fulfilling, dynamic work.

There isn't any point in saying "Well there wasn't any other choice back then," because that's then and this is now. And now is greatly different. The production line is quickly disappearing. All the old dependable businesses are making incredible shifts. We have entered, as Charles Handy has written, *The Age of Paradox*.

Choosing to make your Life Puzzle will be the most effective way of managing this new "age of paradox."

## Attention all Earth travelers: "There is no job god out there!"

This is going to come as a rude shock to many people who think there is some person or place that produces jobs. There isn't one. So if you're busy complaining that there are no good jobs out there to be had, it's time to wake up. Jobs aren't a commodity to be handed out if you stand patiently in line for one.

Jobs are created to meet a demand for product or service. So if you want a job that is just right for you, then perhaps instead of looking for one from somebody else you should go create your own to meet the need for a product or service.

In the next twenty years more and more new jobs will be created exactly like this: make your own job by selling your service or product yourself. Companies will be getting smaller, we'll be sharing a smaller pie. Now that may be frustrating to those of you who want a guaranteed paycheck and lots of perks, but on the flip side, think of the possibilities. Instead of doing a job that doesn't give you much more than a paycheck you'll get to take full responsibility for creating, developing and launching the very thing you want to do!

## Learn, EVERYTHING!

How many times, during your school years did you mutter to yourself, "Why do I have to learn _____? I'll never use it in my life!" That might have been true in the old days of single careers, but in the world you live in now you'll probably have several careers. It is impossible to know exactly what you'll need for all these careers. To be safe, take the stance that you'll need... everything!

Even learn the stuff that you don't like! Don't need to learn computers because you're going to work on cars? Today's mechanics are using computers. Don't need to learn accounting because you're a people-person and you want to be a counselor? Well, what if you're running your own office...how will you know if your bookkeeper is doing the best job if you can't understand a spreadsheet? In today's work world the wider variety of knowledge you have the more valuable you will be...to yourself and your employer.

## But HOW do I know what I should do for my life work?

Yeah, that's a question that just about everybody asks. And right after that you know what most people do? They stick their head in the sand and hope the Job Fairy kisses them on the butt with a wonderfully fulfilling job. Which is why 80% of all people HATE the job they're in. The Job Fairy is lousy at her job...she hates it too!

*Why do so few people pro-actively develop this aspect of their Life Puzzle?*

### Lack of Awareness: What's out there?

Where do most of us learn about what kind of jobs are in the world? From watching our parents or other adults that we know. So if Dad is a doctor and Mom works as a nurse, guess what the likelihood is of you going into the medical field? Pretty good, because it is a world you've learned about. It's less likely you'll become a pipefitter or a helicopter mechanic.

Unfortunately our perspective of the "big world" is pretty tiny as we graduate high school or even college. This makes it difficult for us to make the best choice, even though everybody keeps asking us....What are you going to do when you graduate? Who KNOWS!? Since few of us are comfortable not knowing, we pick anything we can come up with to stop the constant questions. It usually doesn't work well, but it fills in the blank!

### Fear of the unknown: Who do I talk to?

This is an overwhelming fear for many people. The prospect of having to ask somebody for a job is completely paralyzing for many of us. First of all, it leaves us vulnerable to rejection...they can say no. Second, we have to admit that we either don't have a job or aren't happy where we are. Very few of us enjoy this!

How do we find the right person to talk to? Do you just call up the owner or CEO and ask for an interview? How do you find out his or her name? What if you can't get past the secretary? Phew! Just thinking about it all gives one a headache!

These questions become so confusing that lots of people give up and let this fear convince them to take the first job that comes along.

### Fear of leaving a comfort zone.

Those jobs belong to "those" kind of people. Ever heard yourself say such a thing? We all have ideas about how people act in different positions and we often convince ourselves that "those" people aren't like me, therefore I can't be a part of them or, even worse, you convince yourself you don't want to be among them.

This is really about stretching yourself past your comfort zone of staying around the "known". If you're ever going to get anywhere with your work puzzle piece, you're going to have to challenge yourself to branch out, meet different people, take risks. It's worth it.

### Fear of not knowing how to do it.

This is the old, "I need experience before I can get the job, but how do I get the experience without having the job" dilemma!

Whether you are 16 and entering the workforce or 36 and wishing to change positions to a new career field, this fear of knowing keeps many of us from taking the step and exploring new avenues within our work puzzle piece.

For some reason we convince ourselves that we have to know how to do a job before we get hired to do it. This is rarely true. In fact, most employers say they would rather have someone who is still in a learning phase but who has an "I'll learn anything" attitude over an employee with lots of credentials but no enthusiasm. So don't let this fear control your life. Change your attitude and you'll find you can get through the door!

# *Standing up to the FEAR:*
# *Taking responsibility for your work puzzle piece.*

If it's any consolation, look around you now at the different people who might be present at this moment. Everyone— that's right, everyone—has had some of the fears listed on the previous page. It is the absolute rare human being who 1) knows exactly what they want to do in their work puzzle piece, 2) knows who to talk to, 3) is totally at ease with meeting new people and taking on a new challenge, and 4) and is aware of all the opportunities available. So calm down and don't spend too much time kicking yourself.

All fears, however, can be managed if you will take the initiative to meet the fear and overcome it. Otherwise fear will win and your work puzzle piece will end up missing pieces or be filled with "jammed-in-even-though-they-don't-fit" pieces. You don't want that to happen, do you?

The best way to challenge these fears is with information. So get ready to do some reading and listening.

## Take some tests!

There are a number of profile tests that you can take to help you determine what types of jobs you will be most suited for. These are well worth taking. Your local college has them available. Call the Career Counseling department and ask them what they offer.

You might also consider talking with a professional career counselor. They will charge for services but if you get a good one realize that you are making an investment in your puzzle piece and that the money is well spent. Get references of professional clients they have worked with and then call them. Also, be sure you clarify with the counselor exactly what you will do: Live testing, interview skills, and resume writing, etc. Determine exactly what services you want before getting started.

## Ready, get set for the information interview!

The information interview will help you with all your fears of the work world! It will help you challenge your comfort zone as you will talk to people who do things you know little about. It will help with the "who do I talk to" because even if the person you're having the information interview with turns out not to be the right person, more than likely they will give you the name of the right person. Information interviews will give you an idea of what type of skills and education you will need for a particular position you might be interested in. Even if you find out that you are short on a few skills you might discover there is a position that you can get within the same type of business that will teach you these skills or broaden your skills while you are taking training for something else.

And best of all, information interviews will broaden your view. A good information interview will show you all sorts of things that you weren't aware of as possibilities. Many times these unknown possibilities turn out to be the direction you really want to head towards, even though you didn't even know they existed until this person shared them with you.

Every information interview you have will be a great learning experience. I can remember when I started information interviewing; I found it so fascinating I never wanted to stop!

• • • • • • • • • • • • • • • • • • • • • • • • • • • • • • • • • • • • • • • • • • • • • • •

## The Information interview:
## open the gates to knowledge!

Information interviewing is so incredibly easy anybody can do it...everybody ought to! It is the greatest and easiest way of finding out information about particular job fields while beginning your little book of who to talk to.

Information interviews can be done over the telephone but ideally you want to try to get an appointment with a person and talk to them directly.

### Here's how to do it:

1. Determine the field you are interested in exploring. It might be a field you want to enter or it might be a field you know nothing about but want to learn. (Remember, information interviews have nothing to do with getting a job; the goal is simply information).

2. Pull out the Yellow Pages and find the field you are interested in. Start in the index because you might discover that this field has subcategories that you weren't aware of that offer more businesses to talk to.

3. Call up one of the businesses. Usually a receptionist will answer the phone. If you gently explain to him or her what you are doing (see script below) they will usually be most helpful. You might not get directly through on this phone call but often they will give you the exact name of the person you need to talk to. Then you can call directly in a few days and ask for this person. Surprisingly, you will discover that these people are usually quite helpful. Rarely will they hang up on you!

—continued on next page.

## THE SCRIPT: Getting from the outside...

"Hello, my name is _____ and I'm wondering if you could help me. I'm taking a class and need to set up an information interview as part of this class. [You *are* taking a class....the class of life!] I would like to speak to the company president [or the Director of Engineering...use what works for your needs] and see if it would be possible to either meet with him or her or at least talk with her or him over the phone. Could you tell me the name of the president and when would be a good time to contact him or her? This is NOT a job interview, just an information interview."

At this point the receptionist will either give you the name, send you on to the next secretary to leave a message or if you get lucky on the first call, will put you through directly. Once you get through to the person you need try this next script.

## THE SCRIPT: ...to the inside.

"Thank you, Ms./Mr.___ for taking my call. I know you are busy but I was wondering if I could set up a time that I might come in and talk to you about your company and your position within the company. I'm not looking for a job, I'm just doing some information interviewing and feel you could give me some good insight into this field. When might it be convenient for you?"

At this point 90% of the time you'll get an interview!

## The interview: be prepared.

Once you get there be ready to ask good questions: Write them down and have them with you. This will help you stay on target and ensure that you get the information you want. It will also help you with your initial nervousness (we're all nervous).

Here are some sample questions to help you get started. What others can you think of?

1. Will you tell me a little about SYZ Company, like how long it's been in business, how many employees you have, has it always produced _____ ? (The goal here: let them brag about their company!)
2. Can you tell me a little about your position and how you got to it?
3. What type of responsibilities come with this position?
4. What training would you suggest for this field? Can you give me the names of schools for training/knowledge in this field?
5. What type of positions would you suggest to help one get started in this field?
6. What do you see as the future in this field?
7. What professional organizations would you suggest I contact for information?
8. Can you give me the names of others I might contact to further my knowledge of this field?

**At the end of the interview be sure to thank them for their time.**
**Then ask for their business card.**
**When you get home, immediately write them a thank-you note!**

# Work: putting it into the perspective of your entire Life Puzzle

**W**ork takes up so much our life-time. All through high school the message is constantly focused towards getting a job or going on to college and then getting a job. By the time you are 18 you know that you're going to have to "do" something. Whether you walk out of high school into a job, or you head off to college and pick a major—which of course will lead to a job—the message comes through loud and clear: You must get a job, make money and buy things—cars, home and clothes. You're on the way to the rat race!

This work obsession becomes all encompassing and is one of the central reasons why so few of us realize that we have more to making our Life Puzzle than just our job. While everyone asks you what major you've picked for college, no one asks you how the rest of your Life Puzzle is coming along. It becomes very apparent to anyone entering adulthood that getting the right job is a key require-ment of "being somebody". It is a domi-nating focus for everyone.

And so off we go into the paid work world, doing what everybody else is doing and following along. We rarely question this because it seems that even though most people don't like doing it— it's estimated that 26 million workers would like to tell their boss to take this job and shove it!—there doesn't seem to be another alternative.

Or is there? Well, there is if you choose to break out of the mold. This is the very same mold that keeps most people on the 0-5 cycle of the Choosing Continuum—doing enough paid work to get by but at the loss of the other pieces of their Life Puzzle. Look again at the Life Puzzle and you will see that work is but 1/16th of your entire Life Puzzle.

So how do you keep paid work from overtaking the rest of your Life Puzzle-making? Start by asking yourself: What is work? In the old mold, work is the time we must give up in exchange for money. And what is money? Money is what we exchange our life energy for so we can buy the things we need or want. Let's face it, if we didn't need money for things, how many of us would be crawl-ing out of bed at 6:00 a.m. on Monday? (Did you know the greatest number of heart attacks occur around 4:00 a.m. on Monday morning?) The more things we need and want, the more money we must have, so the more paid work we must do. How do you break this cycle?

First, question your needs and wants. We have become a society that is con-sumed with having more and more things. This arose out of the industrial revolution, which needed to sell more and more stuff in order to grow the economy and new jobs. Today, we are at the bursting point as we spend our lives making money so we can buy more things which we barely have time to use since we're working so much to pay for all these things!

Is it worth it? Do you really want to get caught up in the material obsession which forces you to place work as 15/16ths of your Life Puzzle? That is a bold question each of us must ask ourselves. We can all have balance but not if we keep repeating the same old do-what- everyone-else-is-doing mentality.

There are two reasons to break out. One is for your own Life Puzzle-making. Only you can decide how to create a life that includes balance. No one can stop you from choosing this. But it will take courage and effort to break from the rat race, materially obsessed, paid work world cycle. The benefits are tremendous.

The second reason is planetary necessity. Whether we like it or not, we have stretched the Earth to the limits of her productivity. We've tapped her for almost all of her natural resources. The days of making stuff from stuff are coming to an end. We are leaving the industrial age and heading to one of service. This will rock the foundations of the world but will be a necessary part of the transition if we are going to survive on this planet.

## Putting work into perspective.

There are two reasons we work:
1. For money
2. To fulfill our lives: enjoyment, challenge, learning, prestige and status, etc.

The problem for most of us is that the focus of money overrides our need to fulfill our lives. Thus most of us fill our lives with work to make a living but not to make a Life Puzzle. How do we change this? Redefine the role work has for you. The best definition I've seen comes from Joe Dominguez and Vicki Robin's book, *Your Money or Your Life*. This is a terrific book that will help you put paid work into the perspective of your entire Life Puzzle.

They define work as *"Simply any productive or purposeful activity, with paid employment being just one activity among many…remember that our real work is just to live our values as best we know how…jobs [can be] loving our mates, being a decent neighbor or developing a sustaining philosophy of life."*

From this definition, **work becomes any activity that builds your Life Puzzle.** Paid employment may be part of it. but it doesn't have to be the central focus for defining your life. This allows you to break out of (or hopefully never enter!) finding your value at the doors of the rat race and the consumption of things.

## That sounds great…but where am I going to get the money I need?

Paid work of course! But with an appreciation that paid work is not the only work of your life. Understand that paid work is necessary to meet material needs but is not necessary as a way of defining your entire life. What you'll discover is that material needs become much less when you decide that things are not what give you value, i.e., the BMW for status or the 5,000 sq. ft. home to keep up with the Jones. When you realize that paid work is actually an exchange of the time you have to make your entire Life Puzzle, you become much more conscious and selective of how much money or things you need in exchange for your life time.

All of us have a limited amount of time in which to create our Life Puzzle. In order to make a balanced Life Puzzle we must truly question the amount of our time we want to exchange for money to buy things. Which is more important, more things or more Life Puzzle building time? If time is your answer, then you will need less money because you will want, and need, fewer things. Things don't make a happy Life Puzzle; time and energy invested in making your whole Life Puzzle, not just the work piece, brings true happiness.

## Work and your Life Puzzle: Finding meaning and purpose.

Work: any productive or purposeful activity. **Work is your life energy in action!** Thus, loving your spouse, nurturing your children, volunteering at the local fire department, stuffing envelopes for the AIDS charity fund-raiser are all work.

All of these activities add to the world and add to your Life Puzzle building as they give meaning and purpose to your presence on Earth. Sure, stuffing AIDS fund-raiser envelopes may not be the most exciting thing you've ever done. But in context to why you're doing it, isn't it much more purposeful work than stuffing envelopes with an advertising flier for a lawnmower as part of your paid job? The old definition that work must be paid in order to have value would say the advertising flier envelopes

would have more purpose than the AIDS fund-raiser but the new definition challenges this.

The old definition of work keeps many of us locked into jobs that we hate, sacrificing time that we would much rather spend with our families, our community, our church or the Earth. Yes, it is a difficult choice to break away from the ingrained pattern to which you have been conditioned. But it is possible to bring meaning back into our daily lives by adjusting the role that work and money have in our lives.

If you want to break out of the mold, there are three books you should read to help give you the foundation to make this wonderful shift: *Your Money or Your Life* by Joe Dominguez and Vicki Robin. *Downshifting: Reinventing Success on a Slower Track*, by Amy Saltzman, and *Creative Work* by Willis Harman and John Hormann.

## Life is not a "to do" list, it is a "to be" process.

We're born into a world that teaches us we should grow up, get a job, get a house, some kids, two cars, lots of clothes, several TVs, designer sheets and towels and new living room furniture. And many of us do it thinking that this will make us happy and contented people. But the truth is, it is a false "to do" list that brings very few people happiness.

One very common phenomenon that Gail Sheehy noted in her book *Passages* is that this frenzy of filling the above list starts right out of school and continues through our early 30's, at which point a startling number of people wake up, look around and scream, "I don't want all this stuff." After that initial scream some learn to shut off that inner voice and actually take on bigger houses, more cars and luxury vacations with the hope that these things will make them happier. They'll have another scream in their 40's! Those who listen to it in their 30's often find themselves divorcing, breaking up families and running away from as many of the things as they possibly can. Everyone is losing in this process.

Let's stop doing this—to ourselves and the next generation! Life is not a list of things to do and get. A high quality life is a process of building a healthy, well balanced Life Puzzle that lives in harmony with the Earth and the community of people. You've been conditioned to be a "to-doer", will you have the courage to break out and become a "to-be'er"?

---

## Suggested reading list

| | |
|---|---|
| Bolles, Richard | *What Color is Your Parachute?* |
| Dominguez, Joe and Robin, Vicki | *Your Money or Your Life* |
| Saltzman, Amy | *Downshifting: Reinventing Success on a Slower Track* |
| Harman, Willis and Hormann, John | *Creative Work* |
| Brandt, Barbara | *Whole Life Economics* |
| Bolles, Richard | *Three Boxes of Life and How to Get Out of Them* |

---

## ACTION PLAN

**Exercise #1.**
What would you like your life's work to add to this world?
In your journal, write down the answer to the following question:
If you didn't have to work for a living, what "work" would you do?

**Exercise #2.**
Go back to the journal writing from exercise #1. Based on what your ideal "work" would be (and certainly it can be more than one thing), set up an information interview with two people who might give you valid information about this endeavor. Follow the information earlier in this chapter on how to do an information interview. Go for it! You'll have lots of fun with this one.

# *Owning my own…*
# Communication

# Good communication is a conscious act: Is yours?

While you are busy putting together all the pieces of your Life Puzzle, it is important for you to focus on becoming a conscious communicator instead of a reactive one. (Recall the Choosing Continuum). This conscious act of communication is with others and within yourself.

So much of what we say to ourselves and say to others tends to be negative, defensive and protective. This is a result of years of learning to be what I call "duck and weave" communicators. This is the process we learn in our schools and families in order to get around others and…get our own way. We duck and weave when our parents ask us whether we've done our homework or taken out the trash. We duck and weave with our friends when we feel pressured to do something that we don't want to do but don't feel we can say no. We duck and weave within ourselves when we can't confront ourselves honestly.

By the time we've reached adulthood our communication has become a reactive pattern. Now we transfer this reactive communication style to our marriages, families and work. Ask yourself: Do you work diligently to have open, honest communication with your partner or do you just let issues that are bothering you get swept under the carpet? Do you speak up honestly at work or are you part of the group-think…following the status quo even when you know it isn't right? With your children, are you actively engaged in developing communication channels based in trust and openness…or are they learning the same patterns of duck and weave that you did?

If you're going to have a great Life Puzzle, it is necessary to make good communication a daily act of consciousness. This starts by looking within yourself: Self talk. Are you consciously aware of the little voice inside you? Is it always yelling negative things in your ear? Or, have you silenced it altogether as part of your reactive lifestyle?

## You are either your own best friend or your own worst enemy.

The goal of good self communication is to talk to yourself like you are your own best friend. But most of us find our inner communication harsh and divisive—more like an enemy than a friend. This is a definite goal in building your Life Puzzle: Make your self-talk a process of encouragement from your best friend… you.

The conscious act of communicating with others starts here: seek first to understand (and not concentrating on being understood). This is a conscious act of being fully aware of the other person and what they are saying to you. This may seem like a very simple thing to do, but very few of us do it. We listen quickly and then can hardly wait to respond. This results in lots of misunderstanding and miscommunication because no one is paying attention, they're waiting to react instead.

Pro-active communication starts with understanding—truly trying to understand the information that is being sent to you. It requires an open heart and it assumes good faith in trusting that the other person has no hidden agenda. Understanding another doesn't mean you always agree with them, it means you are giving respect to their viewpoint. If you do this with everyone you encounter you'll be amazed at what you can learn. It will give you a broader perspective on the world and much more information for building your Life Puzzle.

## Just dying to get it off your chest? Maybe you should put it down on paper first.

One of the reasons so many of our relationships—whether it's with our marriage partner, children, family members, or co-workers go so poorly—is due to communication. When we hit issues that create conflict, we do not know how to use good communication to move us past conflict and into resolution. As a result, we stuff our thoughts and feelings until they finally come out in a full blown explosion, or we just let them steam inside us for years.

This is a lose/lose proposition for everyone. We can learn to deal with

conflict more effectively by having the courage to learn better communication techniques to help us clear the air. One of these techniques is to write a letter.

If there is some issue bothering you and you just don't know how to resolve it, it is often better to put your thoughts and feelings down on paper instead of starting with a more direct communication process. Writing a letter to the person is a safe way to express your views.

First, it allows you to say everything you want to say without getting interrupted. Second, it allows you to edit and change it before sharing it. This is great because often, when we see what we've written, we realize that it is harsh, critical, and attacking. Biting the head off the person we're in conflict with may make us feel good as we get it off our chests and onto paper, but it usually does not help resolve conflict. After you re-read your letter you'll probably want to do a bit of a rewrite.

Third, writing sometimes helps you resolve the conflict from within yourself. When you see what you've written you might find yourself stepping back and realizing that you are as much a part of the problem as the other person.

Fourth, it allows the reader to fully view your perception of the problem before responding. Many times, when we're talking to someone about a touchy subject they quickly become defensive. Then the communication process breaks down into a brawl of, "No, I didn't say that"…"Yes you did, blah, blah, blah." When it's down on paper the other person can point to a section and say, "Could you explain this?" or "In this section when you say this upsets you do you mean…," but they can't say you did or didn't say something…it's in black and white!

## Rock the boat without capsizing it.

Most of us hate conflict and we'll avoid confrontation whenever possible. This leads to all sorts of problems in our relationships and it can also lead to health problems within ourselves as we let the conflict settle inside us instead of dealing with it pro-actively and then moving on.

Writing letters, even if you never send them, is an excellent way to confront conflict head on without having any casualties. Give it a try.

### He said, She said… men and women in conversation.

Men…you can't live with them and you can't live without them…what's a woman to do?

Women…you can't live with them and you can't live without them…what's a man to do?

Isn't that just about the gist of it? We love each other but we certainly don't understand each other! And that's because men and women truly communicate in such different ways that it is almost like they speak a foreign language to each other.

In building your Life Puzzle it is immensely helpful to fully understand how differently the opposite sex communicates to you…and you to them. This is a two-way process.

While you may shake your head, throw your hands up in air and say, "Men (or women)…I'll never understand them," you need to understand that they are saying the exact same thing about you. However, considering that you are likely to engage in loving relationships, have children of the opposite sex, and probably encounter co-workers, it is really more important to spend your time learning their communication styles than complaining about them.

Imagine if we all did this. Maybe we'd be working in harmony with each other instead of creating so much chaos.

Most of these gender-based differences are, like so many things, rooted in our childhoods. Little boys and little girls are different! Not better or worse…different. In these differences we learn drastically divergent styles for communicating.

For example, little girls share their thoughts and feelings with their friends. This is how they make friends, and they share everything, down to the tiniest of details and most fleeting of thoughts. This is interpreted as a sign of friendship between girls.

On the other hand, little boys do not share their thoughts and feelings about everything with their friends. They keep most of their feelings deep inside because they learn early on that sharing feelings leaves them vulnerable and open to attack from other little boys.

When these same little boys and girls grow up, she keeps on sharing and wants to do the same thing with her new best friend, her husband. And she assumes he wants to share all his intimate thoughts and feelings with her, too. But he doesn't. How many marriages dissolve with her screaming at him, "You never share any of your feelings; you're like a zombie?" And he's staring back at her incredulously because he's provided her with a fine home, cars, etc. How can sharing feelings be that important? She doesn't understand that he doesn't find it important to share his feelings or that it is necessary for a good marriage.

Your Life Puzzle building will be greatly enhanced by learning these communication differences. There are several wonderful books that clearly describe these different processes. Understanding these communication styles will help you in your pro-active marriage, your family, and improve relations at your work site. Read them and then share with your partner, your teenage children, and your co-workers!

*You Just Don't Understand* and *That's Not What I Meant,* both by Deborah Tannen, Ph.D.

*What Your Mother Couldn't Tell You and Your Father Didn't Know,* by John D. Gray.

## Talk to yourself: Intrapersonal Communication

Whoa! What are you saying to yourself?

We are all constantly talking to our inner selves. This internal talk helps us make decisions about our lives. "Should I eat this pound of fudge? Nah, too fattening…ah, what the heck, for tomorrow I shall diet. Oooh, I am *sooooo* bad." Sound familiar?

On and on we go, talking to ourselves. Unfortunately, much of this internal talk is very negative. Is yours?

*Do you constantly find yourself saying:*

- That was stupid, why did I do such a dumb thing?
- I'm such a failure, otherwise such-and-such wouldn't have occurred.
- I just know my boss is going to figure out I don't really know what I'm doing.
- I'm not a good cook, I just can't walk into the kitchen and whip up a great meal.
- I'll never get ahead because I don't have all the advantages other people have: money, looks, talent, etc.
- I'm sure my partner will look for somebody better than me, why would he or she want to be with me when there are cuter, smarter or funnier people to be with?
- I'm such a jerk. Why did I say that? Why can't I keep my mouth shut?

## Change the way you talk to yourself and you will change your Life Puzzle.

Think about it for a second. If your internal talk is constantly negative, how would it be possible to produce a positive Life Puzzle? Since your mind can only be in one place at a time, if you're attached to negative self-talk you can't simultaneously be in positive self-talk. Right?

## Can it be that simple?

Yes, rephrase the way you talk to yourself. Restate these self-talk statements on the left this way.

- That wasn't the best way to handle that situation, next time I'll do better.
- Sometimes things happen that I can't control. That doesn't make me a failure.
- If I focus my energy on doing the best job I can, my boss will support me.
- If I keep practicing in the kitchen, eventually I'll be a great cook.
- I may not be a movie star, but I'll take advantage of the assets I've got and keep working hard at it.
- If I spend my time developing my best self whether my partner or I stay together or not, I'll know I'm the best I can be for both of us.
- I need to learn to think before I speak so I communicate more effectively.

---

Practice positive self-talk…every day! Learning to take full responsibility for your communication puzzle piece inevitably leads to a healthier, happier, more balanced you.

---

## Interpersonal Communication: Talking with others

Ineffective communication between people causes most of the world's problems. Family members murder each other, friends destroy years of caring, and strangers rigidly refuse to be honest with each other, all over ill-chosen words that are misunderstood between different parties.

When talking with others are you having a monologue or a dialogue? A monologue is when one person talks, a dialogue is when two or more people are sharing information. Many times, even when two people are talking, there is only a monologue going on. That's because as each person talks, the other isn't listening; instead, he or she is preparing to talk back.

## The key to good communication: Listening.

Give your full attention to what the other person is saying. It takes effort to do this and one must actually train oneself to give another person 100% listening attention.

This is especially true if the communication involves a sensitive issue. To avoid getting defensive and turning the communication into a battle zone, train yourself to stay focused on listening instead of preparing your defense.

Accept that the other person needs to be heard, *not argued with*. Once you've heard this communication, you have a right to repeat back to them what you heard, to be sure there is no misunderstanding. This way, even if you don't agree with them, or you think they are trying to manipulate you, you can acknowledge that you listened with 100% attention. Only at this point can communication move forward because the other person feels he has had his communi-

cation received. If we know the other personal fully listened, we are usually willing to be disagreed with, as long as we've been heard.

## A good communication process:

1. State your feelings with an "I" statement— I feel, I am, I wish, I want, I think. Avoid blaming others, i.e., you make me feel, you made me mad when…

2. After you've stated your side, ask the other person to repeat what you've said. If, in repeating it, you find the person has misunderstood or misinterpreted the desired message, stop. Take time to re-share your feeling or thoughts, and clarify.

3. Once you feel that the other person has clearly heard and understood what you've said, then give the other person a chance to state his feelings. Listen fully, then repeat to them what you think he has said…"I hear you saying that…"

4. Good communication means both people have had an opportunity to have their thoughts and feelings shared and acknowledged.

5. Keep in mind: first seek to understand, then move to be understood. This takes courage to try to understand where the other person is coming from before you get a chance to be heard and understood.

## Any hidden agendas?

Before you communicate to others, always check within yourself to be sure your intent is honest communication. Your Life Puzzle will be affected by dishonest, manipulative communication games. The art of good communication results in both parties having their needs met. Compromise and honest sharing lead to win/win communication.

## Communication Games: what ones do you play?

"If they really loved me they would know to take care of those things for me!" said Doug's mom as she continued complaining. "Well how do they know what needs to be done unless you share with them? They don't live in your house, how can they know the walls need painting?" I asked, somewhat exasperated. "I know they would gladly take care of those things if you would just tell them what you need."

"No, if I have to tell them then they obviously don't care. If they cared they would take care of them." Barb's face showed pain as she was convinced that her logic made sense.

"Well, your sons aren't mind readers, Barb. They live miles away from you and it is difficult for them to guess what's going on at your house. I know they too get frustrated, hearing you complain about problems that could have been quickly fixed if you had just communicated with them when it first happened. Instead, you don't mention it until it becomes a crisis. This makes them feel guilty because the problem has grown so large it's inconveniencing you—something they don't want to have happen. Why don't you just talk to them?" I said.

"It's just not the same if I have to ask. They should care enough to be there when I need them." Barb's face showed a bottled up anger and sadness. She had committed herself to this position and wasn't going to budge.

"So you would rather be silent, thus denying your sons the ability to help, which ends up with them feeling guilty and you angry and sad. From where I stand Barb, that's nuts. To be blunt, you are the source of your own anger and sadness. You are responsible for it by playing this victim game and refusing to communicate. The result: everyone loses."

Barb's face showed shock and disbelief. She had never looked at the situation from this angle before. She said, "Now that you know, you could tell them, and they'll get better at helping me."

I shook my head and said, "No Barb, I'm not getting involved in this twisted communication game. If you want your needs met, then you have to have the courage, honesty and decency to communicate directly with the people who can help you. If you choose not to do this, don't be surprised if the outcome is less than satisfying. You have the power to change it, not me."

Our conversation ended at this point. I hoped that in time Barb would come to realize that good communication is a personal responsibility. Each of us is responsible for sharing information with others. If we are more invested in playing games instead of directly communicating our thoughts and feelings, despite how others might react, then we will always find ourselves coming up with less than satisfactory outcomes.

If we communicate honestly, even if the other person doesn't like what we have to say, at least we can live comfortably within ourselves—knowing we did our best to share our thoughts and that we refused to play a communication game where there are no winners, builds a healthy Life Puzzle.

# *Understanding your temperament style—understanding others, too!*

**H**ave you ever noticed that not all people see the world the same as you? That's because different people have different *temperaments* or their own way of seeing the world and responding to it.

There's been quite a bit of study done on different temperament types. Carl Jung began the work, and since then numerous people have employed his ideas. Now there is a fairly abundant and reliable source of information on this subject.

You are born with your temperament style, so I often call it one's "soul essence," as it is so much a part of one's way of processing information right from the start of life. For example, I am a twin, and even though she and I grew up in similar circumstances, we do not process and react to the world in quite the same way. My father says this was obvious when we were quite young. We now know that our temperament styles are exact opposites!

There are sixteen main temperament styles and I've included them in this book. If you want to find out your temperament style, I suggest you purchase or borrow from the library the following book: *Please Understand Me,* by David Keirsey and Marilyn Bates.

In *Please Understand Me,* there is a simple test that will help you determine your temperament style. It's also useful to share this with your partner, family members (children older than 12), and co-workers.

## THE MAJOR CATEGORIES
• • • • • • • • • • • • • • • • • • • • • • • •

### Extrovert (E) vs. Introvert (I)
This one is fairly obvious. Some people like to be with other people, others prefer to be alone or with just one other person.
*Extroverts* are energized around others. *Introverts* are de-energized around others.

### Intuitive (N) vs. Sensing (S)
*Intuitive* types tend to be dreamers. They see everything, all possibilities. They have lots of pie-in-the-sky ideas. They are often artists and creative types. They are the people that come up with new ideas and ways of changing the world.

*Sensing* types are practical and analytical. They need to see it, touch it, or hear it in order for it to be real. They see the world in black and white or concrete terms. They are methodical and organized.

### Thinking (T) vs. Feeling (F)
*Thinking* types are rules oriented. There's a right way and a wrong way to

do things. They follow the law and don't like to deviate from it, as they are sure it helps create order in the world. To thinkers, rules were made *not to be broken* by people just because they don't like the rules.

On the other hand, *Feeling* types think rules are good, but not if they are so rigid that they can't be bent when necessary. Feelers see the human side and the extenuating circumstances that require rules to be changed when necessary.

## Judging (J) vs. Perceiving (P)

*Judging* people are those who like closure in life. They set deadlines and meet them. They make a decision and never look back.

*Perceivers* keep life open ended. They like to look at all angles before committing and this can take a bit of time… that's okay. They are not deadline oriented at all.

## The Sixteen Temperament Types

● ● ● ● ● ● ● ● ● ● ● ● ● ● ● ● ● ● ● ● ● ● ● ● ● ● ● ● ● ● ● ● ● ● ● ● ● ● ● ● ● ● ● ● ●

*On the next pages you'll see the sixteen combinations. You are one of them! But realize too, there are fifteen other styles. These are the people you meet each day. When you focus on understanding other temperament styles you build your Life Puzzle communication piece.*

### ● ISFP

ISFP's are gentle, compassionate people who tend to focus on meeting others' needs, especially those less fortunate than themselves. Quiet and modest, ISFP's avoid conflict and seek peace.

At work, ISFP's are team players and work toward bridging people and tasks. They are often in positions that serve others like secretary, doctor, or x-ray technician.

ISFP's enjoy their leisure time and actively seek it out. Living in the moment is possible for ISFP's, who can slow down and see the beauty around them. Leisure activities can be group activities such as picnics or individual ones such as poetry writing or painting.

Relationships are very important to ISFP's and they often arrange their life first for their relationship, second for career. This can, however, lead to trouble as their partners may not appreciate an ISFP's intensity towards the relationship, and the ISFP can be taken advantage of. When relationships end, ISFP's blame themselves and feel their needs were not met.

A caution for ISFP's: Learn to be a little more skeptical of others, less self critical. Learn to nurture your inner self and find your self-satisfaction first from within, second from others. Too often ISFP's do it the other way around and find themselves always looking to others first.

## ● ENFJ

ENFJ's like organization and closure but are tolerant and open to others, often serving them. They are aware of others' needs and seek to assist them in developing plans of action to turn ideas into reality.

At work, ENFJ's are team oriented and focused on improving the world or society. Harmony in the workplace is important, but they resist dullness, seeking new challenges that let them serve others. Clergy, counselor, and teacher are often ENFJ's occupations

Relationships and responsibilities come before leisure and they often mix their leisure with serving others. Thus taking underprivileged kids to the park is a leisure activity.

Relationship equals romance to the ENFJ. They can fall head over heels in love and tend to idealize their partners. They need to be more realistic in relationships. They are highly committed and value loyalty. They have a difficult time when their relationships go through rocky times, seeking to quickly put it back in harmony. Often ENFJ's would do well to take more time exploring the underlying issues versus rushing to "set it right again."

Tending to be extremely loyal, ENFJ's can be disillusioned by those they are loyal to who, being only human, make mistakes. ENFJ's need to balance loyalty with a more realistic appraisal of people.

---

## ● INFP

Ideals are key to INFP's. They are introverts who don't like to sacrifice their ideals, which they quietly, consistently work toward. They maneuver around obstacles and work to get the world to line up with their internal view of perfection.

At work, INFP's want to make the world better, but sometimes have difficulty working with others who don't quite see the "perfect world" the way an INFP does. Counselor, editor, and writer are good occupations.

Play does not come easy to INFP's, and it tends to be solitary: reading, music, gardening, painting. In social situations, INFP's can be charming but they have to want to be there, otherwise they tend to withdraw early.

Love is an extremely deep commitment. Yet it is difficult for INFP's to find a partner, who is often idealized and created as perfection. INFP's have a hard time sharing feelings and letting themselves be known by others.

INFP's can have tunnel vision, leading them to become isolated since they cannot accept others' views easily. To some they may appear out of touch with reality, and this can lead to problems.

## ● ISTP

ISTP's are realists who manage and adapt to situations with expediency and completeness. They are able to see the big picture and gather the necessary information quickly so they can respond. They like managing a crisis.

At work, ISTP's are the first ones you go to when all hell breaks loose because they will keep a steady head and act expediently.

ISTP's enjoy their leisure time, liking practical activities. They pursue their interest thoroughly, and when bored with a particular interest, will move on to a new one on which they will also become an expert. They can enjoy being in a group or alone but once in, they are completely into it.

In relationships, ISTP's show love through actions, not words. They are best in relationships that allow the ISTP to enjoy their hobbies without complaint. If you are involved with an ISTP you'd better learn to join in instead of expecting them to give this up for the relationship. The hobby will win because the ISTP fails to comprehend why you would want them to give up something they enjoy.

ISTP's like troubleshooting, but tend not to set any long-term goals for themselves. They just wait for the next crisis to give direction to their lives. As a result, ISTP's can appear indecisive. Setting short and long-term goals is very important for an ISTP in order to avoid a life that "just happened, I'm not quite sure how".

---

## ● ESFJ

ESFJ's are the great organizers. They place value on harmony and work to keep the peace among their groups. They work well with others and like closure and a certain amount of structure in group activities.

ESFJ's like work that has a practical impact on others and their lives. Speech pathologist, teacher, and choir director are all types of positions an ESFJ might prefer.

ESFJ's like to enjoy leisure time with others but are just as comfortable spending time alone, since they do need to be able to renew themselves. ESFJ's like open dialogue, debates, and stimulating conversations as well as some physical activities. Working with community groups is especially rewarding.

ESFJ's are great partners in love. They like warmth and commitment and will work on their relationships…sometimes past the point of healthfulness. They are dedicated to their partner but can have a tendency to put their partner's needs above their own to the detriment of both parties.

ESFJ's don't like conflict and can ignore that which they find uncomfortable, which doesn't always produce the best results for anyone. Learning to say no and to accept conflict and deal with it are necessary for ESFJ's; otherwise, they can become overwhelmed with pleasing others while losing themselves.

## ● ESFP

ESFP's are part of the crowd! They are where the action is, enthusiastic and fun to be with. Generous with time and money, they have a special touch that brings people to them.

At work, ESFP's are people-oriented but like action and variety. Coaching and teaching are good occupations because ESFP's love to inspire others.

Friends are very important, and an ESFP's leisure time is spent with friends in fun activities such as sports, playing cards, or bike clubs. ESFP's cherish friends and take the time to let people know they are special to them.

Love is a joy to ESFP's as they care for their loved ones with open hearts, yet at the same time they can easily fall in love with many others. ESFP's like their love returned and do not handle criticism well. "If you don't like me this way someone else will"...off they go!

ESFP's prefer socializing and sometimes neglect their commitments of more practical realities. ESFP's would do well to learn to become good time managers and practice sticking with a project even when it isn't as fun as they would like it to be.

---

## ● INFJ

INFJ's are full of ideas, ideals, and inspiration, and spend their lives focused on them. INFJ's can be loners and are perfectly content to be so! The complexities of humans, themselves in particular, are especially intriguing and they spend much of their time learning in this dimension.

At work, INFJ's are big-picture creators...planning for the future while living in the present. They work in fields that involve the human spirit like clergy, social work, psychiatry.

Solitary leisure pursuits are ideal for the INFJ, although interaction with a close group of friends is good, too. INFJ doesn't waste much energy with people who are "just acquaintances," but prefers nurturing a small group of like-minded people.

INFJ's are one man/one woman-only kind of people, desiring to commit fully to just one special person. Superficial relationships are boring to INFJ's. However, verbalizing the depth of their love is sometimes difficult. INFJ's forget that others can't read their minds!

INFJ's can become too isolated and may create an inner world that ignores the basic realities of the one around them. Learning to let go of one's ideals and allow other viewpoints in, is helpful to you.

## ● ENTJ

ENTJ's are natural born leaders with a strong drive to give structure and order wherever they may be. They are policy and goals designers, depending on others for implementation of procedures.

At work, ENTJ's display a team spirit but they can be short tempered with those that are inefficient or nonchalant about their work.

In relationships, autonomy rules. ENTJ's are more practical than emotional and they somewhat expect their mates to run their own lives and not depend on them for lots of little extras. ENTJ's are the clear rulers in the home. Romance is little appreciated, while order and comfort are.

ENTJ's can be wonderful, but if you are in a relationship with one or work underneath one, don't expect lots of pep talks and pats on the back. ENTJ's need to learn to balance their leadership abilities with a bit more humanity.

## ● INTP

INTP's are precision thinkers. Highly intellectual, they are able to quickly pick up nuances that defy reason or logic. Analysis, logic, and thinking are all important to INTP's.

At work INTP's make great mathematicians, computer nerds, and scientists. There is a right and wrong, black and white, and the INTP will always hunt for it. Great for detailed thinking, INTP's see the big picture and can give it a name, but it is up to someone else to build it and bring it to reality. Ideas are started with INTP's but others on a support staff will implement.

In relationships, INTP's are committed although somewhat distant. The social life is usually managed by the partner but INTP's willingly cooperate in this arrangement, happy to have someone else do this for them. However, INTP's need to verbally express love so their partners do not feel taken for granted.

## ● INTJ

INTJ's are unique among all types. Visionary and self-confident, INTJ's see a world of future possibilities created from workable theory. INTJ's are fiercely independent in creating their own lives. Authority and rules of the world mean little to them if the rule does not make sense. They are not awed by titles or good marketing programs.

At work, INTJ's use intuition to help them as much as logic. Creativity is of the utmost importance though the end product must have value or usefulness. They are great in scientific endeavors or as a visionary executive, who, while creating new business concepts within his or her mind, also has what it takes to make sure they get implemented.

Leisure has to have some reason, just to relax is not good enough. They enjoy endeavors that stimulate their brains and allow for creativity.

In relationships, the INTJ can appear distant and cold. They value harmony and order from their mates. They have a difficult time expressing emotions but are very sensitive to rejection. INTJ's can be somewhat wanting in a relationship.

# ● ESTJ

ESTJ's are the "let's get the job done now" type. Using logic and analysis, they roll up their sleeves and dig right in. They stay focused on the task, getting it done in the most efficient manner possible. They prefer actions to contemplation.

At work, ESTJ's prefer organized, logical work. Good at using time and resources, they like making decisions when they have all the facts. ESTJ's make good leaders, managers, and supervisors.

ESTJ's keep work and play separate. Play is usually goal-oriented; thus, just looking at the sunset is less enjoyable than enhancing family relationships, or learning to scuba dive. ESTJ's often need to learn that play doesn't always have to have a purpose!

ESTJ's and love mean stability. Love relationships are logical and steadfast. ESTJ's need to learn to bring in more feelings and be aware that their partner's needs may require more intimate expression than what a typical ESTJ usually presents.

As efficient and logical as ESTJ's are, they tend to decide too quickly, having a tendency to be unwilling to change their mind once it is set. They would do well to bite their tongue or at least leave opinions open longer.

---

# ● ENTP

ENTP's love new ideas and complex relationships. They maintain faith in their ability to constantly improvise in a situation. They hate the routine, always looking to innovate and change. Working within a highly structured environment is very uncomfortable for them.

Analytical, entrepreneurial, and creative are three requirements in the workplace for ENTP's. Status and money pale in importance to being noted for their innovative accomplishments. INNOVATION is all important in their work. If it doesn't provide it...they will create it!

Play is very important as long as it provides new outlets, adventure, and little structure. These are the type of people who can go away for the weekend with no idea of where they are going and what they might come across. Inevitably though, they end up with a great weekend.

ENTP's take a long time in love...they explore a variety of relationships and even after committing to one, they still require independence and freedom. This works well if their mate is also self-dependent; it works poorly for a person who desires a "settled down" relationship.

ENTP's are dreamers, always looking for change and challenge. They need to learn to value others and their input, which ENTP's often discount as being less valuable than their own. ENTP's need to set realistic priorities to avoid taking on so many innovative projects and ideas that nothing gets accomplished.

## ● ISFJ

Key words for the ISFJ are loyal, considerate, and sympathetic. They repeatedly go out of their way to help others. They prefer a world with rules, order, and traditions. They are happiest when in the service of others and are willing to make sacrifices for the greater good.

They like methodical, orderly work that serves the greater good and allows them to pay attention to detail. Bookkeeper, librarian, and social worker might be possible occupations. Playing is somewhat difficult for ISFJ's, as play comes only after all work is done. They have a tendency to put off leisure activities. A good technique for ISFJ's to get more relaxation time is to add it to their "to do " list!

ISFJ's can often be taken advantage of in relationships. Loving to serve and please others can often find them being used by partners who feel they should be served. ISFJ's need to learn to take time to honor themselves in a relationship and make sure that their partners maintain a balance of give and take.

ISFJ's are wonderful people but often are not assertive enough to protect themselves from being manipulated by other more powerful, less self-effacing, types. Taking classes in assertiveness training is a good start.

## ● ESTP

ESTP's are full of action, are outgoing and fun to be with. Practical and realistic, they can take a problem and quickly set the path towards an efficient solution. They can be blunt; not to be mean, but "Heck, that's just what needed to be said to get the job done."

ESTP's can be dramatic and often prefer occupations that allow room for flair. Sales and service are a natural outlet for ESTP's.

Fun-loving, ESTP's like active leisure; a canoe ride down Class-3 rapids is more interesting than taking a rowboat across the lake. Some element of risk is preferable to an ESTP—it's much better than reading a book and listening to Bach!

ESTP's love relationships, but mainly during the good times. On the roller coaster of love, down times, or the typically dull times that occur in all relationships, are too confining for ESTP's. If they concentrate on bringing new adventure into the relationship the partnership will survive, but ESTP's have a tendency to hold their partners responsible for boredom and get pulled in other directions.

ESTP's should remember that they don't have to be busy all the time to be a good person. They need to learn to honor their inner selves which sometimes gets lost by these great adventurers.

## ● ISTJ

ISTJ's make the best people to work with because you can always count on them! Methodical, dependable, serious and hard working is the ISTJ. They like hierarchy and structure, are great with details, and seek to maintain the status quo. In their work environment, a structured setting allows privacy from interruptions, which is important.

Leisure is an earned activity for ISTJ's. It must have purpose and results for them to truly enjoy it.

Love is very important to ISTJ's with commitment, loyalty, and consistency having the utmost value. You can always count on an ISTJ to do the practical things—keep the house clean, pay the bills, and maintain social order for the family. However ISTJ's often confuse these gifts as a sign of love, and they forget to share themselves as part of the relationship.

ISTJ's need to learn to maintain flexibility as they can become rigid. They are great at details but often fail to see how these details fit into the greater picture. Thus, their efforts are spent finishing up details when the bigger picture has changed and the need for those details may no longer be necessary.

ISTJ's tend to be loners, self-sufficient, and assume that others are this way, too. They tend to forget that others need pats on the back once in a while.

---

## ● ENFP

Go, go, go is the ENFP. They are initiators of change who energize and enthuse everyone they meet. They love the start up phase of a project but can get bored after it is up and running. They are always looking for new projects to get involved in. ENFP's bring excitement and joy to all aspects of their lives.

At work, ENFP's are creative. They are very good to put on a new project because you can guarantee they'll get it off the drawing board and on its way. ENFP's are often nontraditional in their career path and are always in a learning phase—no matter where they are. They will gravitate towards positions that allow for creativity, or they will create their own business, often in the service of others but in a unique way.

ENFP's love to travel and read as these two activities open up the door for new possibilities and ways to view the world. Learning is often involved in an ENFP's leisure. Some like physical activity, although most ENFP's enjoy it because of the mental release it provides as a result of the physical effort.

ENFP's can be fickle in love, either overcommitting or undercommitting. Balance in relationships is difficult for them to maintain because of their desire for change and looking for the best fit in many different areas of a relationship.

Though ENFP's are great "idea people," sometimes their lives become so filled with ideas that nothing ever really gets done. ENFP's need to learn prioritization, otherwise too many good ideas will go undeveloped.

## Suggested reading list

| | |
|---|---|
| Stone, Hal & Sidra | *Embracing Your Inner Critic* |
| Swets, Paul | *The Art of Talking So People Will Listen* |
| Keirsey, David, Bates, Marilyn | *Please Understand Me* |
| Tannen, Deborah | *You Just Don't Understand* |
| Tannen, Deborah | *That's Not What I Meant* |

# ACTION PLAN

### Exercise #1. Good communicators are good listeners.

Set yourself a goal: "For the next three weeks I will become a highly conscious, active listener to others and myself."

A. To do this it is helpful to put little reminders around so you will stay focused on this goal. There are several things you can do. Put little dots where you will see them and be reminded to focus on active listening. Or try a little note that says "Shhhh...listening going on!"

B. Make notes in your journal: is active, conscious listening difficult? Do you find yourself dying to talk while trying to listen instead? What about your self- talk? Are you amazed at what you're saying to yourself? How often are you repeating a thought to yourself?

C. After three weeks of active, conscious listening, do you see the world and yourself a little differently? Is it better? Are you better for it?

### Exercise #2. Seek first to understand.

This parallels Exercise #1. When seeking to understand, you make a conscious effort to appreciate, acknowledge, or gather information that will help you understand the other person's perspective. This may involve looking at gender differences, cultural differences, educational opportunities, and the other person's self-esteem level and seeing how it impacts another's communication efforts. When you ask yourself these types of questions it helps you to step into the other's shoes and see it from another viewpoint.

A. Seek first to understand by listening and looking within the heart of the other person.

B. When the "judgement" voice turns on inside you, turn it off. Instead tell yourself: "Focus on understanding this person's point of view."

# Community
## *and the*
# Environment

# *Making your Life Puzzle may start with "self", but it inevitably leads to the whole of the world around you.*

**M**any times while talking with people about making their Life Puzzle and creating a lifestyle of optimal health a comment will come from the audience: "Making my Life Puzzle sure seems selfish. Everything you're saying is about what 'I' need to do in the areas of nutrition, exercise, my feelings, and my thinking. It just seems to be caught up in me, me, me."

My response to this is threefold. 1) Initially, making your Life Puzzle is very centered in the "I". That's because, in the beginning, you are going to have to spend a good deal of time learning, making personal choices, getting started on your exercise program, and making more and more commitments to your daily lifestyle. It may mean that you will have to pull yourself away from the old lifestyle, such as being with certain people who encourage you to stop trying to be pro-active and remain reactive (like them!). This will appear selfish, but you will discover that it isn't selfish at all. In time, this intense concentration on yourself and making your Life Puzzle will begin to taper off. You will have gotten a good deal of the lessons under your belt and it will become a way of life that continues to build on itself.

2) Once making your Life Puzzle has become a comfortable lifestyle and you have begun to receive the numerous benefits that making this change can bring, you will begin the second phase: You will begin to realize that most of the people you are walking with through life are still deeply entrenched in the old model of victim playing. You watch them create reactive lives and within that you remember your self from that time. You remember the pain, the exhaustion, the frustration. As you have learned that it doesn't need to stay this way, you begin to reach beyond your "self" and extend yourself to others, with the desire to encourage them to make their own Life Puzzle.

This is when Life Puzzle making moves out of the self and into the *whole of the community* around you. Because within your own Life Puzzle-making, you begin to realize that a Life Puzzle that remains strictly within the "I", can't be a balanced Life Puzzle at all. Making your own Life Puzzle requires you to reach out to the community because there is an awareness that there is no separateness—every action you take in your life has an impact on someone else and vice versa.

Thus, your Life Puzzle becomes deeply committed to the community as a whole, and you begin to act responsibly with the awareness that your actions impact not just your own life but the community at large. So, for example, you don't choose good nutrition just for your own body, but with the realization that when you eat poorly, you risk creating illnesses such as cancer and heart disease. This will impact the community…which will have to care for you.

3) Another dimension has opened up then within your Life Puzzle-making. If living responsibly aids the community as a whole, then building your Life Puzzle makes even more sense. At this point, you can see that the selfish time of making your Life Puzzle, the time that you pulled away from the community to do your personal work, is actually not selfish at all because ultimately this investment in self will ensure that you do not become a burden to the community as a whole.

## Make your Life Puzzle: an answer to a nation of victims? Rebuilding the Earth community starts with self-responsibility.

Unless you've been hiding for the last 30 years, it's obvious that most people operate from a very selfish "what's in it for me and who is going to give it to me" way of life (but of course, they don't want to have to do anything for it.). This creates an isolated world where everyone withdraws and cares only for their very immediate needs, with little understanding for the community as a whole.

We see this isolated world all around us and nobody is happy with it. Yet there seems to be a belief out there that some "system" is needed to come and fix it. But you can't fix others, you can only fix yourself. All we can do is encourage others to do their own personal work to become self-responsible. This brings them out of isolation, and they too will reach out to their community. In this way the world begins to heal itself.

That's the power of making your Life Puzzle: The understanding that just one human being, by taking full responsibility for his or her life, can have the ability to impact the total community.

How do you make this happen? It doesn't have to be a big, high-tech extravaganza, but through the simpleness of living in balance in the all areas of your Life Puzzle, the message about consciously creating a Life Puzzle is passed on to others.

For example, within your work piece, how can pro-actively making your Life Puzzle affect the community? How often do you hear co-workers complaining about their powerlessness over manage-

> We're all in this together. Start with taking care of yourself so you will have the necessary energy to be able to reach out and help someone else!

ment? How many times do you watch yourself get sucked into this negativity and leave work frustrated? Everyone is talking behind the boss's back, yet nobody is being honest in their communication. This brings the whole group down and, in time, everyone is doing just enough to get by. New projects are overlooked with nobody willing to care. Except you! You refuse to keep this negativity cycle going and you approach your boss. You tell him or her what's happening, what you feel about the situation, and what solutions to this problem you think might be possible. Of course you can't guarantee the outcome of this, but just the act of breaking out of the victim role will guarantee two things: 1) you feel empowered because you have tried to find a solution through good communication, and 2) others will be influenced that there might be another way to live than just standing around complaining.

As you continue to live more and more comfortably within your lifestyle, you'll discover that many other people will notice. You will find yourself encouraging others—suggesting books they might read, classes they could take, and steps they could try. Your Life Puzzle-making has moved well beyond the selfish 'I'!

## Share it with others, then let it go!

Sometimes, after we've discovered the empowerment that making our Life Puzzle can give us, we get a little overzealous in trying to pass it on to others. Now that we know it, we think everyone else should know it and do it. We take it personally when others don't jump on the bandwagon as quickly as we'd like, or at all in some cases.

Before long we become judgemental about others who aren't doing it, or aren't doing it at the level we think they should be. This lack of action by others often incites one to try harder to share it with them!

STOP! If this is going on then you are missing the point about making a Life Puzzle: self-responsibility. You can only change yourself, not others. Believe it or not, you can't make others become responsible for themselves! (Ask any alcohol rehab counselor if they make any of their clients change!) No, self-responsibility is a personal choice, and many of us will steadfastly refuse to elect to take it on. And usually, the more someone else insists, the more resistant we become.

So, when it comes to making your Life Puzzle, if you want others to try it, the best thing you can do is LIVE it yourself. Share it with others if they're interested, and then once you've shared, walk away and let them put it to use in the way that is right for them. As I said earlier, making a Life Puzzle is not about perfection or about being fanatical. It is a simple lifestyle process, lived daily. Get your ego out of it and just live it. When you do it this way you'll be amazed to discover that people who once thought you were completely offbase and a little nutty are suddenly asking you questions, or are actually defending your right to be a little different. Then you'll notice them drinking water at their desk, or excitedly telling you that they tried their first massage or completely goofed off last night even though they had lots of work to do, because they just needed to play…Ah, Life Puzzle-making has come to the community.

## Once upon a time...

Okay, I'll admit it, wherever I work I am often looked at as being a little strange. I eat differently, I exercise regularly and in general I'm refusing to participate in the mile-a-minute, boy-aren't-we-having-fun-as- we're-killing-ourselves work world. I just sort of come in, do my own thing, and when others laugh at me, I just shrug my shoulders and keep on rolling. Because I know what's going to happen.

If I just stay doing the things that work for my Life Puzzle, little by little others are going to ask questions. Or they're going to try an idea I threw out one day when they were complaining about their umpteenth headache. And then one day one of them is going to come into my office, close the door, and ask me what suggestions I have to help with a certain problem. Because, by living a healthful lifestyle, people notice that I don't get as tired as they do or am not as negative or overwhelmed by the problems of the day. I may be weird but I am happy, and after a while others convince themselves that

trying some of that weirdness might not be so bad after all (considering the pain they're in). My "selfish" Life Puzzle has extended to the community and now we're all working together.

## Community is not just people, it is the physical world around you as well.

As you begin to realize that every action you take or don't take impacts the community of humans around you, it isn't long before you become aware that all of your actions impact the environment, too.

The issue of self-responsibility takes on a greater dimension: the survival of the Earth. If all of our actions impact the environment, then continuing to remain reactive instead of pro-active in our lives will have a powerful negative impact on the environment.

It is in self-responsible living that saving our environment begins to become possible again. Simple things, like reducing the amount of driving you do, planting a container garden in your city home, or composting vegetable scraps instead of sending them to the landfill will make a large difference to the Earth! And that makes a difference for all of us.

## Going 90 miles an hour and the wall is just inches away.

Who will save us now? The environment is the obvious recipient of the reactive, "do enough to get by" model. We have just about exhausted all of our planet's resources, polluting the rivers, the ground, the sky. We've allowed businesses to maintain high profits while dumping refuse into a river that has been all but brought to extinction. We can blame the business, but ultimately we are all responsible, because we have turned away from the realization that hurting the environment hurts everyone else.

## Put the brakes on and pull a sharp right, immediately!

What can we do? Individually there are many steps you can take that will help. Each small step leads to another and will surely influence others to start their small steps.

Below are some ideas, but by no means is this all you can do. But you must do *something*! Pick one or two ideas and start there. You'll discover that the next step will present itself and you are on your way.

1. *Write your Congressman, Senator, Governor or State legislator about your concern for the environment.* If there is particular legislation that you have an interest in, write!

2 *Join your community neighborhood organization.* If you don't have one, start one! Use this organization to confront environmental issues within your community. It could be as simple as having a Saturday clean-up in the spring or fall to pick up litter or to confront an environmental hazard created by a current policy that needs to be addressed. There is power in community groups!

3. *Recycle everything possible.* Also, work with your community to find out what is being done with the recycled material. Is there a way you can support this by purchasing these recycled products? Recycle at the office, even if it's inconvenient.

4. *Make your home a caretaker of the environment.* Turn off lights, run the dishwasher less, add shower nozzles that conserve hot water, put a brick in the toilet to use less water, and lower the heat in the winter, and raise it in the summer to use less heating and air conditioning.

5. *Reduce and reuse.* While recycling is good, reducing the amount of stuff you use in the first place is better. Ask yourself, "Do I really need this?" Also, reuse what you have. Purchase items that can be fixed versus thrown away.

## Suggested reading list

There are so many books that deal with your relationship with the community. From books on volunteerism, ecological and environmental issues, political action, or how to start a non-profit foundation to help save a 300 year-old tree in your neighborhood, the list is endless. Below are a few ideas but if none fall into a category that you are personally interested in, keep searching.

| | |
|---|---|
| Makower, Joel | *The Green Consumer* |
| Hollender, Jeffrey | *How to Make the World a Better Place* |
| Erlich, Anne H. & Paul R. | *Healing the Planet* |
| Carson, Rachel | *Silent Spring* |
| Gore, Al | *Earth in the Balance* |
| Hawken, Paul | *The Next Economy* |
| Hawken, Paul | *The Ecology of Commerce* |
| Henderson, Hazel | *Building a Win-Win World* |
| Elgin, Duane | *Voluntary Simplicity* |

---

# ACTION PLAN

Below are some ideas you might want to try in order to become more involved in your community. However if you are in the early stages of building your Life Puzzle and just getting into areas such as exercise and nutrition I would suggest you put off taking on a community project at this time. The reason being that many of us get ourselves so involved with this type of project we ignore our personal growth work. Community work is easier in many ways than taking responsibility for our daily lives. But a person who does the personal work first is much more effective at creating community change than the person who is out of balance.

### Exercise #1. Choose a project of concern, make a call!

Getting involved in a project that you feel personally committed to is quite easy. Usually a few phone calls will put you in touch with people who can show you where to go and how to become part of the solution.

Look in the local newspaper for volunteer requests. All newspapers carry them, and if you pay attention you will quickly see what days these announcements come out and that the phone numbers will be listed there. One great thing about this section is the awareness it will bring you of the wide variety of community projects that are currently going on but which you may not be aware of. You might discover one that you hadn't thought of before. Give a call!

**Exercise #2. Create a family project as part of your family mission statement** (see Chapter 14, Family/Parenting's Action plan).

One of the best ways to teach your children is through a hands-on approach to finding solutions to the world's problems. At a family meeting, start a discussion about your desire for everyone to become involved with a community project as a team. Depending on the ages of your children and their interests, work together to find a project that everyone feels committed to supporting.

I can remember reading about a family where the two teenage sons were so disturbed by the homelessness issue that they asked their parents if they could distribute food from their own kitchen. This became a nightly family project of making sandwiches and drinks and sharing them with homeless people. It bonded the family in a cause they wanted to change.

**Exercise # 3.**

If you don't have children become a Big Brother or Big Sister to a child. Once you've established your relationship with them, the two of you can work together to find a community project you can share. You will be helping this child learn the value of community and sharing as well as becoming part of the solution!

# Re-creating yourself through Play

# *Playing is a part of my Life Puzzle? Oooooh, what fun!*

**P**lay is a vital part of making your Life Puzzle. In the process of playing, you actually re-create yourself. Unfortunately, many people view play as a waste of time because nothing "valuable" comes out of time spent in play.

Think again!

First, let me define play: Play is any activity one engages in for pleasure. So one man's play is another man's work, because what may be pleasurable to me may not be pleasurable for you. Thus there's no set criteria for play.

Play activity does have a few preconditions to help you know when you are playing, and when you are not.

1. *Play activity is performed purely for the joy, not for the outcome.* Thus playing a softball game is play whether you win or lose. If winning is the primary goal of your softball playing then it is no longer play.

2. *In the process of playing one feels open and trusting to be oneself.* There is no judgement going on, either by yourself or others. When you are doing an activity that leaves you feeling inadequate, or vulnerable you are not playing.

3. *After engaging in play, one feels relaxed and rejuvenated.* Mental tension has been reduced. That's not to say that after a great game of basketball, or a 20-mile hike with full backpack you have to feel "light and airy" in order to call it play. Exhaustion can be relaxing and thus play. The real key is mental relaxation. Have you removed yourself from your problems? Or at the end of the activity are you more stressed than before?

Play can be anything as long as it is fun for you! Again, fun is a subjective thing because each of us finds different activities enjoyable.

The important thing in using play as a valuable part of making your Life Puzzle is to be sure that you include it as part of your life. Play is not wasted time. It is timeout for your body and mind from the stress of the day. This play time—whether it is sitting down and reading a book, going fishing, taking a leisurely walk, or simply enjoying a favorite CD on the stereo—is very necessary.

When we bring play regularly into our lives it rejuvenates the body and mind. This rejuvenation is vital as it restores the mind, thus allowing the time we are spending at work to become more

> Perhaps if we played at life more, we'd get more done!

## Oh, play…well that's just kids stuff!

You're darn right it's kid stuff! And since adults are just kids in big bodies it means it's stuff for you too!

Actually, in studying children, it has been discovered that children learn best while playing. For example, if you are trying to teach children about geography, they will learn the same set of facts faster if you provide it to them in the environment of a game instead of the typical fact sheets. That's why "Where in the World is Carmen San Diego?" is so successful.

During this "learning play," participants aren't concentrating on learning facts, they're focused on getting from one place to the other. They're not concerned with the work of learning, which requires them to come up with the right facts. Children will learn the facts, because they need them to play the game. Thus the facts "happen" in the process of play. When the game is over the facts will still be there, but they will have been learned in an enjoyable, non-threatening way.

This is the opposite of how most of our learning is presented. We think learning has to be hard, and serious but the research shows the opposite! The lighter, less serious, and non-threatening you can make the learning environment, the quicker and more permanent the learning will be.

productive. Without play our bodies and minds become overloaded because we never gives ourselves a break from the normal stresses.

Go for long periods without play in your life and your mind will literally short-circuit. If you have convinced yourself that play is wasted time you should readjust your thinking on the subject. Without play you will exhaust your body and mind. This results in burnout, and you will discover that your work time becomes less productive, you may end up physically ill, which will force you to take time away from work while you rest, relax and recover. Wouldn't it be better and easier to just play and recreate yourself this way, rather than getting yourself exhausted and sick?

*I used to be quite serious, but then I learned to love being a fool. It's the best thing that ever happened!*

It's true! When I gave myself permission to play my life took on another dimension entirely. I started laughing at myself, and gave up always having to be serious, orderly, in control, under management, and productive at all costs.

All that seriousness made me quite rigid and it also made life a chore. I was always trying to accomplish something, showing the world I had it all together. Of course I didn't have it all together, so in order to make the world think I did, I had to spend all my time working at life. This was exhausting.

In the midst of a life crisis, circumstances presented themselves such that I couldn't control it, no matter what. And for some reason I decided to play instead of work at controlling. It was great! Instead of hiding from the world I decided to just live in it, with all the good, the bad and the ugly. And you know what? The world didn't end, people didn't stop liking me, and I didn't get fired for not being perfect.

So I've decided to play for the rest of my life. I don't mind tripping on sidewalks, or having my dinner guests laugh at my latest test dish which isn't going to make the next cookbook because it was awful! Allowing myself to play has opened up my life to a tremendous amount of new learning. Playing at life allows me to re-create myself, opening my life to lots of possibilities. Playing provides a safe environment to try out new ideas.

## Bring more play to your life!

One key element of play is that during the process we don't judge ourselves or the activity, we just do it. In many ways then, we can turn simple, daily processes into play if we stop judging, and start playing.

## Turn daily chores into PLAY!

One day, while arguing with the toilet I was cleaning, a little voice inside yelled, "STOP! THIS IS NONSENSE! Here you are making the simple act of cleaning a toilet a real drudgery...why?" My answer was, "Well I hate doing this, it's boring work." And the little voice responded, "Then turn it into play!"

And I did. Instead of making it a horrible time, I made a game of it. I turned the stereo up nice and high, (now I wait until everyone's out of the house or I kick them out!), get all the cleaning stuff out, turned off my way too serious brain, and I got goofy.

The great thing about cleaning is that it doesn't require intense mental concentration—heck, vacuuming and dusting are one of those "auto-pilot skills" the body just knows what to do...move all the trinkets from this shelf to that, spray, wipe, done.

Cleaning is mentally relaxing to me, thus it is play. Listening to music allows me to play. While letting the music get inside my body I sing, I dance, I get happy!

And at the end of the play time, without even really caring, I end up with a clean house!

## Play at LIFE!

Watch a young child walk down the street. Every step is one of play and the joy of discovery. They see the flowers, they find funny ways of looking at normal, logical things, turning them into a brand new concept. Children learn while doing this play of life. So can you!

Why not hopscotch or skip down the street as a way of reminding yourself of your inner playing child? Maybe it will jar your mind back to your childhood days when play was a normal part of your day.

Add a smile and discover how it opens you to play. Walk down the street and give a big, *look 'em straight in the eye* smile to everyone you pass. Then watch how this playing helps to transform total strangers. If something so simple can improve the day of even one person, especially yourself, doesn't that make play a valuable part of your Life Puzzle?

## Play at Work!

This may sound funny, but actually if you would bring a little play into your work day, you'd discover that you'd become less tired, more productive and open to seeing new avenues or ideas that you could use to make your work day more enjoyable.

For example, do you do a repetitive process every day, such as stocking grocery shelves, plugging data into a computer program, or filling out the same type of forms for the public day in and day out? Could you bring some play into this? Could you play a "race yourself game" and get the shelves stocked faster by figuring out different patterns which might save time? While doing this you'll discover the shelves still get stocked, but instead of focusing on just getting the shelves filled in, you'll find that the time flies by as you challenge yourself to uncover new ways to play the game of stocking.

Ready to scream if you have to fill out one more form? Could you add a personal expression to lighten the day of the person who is going to receive the form and process it? A smiley face, a red dot, an anonymous signature? The mystery form-filler! Keep the processors guessing who's doing this by changing the anonymous signature now and then. This game will engage many others in your play! And what the heck, the form is still filled out and sent on its way to do its work!

---

## Suggested reading list

London, Peter      *No More Secondhand Art—Awakening the Artist Within*

Jones, Michael      *Creating an Imaginative Life*

*Enough books…go play!*

# ACTION PLAN
## Bringing play back into your life!

### Exercise #1.

Is there any play in your life? Take a few moments to make an inventory of the play in your Life Puzzle. Can you name something you play while outdoors or indoors? When alone or with others? Do all the things you do for play cost money? Do they require large amounts of time in order for you to do it? Are you able to be spontaneous with your play?

What I do for play:

Now ask yourself...is there enough play in my life? Or is there too much work and not enough play? Now that you can see it in black and white it's time to change.

### Exercise #2.

Open up your eyes again...see through the eyes of your child inside.

When we grow older the serious adult sees a pretty harsh world. Children, on the other hand, can create a wonderful world from nothing more than a sandbox and a couple of blocks. In this exercise, take the next 15 minutes of your life and try to see the world as if you were a 5 year-old child. You might try going outside and walking around. Look at the flowers as if you've never seen them before...now really look at them. If you notice a playground on your walk, go sit on the swing and give a good push. If you're inside at your desk, look at everything that's sitting on it. How might you use it differently if you were a 5 year-old? (As I sit at the computer writing this I see a pad of Post-It notes and can imagine my 5 year-old self drawing pictures on them and placing them all over the walls.)

Commit at least 15 minutes a day to seeing your world through the child that lives inside you. In time you will discover that you see a much more wonderful world than the serious, work-oriented one in which so many of us get caught up.

# Relationships
## *and*
# Partnerships

# *Can't live without those relationships!*

As a dynamic dimension within your Life Puzzle, relationships are likely to play an important part. Whether it is with the neighbor across the hall or a partner you will spend the rest of your life with, relationships are everywhere. Relationships based on a pro-active model (i.e., self-responsibility), are an on-going building process that you can design.

Sadly, few of us seem to think of relationships as something we create from within as much as something that just sort of happens. Since there is always *someone else* involved, how do you go about designing a relationship, since you can't control other people and their actions?

Many relationships and partnerships become entities that appear to have a life of their own. The participants spend more time adjusting to the relationship rather than the relationship adjusting to meet the needs of the participants.

Think back on an important relationship that ended and broke your heart. Remember how much time you spent wondering how the relationship was progressing? You were not quite sure, and yet not quite able to ask the other person how he or she was feeling. Did you feel out of control? Did you find yourself doing actions that seemed crazy or silly or even self destructive in order to keep the relationship going? And most important, were you at peace within yourself during the relationship or were you unsettled and anxious?

Most of us can recall a relationship that in retrospect was filled with fear— fear of losing it or fear of getting strangled by it. And while this was happening we were desperately caught up in the reactive process.

We weren't making pro-active choices, we were waiting for the next crisis. "She broke up with me, I'll do anything to get her back"…"He promised he'd call, why does he always break his promises?" "What can I do get him to see how much I love him? Why does he treat me like this? " We were confused, overwhelmed and wondering how to make these relationships work, but not once did we ask ourselves why we were turning our lives upside down in order to make this happen.

We continually convinced ourselves that we couldn't live without this relationship when the truth was we weren't really living because of it!

## It's time to get involved!

First of all, relationships do not just happen. Well, actually I take that back, for the majority of people, relationships do just happen. That's because no one teaches us as children how to have a good quality relationship with another person. So puberty hits and the societal messages start flowing and each of us knows that we should be finding someone "special". The problem is we get so caught up in finding that other person, that we forget to ask ourselves why we want the relationship at all.

With hormones raging, we get on the merry-go-round and find ourselves going 'round and 'round with these other people, ending up rather dizzy but not at all sure how to develop an honest, healthy relationship. Think how many hours girls sat together discussing "those boys" and trying to figure them out, consoling each other on the latest crisis over one of "them". On the other side, boys were just as confused. Sometimes they discussed it with their friends, often as not they'd just muddle through the relationship until something happened that either ended it or they went off with someone else.

As a teenager, there were very few people you could actually go to and discuss the way to create a meaningful relationship with another. Like becoming a parent, being in a relationship was one of those issues that was assumed you would "just figure out after you get there." Amazing, isn't it?

Even more amazing is the fact that it doesn't get any better in our adulthood! Developing a relationship at age 35 is as unnerving and confusing as it was at age 17! Ask anyone who has been divorced and is out on the dating circuit again and they will tell you it's awful. The whole process leaves most people feeling extremely vulnerable and unsure of what

is happening. Again, the relationship runs their life and leaves them out of control and at the mercy (victimhood?) of it.

But if you had stopped and asked yourself, "*Am I developing this relationship as a conscious part of my Life Puzzle?*", the answer for most of us would be…*No*. In the pain and confusion of our teen and early adult years, we all disempowered ourselves in order to have the relationship. And in many cases, just to have any relationship at all—no matter how bad— seemed better than being alone.

It's time to break this cycle and shift instead to relationships that you are pro-actively creating as part of your Life Puzzle. Let's examine this.

### "We" doesn't exist: two "I's" do not equal "We", *ever.*

A relationship begins. Once this happens, think how quickly this relationship starts to take on a life of its own. While only days before you were making plans for your life, suddenly you shift all your focus to the relationship. This process usually disempowers both members as they begin the dance to keep the relationship moving. Then, *I* becomes *we*. Only *we* doesn't actually exist, even though the two people repeatedly act as if *we* is a thing of its own.

The problem with *we* is that each person's view of *we* is individual and separate from the other person's *we*. This will become a source of problems as one person acts on his or her interpretation of *we*, yet misunderstands the other person's view of *we*.

When that happens, relationship problems are about to explode! Friendships break up because one person can't believe what the other person did based on an assumption that the *we as friends* comes before, *I as an individual.* And it is seen repeatedly in marriages or partnerships when one person is blaming the other for all the problems in the relationship because he or she isn't doing the right things for the *we* even if it creates a conflict for the *I.*

The problem with running relationships from the *we* model, is that no one ends up being responsible for designing a relationship that meets the need of each individual's full development. It is the belief that if each of us puts in 50% *I* then we'll end up with a 100% *we*. Not true. What we end up with is two half-people with a poor relationship.

It is unfortunate that this is the model we see around us, but it is the norm. Luckily, it doesn't have to stay this way. We have only to look within ourselves to begin the shift away from these types of relationships. It is well worth it, considering how dissatisfied people are with them.

## Join the 100% Club

Stop for a second and think about your current relationship.

- Why are you in it?
- What needs are being met for your Life Puzzle?
- What needs are you fulfilling for the other person and their Life Puzzle?
- Are you able to communicate openly and honestly in this relationship?
- Do you take responsibility for sharing your feelings with your partner? Or do you assume he or she should just know them?
- Do you wake up each morning with the desire to work and play in your relationship so that each parties' needs are being addressed?
- Are you always waiting for your partner to do more for you?
- Have you taken responsibility for your life? Are you in this relationship because it is the best choice for you?

***Only you can decide if you're a 100%er, first in your Life Puzzle and second in your relationship. What do you think?***

Answer these questions and it becomes apparent whether or not you are part of the 100% Club. Very few people are, but you can always choose to be. And there are lots of perks that come with this Club membership:

- A healthy, well-balanced Life Puzzle.
- Living in peace with yourself.
- Relationships that operate from truth, trustfulness and self-responsibility.
- A dynamic, growing relationship that is conscious of all parties involved.
- An example to your children of a healthy relationship between loving partners.

## Most folks are 50%ers

As it is now, few people are very good at running relationships that are pro-active and based in self-responsibility. This is evidenced by the fact that 50% of all marriages end in divorce and that you are more likely to be killed by a family member, spouse, or friend than you are by a stranger. It becomes obvious that we don't handle relationships very well. However, we do reactive relationships quite well!

Reactive relationships end up with both partners feeling like victims. They are rarely based in true self-responsibility. Instead, partners use each other as a way of avoiding taking full responsibility for their own Life Puzzle. These relationships quickly fall into the "do enough to get by" category. They are relationships that end up in counseling just before the divorce papers get signed. They are relationships that leave friends and partners screaming at each other, "How could you do this to me and say you love me?"

If your current relationship is two 50%'s trying to make a 100%, it's time for a change. This math will never add up! It will take some effort on your part but it is well worth it. Your partner may not be ready for this shift and you will have to accept this. Your job isn't to make him or her a 100%er. Your job is to concentrate on shifting yourself and become your own 100%er…first in your Life Puzzle, then in your relationship.

When you fully accept owning, creating and designing your Life Puzzle, then the natural consequence will be a shift in your relationships. They will not be something you disempower yourself to, nor are they a process of using someone else to get what you want. Your relationship becomes a reflection of your investment in developing your Life Puzzle. You actively participate, choose, question, stimulate and grow the relationship. The relationship doesn't "just happen", but is something you develop through conscious effort.

## What was your role model?

Few of us were taught how to develop healthy relationships. We learned instead to model the example put before us: our parents' partnership.

Understand though, that your parents' relationship came from watching their parents' relationship. And until just recently the norm for most relationships was as simple as this: each person had a part to play in order to keep the relationship going. I do this, you do that, and we'll both be happy. But were they?

Maybe some were, but many earlier relationships ended up in loveless marriages that stayed together for the children, yet they blamed each other for the lack of enjoyment that the actual relationship offered them.

Since most of us model what we grow up with, it is time to examine what you learned about relationships and begin to challenge it. You will have to confront a lot of misinformation and make the change to a relationship based in self-responsibility.

The history of relationships has only recently brought us to the point where we can choose to create a pro-active partnership. Until the mid-1900's, most partnerships were based on fundamental needs: food on the table, the production of children, a roof overhead, safety from the world. By the time all of this was taken care of there wasn't much time left over to build meaningful, loving, growing relationships. We take being in love for granted, assuming this is the start of most relationships. But history proves otherwise. Until the last 100 years or so, it was practical realities and power games that created most relationships. Thus, for most of our recorded history, the role model for a good relationship was not mutual love and respect, it was duty and power games. (New research shows that relationships based in equality were the norm in societies 5,000 to 9,000 years ago. These were lost when these peaceful communities were overrun by invaders.)

But times are changing and we do desire better, more meaningful relationships that are not just exchanges of duties between people. It won't just happen by itself. You will have to consciously teach yourself to create it. You will also have to understand that almost any person you choose to create a relationship with *has had as poor a role model as you did*. This means the two of you will have to actively work to create a new model of a healthy, pro-active relationship!

## Homosexual partnerships: The right path for some people.

It is at puberty that our awakening to our sexual identity begins. For about 10% of our population that will mean a homosexual awareness. Though many people consider it controversial, the research clearly indicates that homosexuality is genetically determined. Thus, at age 11 or 12, when a child is first becoming aware of the opposite sex, for this group, their attraction is for the same sex.

Homosexual orientation has been present through all of human history. It is normal and natural in the animal kingdom, of which humans are a part. Unfortunately, because it is rather rare (10% is a very small part of the population), it has had a difficult time being accepted by the majority of people. Thus homosexuality has stood out and been used to justify abusing other human beings because of this difference.

However, I am writing this section because I believe homosexuals have to be recognized as being no different than any other human being. They deserve to be treated with respect as is any human being who walks this earth. Just as you are a human being who is busy trying to put together your Life Puzzle, so is someone with a homosexual orientation.

If we acknowledged that every human being is working on his or her Life Puzzle, then we would accept that one's sexual orientation is just one piece of the Life Puzzle. Each of us must attend to it as it is right for us. Beyond that, no one need spend any time bothering themselves about another's sexual orientation.

Because our society is homophobic (fear of homosexuality), children who discover at puberty that they are oriented towards the same sex find themselves in a quandary. Unless the child is fortunate enough to have supportive family and friends, he or she will often have to deal with the issue by himself. Let's face it, puberty is hard enough in a heterosexual society, but add homosexuality and a child's fragile self-esteem can be sent into a tailspin.

A person with a homosexual orientation desires a partnership just as much as any heterosexual person. Partnerships aren't just about sex, they are about friendship, support, caring and lifestyle choices.

If you are homosexual, creating a partnership with another is a normal part of your Life Puzzle. However, it is unlikely that you have had any better role model for doing this than anyone else. Your potential partner won't either, which leads to the likelihood of a stressful relationship. Homosexual partnerships have the burden of additional societal baggage heaped onto the psyche of a child. This baggage shows up in the relationship unless the individual has done his or her own inner growth work before entering a relationship.

But you will have to teach yourself. You will have to strengthen your boundaries. You will have to create the new role model for yourself and share this with your partner. No, it won't be easy and yes, you will have the millstone of a society that is still confused and conflicted on this issue. But it can still be done if you choose to become 100% self-responsible for your Life Puzzle.

As you read this book, whether you are homosexual or heterosexual realize that you are a human being. You are responsible for putting together a healthy Life Puzzle. That's the short and long of it for all of us. Partnerships and your sexual preference is but one dimension of your whole Life Puzzle.

I hope there will soon come a day when the issue of sexual orientation—just like race, gender, and religion—will no longer be used as a justification for dividing us against each other. We are all Life Puzzles under construction and while no two Life Puzzles will ever be the same, no one Life Puzzle is better than another.

Until we shift our perception, homosexual men and women will find themselves fighting for their right to exist. This is a loss for everyone because so much time is spent fighting each other instead of concentrating on growing our healthy, self-responsibility based Life Puzzles.

## All good relationships start with "I".

"I accept the responsibility of bringing 100% of my true self to this relationship." Great relationships, be they friendships or partnerships, begin with each person taking full responsibility for 100% of the relationship. That is, individuals take full responsibility for creating a relationship that meets their own needs.

Oops, I just heard you thinking... *"Well, isn't that awfully selfish?"* No. Your thinking process assumes that only one person's needs will be satisfied and that the other person will be used to meet the needs of the first person. But think it through a little bit further and you'll realize that if both people come to the relationship accepting full responsibility for designing a relationship that meets their needs, then it would be impossible for either person to use the other.

Instead, each person is in the relationship because they truly want to be, based on the fact that they are responsibly choosing to participate. In this way the relationship can grow, change, ebb, and flow and neither person can be used by the other.

It also prevents many problems that plague most relationships. When you enter with 100% responsibility for yourself you get involved. You open lines of communication to clarify feelings, ideas, and goals. You don't wait for a crisis to force your relationship to deal with these issues, you bring them up yourself. And most important of all, you get out of the "blame the other guy" game. If at one point you find that the relationship is not working for your Life Puzzle, then you can responsibly close a relationship through honest communication. Isn't this a better way to run a relationship?

Few relationships operate from this responsible "I". This is evidenced by the large amount of abuse—physical, sexual and emotional—that we see in so many relationships. As mentioned in the earlier section on boundaries, abuse is the result of two people with poor boundaries. The one who is being abused allows the other person to overpower and invade his boundaries, resulting in the hurt, degradation and pain that further weakens one's boundaries, and on and on it goes. But remember also that while it is obvious that the boundaries of the one being abused are being violated, the one who is doing the abusing has just as weak a boundary. When you are an abuser, it is because you operate from a lack of good boundary of self. This poor boundary is a deep insecurity that you cover up by overpowering another person. This abusive power gives you an illusion of strength and security but inside you know you are weak.

If it happens to be your spouse that you are beating up, sexually assaulting or verbally abusing, it is clear that you are not operating the relationship from a "true self", that is, working towards a balanced and healthy Life Puzzle. How could you be? Would anyone who is self-responsible and self-loving be able to accept and approve of themselves while they abuse another?

Yet this is how so many of us have watched people act in relationships. Individuals, instead of operating from self-responsibility and self-love (the I), come to the relationship unsure of who they are, vulnerable to having their emotional, physical, thinking, sexual and spiritual boundaries invaded or overpowered by another. Before long, the bliss of love has turned into a power dance. They find themselves dancing around each other, waiting to see what the next move will be but never feeling capable of stopping or changing the dance without upsetting the other.

When you operate from the *I*, the relationship dance is one where both partners choose to dance together, where each has the right to suggest changes when necessary and the other respects the input. The dance takes practice and effort by both people. Each accepts that mistakes will be made, but in a healthy relationship centered in I, each person comes back to the dance floor after a mistake, accepts their part in it and agrees to work on it some more.

In so many of the relationships we see today, when mistakes are made, one blames the other. Screaming, shouting, fighting and abuse becomes the dance, and before long neither party wants to be there. These types of relationships work for no one, yet so many people continue on with them year in and year out. This could change if each person would take 100% responsibility for his or her own Life Puzzle.

It's important to understand as you read this that accepting 100% responsibility for your Life Puzzle and for the quality of your relationship means ceasing to participate in abusive, power game relationships. However, that doesn't mean that your current relationship has to end. What it means is that your current relationship has to change.

As you change yourself you'll discover the response from your partner will also be different. If the two of you are accustomed to long fights where you don't talk to each other for a week, imagine what would happen if instead, after a fight, you wrote your partner a letter sharing your responsibility for the problem, offering healthy solutions and committing to try again. Now what would your partner do? When we change ourselves, the change it creates in how others *interact* with us can be incredible. Remember, you can't change others…you can only change yourself. Change yourself by accepting 100% responsibility for your Life Puzzle.

## When I have found my one true love, then I will be complete!

If you think that finding the right partner will make you "whole" or complete, you will fail in all your relationships. And YOU will have set them up for failure right from the beginning. A partnership with another person will not make you whole, will not make you

complete. If you're waiting for that to happen you will be looking for someone who you will never find your entire life.

The only person who can make you complete is you. Oh, a great relationship can enhance that wholeness, but it can't give it you. The best that a good relationship can give you is the encouragement and support to work towards becoming your most whole self, by doing the self-exploration and personal growth work that we are all responsible for if we are going to build a great Life Puzzle.

Too often, though, we use our relationships as an "out" to doing our personal work. We give ourselves up to the *we*, thinking that it will be easier to do than the *I*. If we just find the right partner we will gladly put ourselves second in order to love the other person right and then magically end up being whole as a result.

## No Swiss cheese relationships, *please!*

Let's face it, very few of us, especially during our teens through late 20's really think we have our act together. We are not are confidently running our lives from the point of making a healthy Life Puzzle. It's a very scary time in our lives, when it seems there are just so many

questions we are asking ourselves, that it gets down right exhausting!

Things like: What shall I be when I grow up? Will I make it through high school or college with a diploma? Will my body ever stop changing? Will I make any money? Where will I get a job? Will these zits ever end? Will I be able to make it out in the big world? Who am I? Why do I have flat feet? Will anybody like me with this big nose?

Just when you think there are so many pieces missing in your Life Puzzle and you can't imagine that anyone could see you without looking completely through you, you meet somebody. Despite all these holes (much like a piece of Swiss cheese) this person is sticking around. And in the bliss of this "he or she likes me" it is very easy to believe that the addition of this person into your life has actually covered up your holes and you begin to forget about them for a while. But forgetting about your holes is not the same thing as making them whole. Answering all these questions are the source of developing a *whole* self.

But these questions, and finding the right answers can seem overwhelming to most of us. If we only had to work on one at a time, then maybe we could handle it, but all at once…too much. So, in this overwhelmed state we start seeking a way around all the questions. Ah, what about a partner?

A Swiss cheese relationship has just begun.

## How do you prevent Swiss Cheese relationships?

Start with *I*. Take full responsibility for having a loving relationship with yourself. Then, accept yourself with all your holes. (Here's the good part, your partner comes with holes too…we all have them!)

Build your relationship from this understanding, and the two of you can spend your time not covering or ignoring your holes but instead encouraging and supporting your partner to work on their holes. At the same time, you accept your own holes and ask your partner to encourage and support you in working on them. Thus each person comes to the relationship with the same foundation: self-responsibility. From this point, growth of a true relationship can begin; one based in honesty and trust.

Do you ever remember yourself saying to friends at the start of a new relationship; "He (she) is just perfect, I just love everything about him (her)." And in the bliss of this new love, you feel like you're glowing? But after a few weeks, months, or a year or two, the glow is gone and this once perfect person has two left feet and the personality of driftwood. What happened? Where did Mr. or Ms. Perfect go?

Typically what has happened is this: the glow that is created is not based in truth. It is a false feeling that we create inside ourselves to temporarily mask our own feelings of insecurity. We deceive ourselves into thinking that our life is now suddenly perfect with the advent of this new love. All we ever really needed was Mr. or Ms. Right and our lives would suddenly come together. But as happens in all relationships, this glow passes, and inevitably we wake up one day to discover that we are the same old person, that we still have many of the same old insecurities or holes and this person… the love of our life…is not the answer after all.

At this point it is easier to accuse and attack our partners than to look inside ourselves and acknowledge that we were using the other person to cover up our holes—all the ugly feelings of insecurity that each of us have.

Depending on our partners to fill in any missing pieces of our Life Puzzle is to ensure failure in a relationship. Before you begin any relationship with another person, ask yourself: "Am I entering into this relationship to use this person to make me feel good about myself?

Before you start any relationship, be in love with yourself! This is the cornerstone of every great relationship. Not egotistical, narcissistic love that is consumed with the self, but a love that is accepting of who you are today while acknowledging that there is still much growing to do.

If you are depending on your relationship to provide you the approval for self-love you will be at the mercy of the other person giving or taking love away from you. This leaves you walking on eggshells as you focus on waiting for the other person to give you approval and love in order for you to feel okay. It is a very painful, scary way to live. Your entire life becomes wrapped up in the relationship and the response from the other person. *Jealousy, possessiveness, fighting, abuse, depression, tension…* these are the emotions that result when you operate a relationship that is not centered in self-responsibility and self-love. This is time and emotion that would be better spent learning to love, accept and grow within yourself.

Swiss cheese relationships are the norm in our society. We use our partner to cover our holes instead of taking responsibility for our Life Puzzle. Remember, a healthy relationship grows from within while each partner gives and receives encouragement to keep making their Life Puzzle.

If you are in a Swiss cheese relationship, don't blame or attack your partner; start looking at yourself. If necessary, seek counseling to start this process. Forgive yourself and your partner— neither of you were taught to create a healthy relationship, so why should you be mad at yourself for not having one?

Don't waste time attacking yourself or your partner. Accept where you are now and begin to grow your Life Puzzle.

*But if a partner or relationship is a part of my Life Puzzle, don't I have to be loved by somebody to make this part of my Life Puzzle?*

NO! You don't have to have a partner to be whole. It's true that a good partnership adds a fuller dimension to your life, but remember, wholeness comes from within, not from others.

You're better off being whole without a relationship than being in a poor relationship that's full of holes!

## New Law: No marriages before age 30!

I say that because too often marriages are made at very vulnerable times in our early lives. This is so sad because we often wake up in these early marriages and say to ourselves, "What in the world was I thinking!?!?!" Ah, but that's the problem, you weren't thinking. You were reacting to the fearful and crazy world out there makes us seek comfort in relationships as a quick out to all the questions that lie ahead in our lives.

Just think, if we couldn't get married before the age of 30, and long term relationships weren't permitted during our 20's, then we'd be forced to spend more time and care on making our Life Puzzle. This would make us much more capable of creating better relationships once we were free to have them.

Of course, I can say this since I'm past the age of 30! But for now, relationships and marriages aren't outlawed, so we all keep groping along. I just hope that after reading this section you will view your goal of having a relationship as being a pro-active choice versus the typical reactive process which leads to so many poor relationships, and marriages that fall apart leaving children without two parents.

## Hear it on the radio: Love is heartache, loss, and abandonment more often than it is joy, happiness and wonder.

Why have we come to believe that it is normal for our love relationship to be filled with lots of heartache? Listen to the radio for a day and it would be difficult to convince oneself that love is a wonderful thing!

Most Top-40 songs, and country songs sing about loss, jealousy, cheating, deceit and abandonment that occur in many relationships. On a very unconscious level we learn to accept that love is an issue of dependency: "You left me now I'm worthless, I am nothing without you, How could you do this to me and call it love?"

Over and over again we listen to this. As an adult you might be able to filter out this subtle message, but as a teenager listening to these songs it is very easy to fall into their message.

All of us can remember having a teenage break-up and hearing a song on the radio that completely matched our broken-hearted feelings. Our lives were consumed with our loss and our reality became connected to the song that defined our lives! If our self-esteem was fragile (and what teenager's isn't!), this loss reinforced our low self-esteem.

Stop a moment and listen to the radio today. What do you hear? Self-responsibility and love or victimhood and dependency? This heartache certainly sells records and it fits neatly in the relationship model that many of us have come to expect. But it is time to challenge this message.

The expectation that love between two people is as dangerous as a diamond in the middle of a big fire—all yours if you can brave the flame—is ridiculous. Healthy, self-responsible relationships are possible if you choose to create one. Remember, it starts with you not any one else.

As a responsible person, you wouldn't walk through fire to get to the diamond of love because you know you'd be burned. Instead you would responsibly put out the fire first, then walk through like a healthy, sane person and pick up this diamond. This way you can enjoy its beauty without those third degree burns. Top-40 radio convinces you it's normal to get burned! That's true if you are playing the victim game, but not true if you are responsibly making your Life Puzzle.

## Why do we like those Soap Operas?

Watching soap operas can be very addictive. Why? If you step outside of what's going on during a soap opera like *All My Children* or *As the World Turns*, you'll discover you are watching a continual onslaught of victim relationships. They certainly aren't a healthy model of people taking responsibility for their own lives and then treating others with respect. Instead there is a constant weaving of deceit, game playing, poor communication, abusive relationships, selfishness and greed. So why do we watch?

Maybe because it reminds us of our lives just enough to bring joy and relief from watching others get hurt like we have been. Because so many of us are running reactive lives and playing victim to the world around us, watching soap operas makes us feel normal, even if we don't have quite as much drama (or the wardrobe!) as the soaps.

Everyone in a soap opera is a master of the victim model. Their entire lives are caught up in reacting to the latest plot twists. Rarely do you see people taking full responsibility for designing their lives pro-actively.

I caught a classic example one day while I was at the gym. It was mid-afternoon and the television was on. I was on the floor stretching and *General Hospital* was on. One of the male characters was complaining to his grandmother that he was doing everything possible to win back his estranged wife. He was being the model of perfection—sweet, courteous, patient, sending flowers—but it wasn't working. His grandmother suggested he give it a little more time and then trotted off to some other room of the mansion.

Then, just as the scene is about to end, he cries out "I know what's wrong, I'm going about this totally backwards! I know how to get her back...the same way I lost her! I'll use all my talents to deceive and manipulate her, and before you know it, she'll be mine again!" The look on his face was a diabolical smile that made you know his logic was just perfect...this would work. Forget honesty and fairness, deceit and cunning were much more effective. I couldn't help but laugh, the whole thing seemed so ridiculous. But I also wonder how many teenagers, college students and young adults watch this and pattern their lives this way?

## Stop watching them!

If you are currently addicted, stop watching. You'll be amazed at how much time you will get back into your life, but you'll also discover that by not watching them you clear your mind and heart of the bad example of poor, supposedly normal, relationships. There is another way to live life, but you will have to break away from the typical view presented on television which constantly portrays people playing lives of victimhood.

You may not believe that these dramas are affecting your daily life but if you watch them continuously, these shows teach a subtle message that being a victim is normal and acceptable. We know that children are affected by the amount of violence they watch. Children's aggression rises after watching these violent shows, even though we teach them that hitting other people is not good. So too, is it any wonder that watching characters playing the victim game over and over again becomes a subtle model for adult lives?

Imagine instead if you watched show after show that presented characters who took responsibility for their lives, who had healthy relationships, who had open dialogues of honest communication as a problem-solving method. Don't you think you would use that as a role model? Perhaps when a similar scene came up in our life, you might act from this pro-active model? If it makes sense that you might use this visual example of a healthy television drama, it would also seem true that the continual viewing of unhealthy television drama—be it soap operas, evening sitcoms or mini-series— could be used as a visual example of how to live your life? Is this what you want to choose?

Then turn off the television.

# *What do men want? What do women want? Let's make peace.*

There's no doubt that relationships are a very important part of one's life. All of us invest large amounts of time in them as well as our hearts and minds. Yet they remain a mystery for most of us. Women can't seem to figure out how men tick, and men are ever confused about the wants and desires of the women in their lives. For all the energy we put into our relationships you'd think we'd have reached a level with more balance and understanding than is currently displayed.

Maybe the reason we're finding it so difficult is that we keep putting our focus in the wrong place. Women are trying to understand men; to figure them out and twist themselves around the relationship to make it work out right. Men do the same thing. As each of us does this, the whole picture gets muddled up and individuals find themselves walking around, shaking their heads saying, "I guess I'll just never understand women [men]...you can't live with them; can't live without them."

It doesn't have to be like this, but it certainly is in the world where we grew up. We watch our parents shake their heads at each other, throw up their hands and go to their corners. This sets up the friction that we see so often in relationships. But isn't this friction a result of being reactive instead of pro-active? As we enter relationships we quickly give up responsibility for our own Life Puzzle and mix it into the relationship Puzzle. Now everything is a mess!

> 10,000 Puzzle Pieces
> +
> 10,000 Puzzle Pieces
> =
> One jumbled mess

Think of it this way: You have your own 10,000 piece Life Puzzle and so does your partner. Until you entered this relationship you were busy working on your Life Puzzle. Then the relationship starts and you dump your 10,000 pieces in with their 10,000 pieces and the two of you start to work on this new puzzle. What kind of puzzle are you going to end up with? Two healthy Life Puzzles or one jumbled mess?

Most of us end up with the mess because we mistakenly believe that a relationship becomes the more important focus of our Life Puzzle. So you can see why relationships end up so confused. Mixing two Life Puzzles together to make a merged puzzle creates a mess. There is no clear outcome for this mixed puzzle and inevitably each person puts pieces in places that the other person doesn't understand and can't use. Instead of appreciating each of them for the unique pieces that they bring to a relationship, it isn't long before there is fighting and confusion about these different pieces being placed in this mixed-up puzzle.

One partner can't understand why the other wants to fill the mixed puzzle with pieces like having a sports car for the play piece, has issues about being short as part of his or her special challenge, uses sex as a way of communicating frustration instead of love, or has a closed style of thinking about new ideas. So this partner tries to change the other by kicking out a few pieces, or trying to place others in different, less noticeable areas of the mixed-up puzzle.

On the flip side the other partner can't understand his or her partner's choices for the mixed-up puzzle either and does his or her own moving and changing of pieces. Are these two building a healthy puzzle? No way.

Because they are focused on changing each other to meet the relationship puzzle, each finds his or her own Life Puzzle becoming mixed up, confused and lost in the merged puzzle. They have stopped taking responsibility for their own Life Puzzle and have given it up to the relationship puzzle. Inevitably, both become confused as to how to make this merged puzzle look and feel right for their own Life Puzzle and they begin blaming their partner for this.

You can stop this by standing back and realizing that neither men nor women know how to mix their Life Puzzles together to magically create a relationship puzzle. That's because there is no such thing as a relationship puzzle…so stop trying to make one!

If men and women would enter a relationship with the appreciation that the other person is different from them, and should be different, we would realize that the goal isn't to change others but to understand them. And the way we understand others is by reaching out, communicating, sharing and asking questions—it is not by treating the other person like some foreign invader that must be controlled, manipulated and managed.

We can understand our partners by opening our hearts and listening. When you do this you will discover a human being sitting across from you who is just as confused as you are about creating his or her own Life Puzzle and who is just as confused about you as you are about him or her. Men do not magically know how to make a good relationship. Women do not magically know how to make a good relationship. We must come together and open the dialogue.

If you accept responsibility for your Life Puzzle and realize how much effort this takes, then you can look across at your partner and realize that he or she is doing the same thing. You may assume that it looks much easier for your partner, but I can assure you that it isn't true. Making a Life Puzzle is difficult for everyone. Men's Life Puzzles are different than Women's Life Puzzles; each of us needs to appreciate this and work together to understand and support our partners to do their own work on their Life Puzzle, and in this process, we will discover our relationship grows in peace and cooperation.

## Relationships didn't always look like they do now.

The war between the sexes appears to have been going on since the days of Adam and Eve, so that today we assume the power struggle between men and women is both normal and the way it has to be. We laugh at it, and others cry about it, but the patriarchal or male dominant system that is at the center of this struggle is not, contrary to popular belief, the way that men and women have to be or have been through most of mankinds time on earth.

In fact, patriarchy is only about 3,000 years old. Considering that man has been on earth for millions of years, that's not very long. Recently we have been able to research and reconstruct societies from 5,000 to 10,000 years ago and it is very clear that these people did not exist in a patriarchal system at all.

You might then assume that if it wasn't patriarchal then it must have been matriarchal, or female dominant, but that assumption is also wrong. In these well developed, progressive societies it wasn't a system of domination at all but one of equalitarianism; men and women saw each other as equals and they created a society that reflected this.

A key component of these cultures was a respect for and worship of the goddess in relation to her role as a creator: Mother Earth. However, this goddess worship did not exclude men or relegate them to minor positions underneath the females. There were priestesses and priests involved in the spiritual and political functions, so the power games that we see so prevalent in our religious and political institutions of today did not exist. These groups did not have to pride themselves on a woman's right to be an ordained minister in the Presbyterian religion or lauding the first woman in Congress. In these societies, it wasn't necessary because both men and women knew they were equal to each other.

## Can we return to these times?

Why did this equalitarian system end? Riane Eisler, in her groundbreaking book *The Chalice and the Blade,* places the shift approximately 3,000 years ago with the influx of invaders from the Northern steppes. These nomads overpowered the creation-centered groups who were not prepared for war. (Why do you need war when your society is centered on the creation of life? Considering that war is centered on the destruction of life, it would have been unnecessary for these groups to spend time and energy on preparing for war when they found no reason to kill each other). Some people believe that it was the Bronze Age, and the subsequent ability to make weapons, that allowed these Northern invaders to be successful, but Eisler shows this isn't true. These earlier societies also had the ability to make and shape bronze, but they chose not to develop them into weapons, instead using it to fashion works of art and to worship the creatrix.

This shift from being a creation-centered to war-centered society affects us all. We have been raised and encultured in it. The power/dominator model is based in fear and leads to relationships in which neither side wins because they can't see each other as equals. It is male dominant, but both sides lose with it.

You can change this for you, your partner and most importantly, your children. But again, it takes effort to break out of the idea that "this is the way it is" between men and women. As Eisler shows us, there is another way and it is centered in equality.

## You can't change others, so change yourself.

Fine, no one has taught you how to have a healthy, well-balanced relationship. Certainly there are few role models for us to look up to, which means you will have to become your own role model.

That's okay! Just step back and relax and realize that you are capable of learning how to create a healthy relationship with someone else. But it is a learning process that you will have to initiate and then keep sustaining the growth process.

This learning process starts within yourself. You will have to confront and change many of the views that are deeply ingrained. Take responsibility for your Life Puzzle. Strengthen your self-esteem and boundaries. Look within to decide what type of lifestyle you want to create for your life journey. As you do these things, you will discover that when another person enters your life as a potential partner you will be able to decide from a standpoint of empowerment whether or not you want to add this person into your life.

The other side of this is that you will approach your partner with the understanding that he or she also is trying to grow himself or herself. This brings compassion to the relationship as you realize that your partner is searching and building his or her Life Puzzle, too. Now the two of you can work together, not changing each other to maintain the relationship, but changing oneself as part of one's Life Puzzle. As you grow, you invest in the relationship from a point of self-responsibility and self-love. If the relationship is not working to meet your needs you don't get stuck in the blame/victim game. Instead you pro-actively work to address the issues with your partner. This creates a win-win relationship for both of you.

This may sound too ideal but it does work. I've seen many couples confront the blame/victim game by individually taking responsibility for their own lives and then renewing their partnership from this foundation. Marriages that were once heading for the rocks are now on solid footing with each person standing on his or her own feet...not their partner's feet (ouch!).

## Making it last: Great relationships sustain because it comes from within.

There's been quite a controversy lately as to whether it is possible for people to actually make a relationship last for 30, 40 or 50 years. Some suggest that man wasn't meant to be monogamous but is genetically scripted to change partners fairly often. Others argue that since death came early few people lived past the age of 30 until after the 1800's,—long term relationships weren't an issue; you would likely die within 10 years or so of your marriage anyway.

People can argue this point forever, but the bottom line is we belong to a society that honors marriage till death do us part. So whether it's a part of man's fundamental make-up or not, our society has committed to it. So the question is, how do you create a long-term dynamic relationship that can run for 30 to 50 years?

Look within yourself, not your partner. If you are committed to making your relationship last it will be directly attributable to your investment in your Life Puzzle and this piece of it.

One clear fact can be ascertained from studies of relationships that have run for a long time and been happy: In these successful relationships, each person stands out as a unique individual, respecting each other for the individuality that compliments their union. There are no power games going on. Though you may often find traditional work division in the relationship, such as one doing the dishes and the other doing the yard, the respect they have for each other's wants and needs is mutual. Neither party serves the other at one's expense, they serve each other out of a commitment to their own selves. In this way, the balance of giving shifts back and forth as necessary.

These are two people who know that their relationship will be as great as they individually decide to make it by investing in it daily. This daily awareness is the commitment to building their own Life Puzzle, of which the partnership is a very important piece. When you're committed to your own Life Puzzle, making your relationship last a lifetime is an active part of this life-long process!

## Suggested reading list

| | |
|---|---|
| Keirsey, David & Bates, Marilyn | *Please Understand Me* |
| Paul, Jordan and Margaret | *Do I Have to Give Up Me to Be Loved by You?* |
| Lerner, Harriet | *Dance of Intimacy* |
| Whitfield, Charles, M.D. | *Boundaries and Relationships* |
| Marcus, Eric | *Male Couples Guide* |
| Gordon, Lori, H. | *Passage to Intimacy* |

# ACTION PLAN

## Exercise #1. Great relationships start with "I".

Look at yourself first. Answer the following questions to see where you are centering your relationship in *I* or *We*.

On a scale of 1 (low or no) to 10 (high or yes), answer these questions.

_____1.  I am in this relationship because it is good for me.

_____2.  Each day I am at peace within this relationship

_____3.  When conflicts arise I am able to discuss them with my partner.

_____4.  If I asked my partner to sit down with me to discuss long range goals for our relationship, I know he or she would be agreeable to this.

_____5.  If I would like to change a personal goal of my Life Puzzle (such as work, parenting, or community) I know I could discuss this and ask for support from my partner.

_____6.  I don't talk negatively about my partner and our relationship with friends. I go directly to my partner when I have conflict.

_____7.  I don't ignore issues that upset me about my partner. I communicate appropriately to seek a healthy resolution.

_____8.  Emotional and/or verbal abuse is not acceptable by me or my partner.

_____9.  I treat my partner as I would my best friend.

_____10. My partner treats me as he or she would his or her best friend.

_____11. I know my partner feels I am open to listening to his or her needs and is comfortable starting a conversation with me.

_____12. I am able to discuss financial issues with my partner, including long-term financial goals, monthly budgeting, purchasing life insurance, etc.

_____13. I respect my partner and encourage him or her to build his or her Life Puzzle.

_____14. My partner respects me and encourages me to build my Life Puzzle.

_____15. I take responsibility for my sexual needs in this relationship. I can discuss my needs with my partner and feel comfortable showing him or her what I like or don't like.

_____16. I feel I am in charge of my life. I have taken full responsibility for it.

_____17. I am not dependent on my partner for my happiness.

_____18. I think my partner is happy to have me in his or her life.

_____19. Having my partner in my life adds happiness to it. I wake up eager to share my life with this person.

_____20. I feel I have not compromised my Life Puzzle in order to maintain this relationship.

Now go back and add up your total score_____

1-75 points:       Victim/Dependent relationship
76-120 points:  Just getting by relationship, not a dynamic one.
121+ points:     Self-responsible: choosing and creating this relationship as part of a
                         healthy, well-balanced Life Puzzle-making.

What did the previous exercise show you? Were you surprised by the results? What changes can you make within yourself to improve this situation?

## Exercise #2.

Share the previous questionnaire with your partner. Compare your results and use this as a starting point for discussion.

## Exercise #3.

Look at the following list of words. Circle those you feel describe your current relationship. If you are not in a relationship at this time, circle the ones that were present in your most recent relationship.

| | | |
|---|---|---|
| Peace | Joy | Appreciation |
| Honesty | Freedom | Fear |
| Tension | Disrespect | Emotional abuse |
| Fighting | Deceit | Physical abuse |
| Bickering | Mistrust | Sexual abuse |
| Respect | Sharing | Balance of responsibilities |
| Trust | Goal-setting | Control |
| Openness | Mutual sexual pleasure | Good communication |
| Happiness | Love | Anger or hate |
| Disagreements voiced | Lack of communication | Imbalance of responsibilities |
| Duty | Boredom | Alcohol-affected |
| Disgust | Excitement | Drug-affected |

Look at the list of words you circled. Are these the attributes of the relationship you were dreaming of when you partnered with this person?

What changes could you *make within yourself* to improve the description of your relationship?

## Exercise #4.

Based on the description you circled above, write a letter to your partner and share what you've discovered about your view of the relationship. Express to him or her what you feel you are responsible for and the steps you might take to improve the description.

You may choose not to give this letter to your partner. However, in just the process of writing this letter you will discover things about yourself and the desires you have for this relationship within your own Life Puzzle.

# Coming to terms with your personal Sexuality

# *Your personal sexuality.*

**S**exuality. Probably no other word in the human language can create more controversy than sex. Everybody has a sexual self, and yet in the United States it is a most confused issue. Why? Why would human beings take a very natural part of themselves and turn it into such a mess!?

What messages did you receive about sex? Was it masked in shame? Was it dirty and disgusting? Did most of your sexual education come from Playboy magazines and movies with sex scenes instead of your parents? Did the "little talk" you had with your parents leave you mixed on what you were supposed to feel about the value of sex in your life? Was responsible sex clouded in the issue of illness and disease that comes from fooling around with the wrong person?

## Stop a moment and think about this.

The early messages you received about sex are living inside you today. Isn't it time you went back and examined how these messages are now affecting your life? Are they preventing you from enjoying this part of you? Do you enjoy this part of yourself on a physical level yet are dissatisfied on the emotional level?

Re-examining our sexuality can be very difficult to do. The images that become connected to sex when we are quite young create our fantasies about sex and are such a part of us that it seems impossible to separate ourselves from this early connection. Some of the influence on your sexual definition came to you long before you were aware of even the remotest aspect of your sexual self.

For instance, very young children— even toddlers (2-3 years)—will masturbate, (even though they do not understand that's what they're doing!). These children may use this physical release to help them fall sleep, or when they are stressed by some activity going on around them. It is a very calming process for young children. At the same time, this early experience can subconsciously tie sex to being a stress reducer in an adult. You may be shaming yourself with messages that say, "When I'm stressed out, I am bad to also want sex," when in reality you have been conditioned from your earliest days to have this physical and emotional need.

Maybe as you read this, you're saying, "Well, don't we have free will to control our sexual urges?" Yes, of course we do, but sex is one of the most primal urges and can be powerfully demanding on both an emotional and physical level.

This is especially true when we have not consciously come to terms with our genuine sexuality and are not at peace with this part of ourselves. If we are still responding to messages received by movies and the media—or by a mother, father or other family member who may have had their own sexual identity problems—it can be difficult to manage these strong urges in the midst of our confusion.

This is clearly seen in the sexual transgressions made by people such as Jimmy Swaggert or Jim Baker, or a sex offender who preys on young children. Their urges, in theory, could be controlled, but their internal self-confusion renders them out of control. This is not to say that we should excuse their behaviors, but it is to say we can try to understand and help by encouraging them to confront their confusion and discover where it was first created.

## Isn't it better by now?

While teaching a sophomore level psychology class I asked my students, who were in their early 20's, "How many of you sat down and had a quality discussion about sex and sexuality with your parents?" Now I'm thinking to myself, this is the 90's, which means these children are the offspring of the "sexual revolution" generation. Surely this group is having open, honest communication with their parents. Out of 42 students only 1 raised her hand!

## New beginnings: realigning your sexual self-definition

Now that you've taken some time to re-examine your initial sexual self-definition, let's begin to reacquaint you with your sexual awareness.

Understanding your sexuality is a slow building process. First it starts with an awareness of your body, the ability to touch and look at your body with comfort, joy, and most of all trust. When we were very young, we trusted our bodies...babies run naked without a care in the world. They have no shame about being seen by anyone, because as far as they're concerned, it's just a body!

Unfortunately it won't be long before the messages to hide from our bodies comes through loud and clear. After about the age of 11, when puberty begins, the messages are quite confusing (especially post-1980). Yet this should be the time that adults are teaching their young children to know, respect, honor and take responsibility for their bodies.

Instead, children of this age receive a mixed message: according to the media sex is everywhere and everyone is very comfortable with it, while the home, church and society message is that if we ignore it, it'll go away. Mix this confusion with hormones going crazy within the body and it's a disaster waiting to happen.

## Only you can take on this responsibility!

It's up to you to develop awareness, trust, love and respect for your body. Many assume that others give us this respect through sex, but that is not true. If you do not first have respect, honor and love for your body before becoming engaged in a sexual relationship, you open yourself up to being abused and becoming dependent on others for your sexual self-definition. This is a reactive way of living this part of your Life Puzzle.

### A simple test to determine whether you are comfortable with your sexual self-definition: CAN YOU TALK ABOUT IT?

When you operate from the level of taking full responsibility for your sexual self, this gives you the comfort of loving and honoring your body. You live naturally, at peace with your body, and when experiencing sexual relations with another you are able to talk openly and honestly about your wants and desires.

If you can't talk openly and freely with someone about your sexuality—especially a person you would consider sharing your body with—it is a clear sign that you need to take more time to learn and nurture this part of yourself.

### Ah, it's all in your head anyway!

Actually, that's kind of true. Sexuality is mostly in the mind. Too many people confuse their sexuality with sex. That

· · · · · · · · · · · · · · · · · · · · · · · · · · · · · · · · · · · · · · · · · · · · · · · · ·

## What do men want?…What do women want?

Read almost any nationally advertised magazine, from Cosmopolitan to Sports Illustrated, and the issue of sex is entrenched within the pages. Whether it's the swimsuit issue with photos which border on porno shots, or the cover of a women's magazine which shouts headlines such as, "Ten sexual secrets to entice your man," clearly there is deep confusion about what pleases the other sex!

Most of this confusion is deeply seated in the lack of knowledge that is shared from the start of puberty. Remember junior high school? Everybody was doing "it" or at least pretending they knew what "it" was. Of course, nobody could admit that they didn't know what "it" was or especially how to do "it". Phew!

This confusion is present as we shuffle into our adulthood. I've run self-help groups and worked with private clients, and I have never heard anyone tell me that their first sexual encounter was done with the full knowledge of what they were doing. Men tell me they were strictly focused on accomplishing the act, while women generally express a desire for love which they traded for sexual intercourse. Rather sad, isn't it?

WHAT WILL MAKE YOU LOVE ME?

Is it any wonder sex sells? Adults desperately continue to seek understanding about this very important aspect of themselves. They buy magazines hoping to finally get a clue about what the other sex wants, and somewhere in there, what they want, too.

Get out of the media. Learn to define your own sexual needs by learning about yourself. Read quality books, take a class, talk to a counselor, but do something active to end the confusion!

happens when only their physical side is developed and the emotional side is ignored.

*It is possible to go through life and never develop your emotional sexual self.*

This often occurs when we have physical sex too young. We get caught up in the act of sexual intercourse and figure that if we just achieve orgasm then we're doing pretty good. But this is different than the sexual union that results when you are aware of the emotional aspect of your sexuality.

One way this emotional side is experienced is through masturbation, when one is joyously at peace with one's sexual identity and chooses to express it when so desired.

Another way it is created: when two people are engaged in deep and loving sexual relations which lead to a full bond between them as partners. At this level, the sexual self is mainly in the mind, with the body coming along. It is the opposite of the strictly physical sex that has very little emotion and often leaves a person feeling rather empty.

## Sexual boundaries

As discussed earlier in the book, each of us has a physical and emotional boundary around us. This boundary

• • • • • • • • • • • • • • • • • • • • • • • • • • • • • • • • • • • • • • • • • • • • • • • •

## To Score? ... For Love?

WHAT WILL MAKE YOU LOVE ME?

Due to the variety of messages we receive, sex is a very confusing issue for most of us. Sex is rarely an encounter between two people who are operating from a position of self-love and self-responsibility. If they were, there wouldn't be nearly as much confusion between the sexes because we would be able to talk openly and honestly with each other.

Self-responsible sex is when you accept full responsibility for your sexual needs while respecting and honoring your partner, resulting in safe, loving sex. When one considers the scenario of increased sexually transmitted diseases; when safe, protected sex is the exception, not the rule; when rapes become commonplace and teenage girls engage in sex in order to produce a baby that will make them feel warm and loved, it is obvious that sexuality based in self-responsibility and self-love is a rarity.

What a loss for the entire human race! Honest, true communication is the solution to this problem. But you, in making your Life Puzzle can accept responsibility for your own sexuality. Begin the communication with yourself, your partner, and your children.

NO MEANS NO

defines us as being separate from all others, with the complete right to run our lives as we see fit as long it doesn't violate another's boundary.

As part of your physical boundary, sexual boundaries are there to protect you and your sexual self. No other person has the right to cross your sexual boundary unless you choose to allow it, and you do not have permission to cross someone else's sexual boundary unless you are given this permission under peaceful terms.

Sexual abuse occurs when someone crosses your sexual boundary without your permission or you cross someone's sexual boundary without their permission.

It is this complete lack of understanding about our sexual boundaries which opens the door to sexual abuse. This unfortunately has been quite pervasive in human culture for a long time. Child sexual abuse, though only now becoming known, was actually quite common in early American and European cultures. Children were routinely used for sexual pleasure. That is because they were not respected as anything more than chattel to be used by adults. (Think about the fact that it wasn't until the 1920's that laws came into existence preventing children as young as age 5 from working 12-hour days in factories! If adults could do this to children with no remorse, why would they consider that children weren't there for their sexual pleasure as well?)

This abuse has been going on behind closed doors for hundreds of years! And then it gets passed onto the next generation. The child grows into adulthood and perpetuates the same boundary violation on the next generation. This must stop!

But it won't stop until we adults teach ourselves about our own sexual boundaries by learning to honor and trust our bodies, and at the same time acknowledge and honor everyone else's sexual boundary. When you have done this, then it is time to pass it on to your children, and hopefully the cycle of abuse, rape and other sexual crimes will stop once and for all. It is imperative that this knowledge be shared so we can go through our lives with respect for every human that walks this earth.

## Suggested reading list

Tieffer, Lenore          *Sex is Not a Natural Act*

Comfort, Alex, M.D.      *The New Joy of Sex*

Selby, John              *Peak Sexual Experience*

Lloyd, Joan Elizabeth    *Nice Couples Do*

# ACTION PLAN

## Exercise #1. Learning to love yourself.
## Loving our bodies as they are.

Stand in front of a full-length mirror. Slowly remove your clothes and look at yourself naked. Are you familiar with this body or are you constantly hiding from it? (This may be difficult for many people to do. So if you find it uncomfortable, that's okay. You can choose to stop if necessary.) One lady who did this exercise shared with me that she had not looked at her whole body, naked for at least 20 years. (She kept her eyes averted in the shower and she had removed the mirrors from the bedroom where she dressed. She was so sure she wouldn't like what she saw that she just didn't look. When trying on clothes in the store, she turned her back to the mirror until she had redressed.)

Write about your feelings in your journal.

What messages have you learned about your body? Can you renew a relationship with your body and honor it as a joyous part of you?

## Exercise #2. Journal writing.

What were you taught about sex? What have you shared with your partner about this early learning? How has this affected your current sexual relationship? How do you wish it might be different? What is keeping you from owning this part of your Life Puzzle?

# Parenting *and* Family Building

# *Being a parent is the toughest job you'll ever do. Make sure it is a job you really want!*

**Y**ou have to have a license to drive, fish or hunt, but heck, anybody can have a baby!

Making a baby is not what parenting is. Face it, just about anybody can make a baby. People have been making babies for millions of years, so apparently that is not a very hard thing to do. Every day thousands of babies are born which means that a lot of people figured out how to make a baby.

Parenting a child is much, much more than making a baby. Making a baby is all about biology…put two parts together and, whammo, the rest is pretty much done by itself. But parenting a child is a CONSCIOUS DECISION TO SPEND THE NEXT TWENTY YEARS OF YOUR LIFE (or more if you have more than one child) DEVOTED TO TEACHING ANOTHER HUMAN BEING HOW TO BECOME A FULLY RESPONSIBLE PERSON.

If you don't want this job you don't have to take it, but at the same time you have to understand that means you can't make a baby. Making a baby is a *pro-active decision* to become a parent. If you make a baby and reactively discover that you are going to become a parent, then you've acted irresponsibly. This is unfortunate, because this reactive process of making a baby is going to affect a lot of people besides yourself.

I cannot stress enough the importance of thinking through the decision of making a baby and becoming a parent. As part of your Life Puzzle, choosing to have a child can add a wonderful dimension of your life. But it needs to be a decision of *choice*, not a reaction of "Oops, I'm pregnant. How did that happen?" or "Well okay, we've been married three years, I guess the next step is to have a baby," or "Our relationship is having some problems, maybe if we have a baby things will get better,"or "Let's go ahead and have a baby and get it over and done with," or, "My parents are waiting for grandchildren, so let's have a baby" or "If it happens, it happens, and then we'll deal with it."

## Your child: A Life Puzzle under construction.

Children must be taught everything! You may think that children instinctively know how to grow up, but they don't. Children must be developed into their full human potential by the adults around them.

Even learning to walk requires some level of stimulation from the adults around them. A child that is never lifted to its feet and played with, who is confined and not able to stretch out and pull itself up, will not walk!

With children, you can't take anything for granted. They will need your support and discipline every step of the way. Will you be there?

As you examine this part of your Life Puzzle, realize that as you choose to bring children into this world you are taking on a large responsibility; that you are making a decision to shape your life around the needs of this child. Even more importantly, you are making a decision about the type of lifestyle you will create with your Life Puzzle.

## How many people want to have a baby someday?

Just about all of my community college students' hands went up, with heads nodding, faces smiling. You could just see their faces registering the pleasure that having a baby would give to their lives.

## How many want a 13 year-old?

All the hands except two or three went down. Faces now registered a whole different story, "Geez, anything but a 13 year-old. Who wants to be around that?" Smiles turned to rolled eyes and comments of "No way, I hated being 13. I sure wouldn't want to hang out with one."

## Then why do you want to be a parent?

This comment shocked my students but it's true. If you don't want the 13 year-old as much as the baby then what you're really saying is that you don't want to be a parent. What you are after is something warm and fuzzy that will make you feel good about yourself. In which case, get a cat or dog instead and everyone will end up happier!

You won't bring a child into this world that will eventually become neglected. You won't frustrate yourself by realizing that a lot of your life is going to be spent around children when you would rather be doing something else. Society and the world will be happier because they won't have to deal with a child that is neglected by its parent.

If you only think about having a baby you will be sorely disappointed, because the baby stage of the child you bring into this world only lasts about four years. After that, children begin having minds and lives of their own and will begin to separate from you. At the same time they'll require tons of your money and time.

Please, for the sake of your child, for the sake of your life, do not have children unless you examine and choose proactively to make parenting a part of your Life Puzzle.

## Too many are neglected.

It may seem to you as you read this chapter that I am encouraging you not to have children, but that is not true. I am encouraging you to be very certain that you make this a conscious, pro-active, well thought out decision for your Life Puzzle. That's because there are too many children today who are born and then basically abandoned by their parents. This has led to a world-wide population problem and a huge number of children having children. In 1995, 500,000 children were in foster care in the U.S.!

In 1965, when I was 11 years old, I overheard a CBS Newsradio report that said, "At the current population increases in America it is estimated that by the year 1990, there will be millions of homeless in the street and insufficient low income housing for these people." I remember being shocked as my child's mind could not comprehend how something like this could happen? It made me very conscious that having a child went way beyond "I want a baby." It had a serious impact on the world at large.

The most shocking thing to me now is this: In 1995, when I was 40 years old, *there were millions of homeless in the street and not enough housing—that horrible prediction had come true.*

## Families aren't born, they're made.

Does throwing three or four (or more!) people together in one house make them a family? No, not necessarily. Creating a healthy family doesn't just happen, it takes every member making an effort to work together to make a family. Otherwise you'll just have a bunch of people sharing a house but not building a family.

Building a family is an ever-changing process. As children grow into different stages of their lives, the responsible adult must also change to assist and guide the child into the next stage of growth. When you have more than one child, parents have to be able to juggle their actions to assist different children who are at different stages, all at the same time.

Parenting and family-building is tough stuff. No two families are ever the same, just as no two children are the same. Stop for a moment and think about your own brothers and sisters...are you just like them? Of course not. Neither will your children be...nor should you want them to be. The addition of each new child will dramatically change the family that is being built.

## Learn how to be a parent! Take a class.

If you stop and think about it, it's kind of ridiculous that anyone would have a child without first taking a class on parenting. Considering the responsi-bility you're about to thrust on yourself, wouldn't it make sense to take a class? Yet very few people do this, almost as if there is a shame in taking a class because it might mean that you don't instinctively know how to raise a child. *Raising children has nothing to do with instinct.*

Many people have children and just assume that the child will know how to grow up. But they don't. Children have to be taught to be human. Yes, they have to be taught to be human.

You wouldn't hop in a car and instinctively know how to drive, heading out to the freeway five minutes later? Of course not. You'd take a course and have someone teach you. Doesn't it make sense that you'd want to *learn to be a good parent? Then take a parenting class!*

## Building and letting go.

The long term goal of all family-building is to raise the children to become responsible to run their own lives without dependence on their parents. In other words, if you're good at parenting you'll put yourself out of a job in 18 to 20 years. If you feel confident as your children leave home that they are now capable of running their own lives then you've done a great job. If instead your children are running home every time they have a problem, if they are calling you to bail them out of their latest fiasco, then something didn't go right. (Go back to the boundary section of this book.)

Letting your children go, little by little over the years of their lives, is the art of parenting. Teaching them how to run their lives is difficult enough, but having the courage to push them out of the nest and trusting that they will put to use all the knowledge you have taught them in order to run their own lives is the heart of being a pro-active parent. In effect, what you will have done is to teach them to design their own Life Puzzle; to be self-responsible. By showing them—through making your own Life Puzzle—the process of becoming totally self-responsible for creating one's life, you will have provided your children the greatest gift possible: freedom to live responsible lives.

# *Parenting and children—not a pretty history. Will you break this cycle?*

**A**s noted earlier, many adults walk this earth with very low self-esteem as a result of a childhood that was filled with abuse and neglect. This has been going on for generations. After reading this book I hope you will break this cycle of poor parenting by first building your own Life Puzzle and then passing it on to the next generation. Only then will the deplorable history of children being victims finally be reversed.

Why did people have children in the past? First, there wasn't any birth control, so the only way not to have children was to never have sex. Very few people opted for this and thousands of babies were born as a result. These children weren't planned; they just showed up!

The second reason most people had children, up until the early stages of the Industrial Revolution, was to produce workers. In the agricultural age, when most of the population lived on farms, making babies was really making field hands. The more children you had, the more farm you could work, own and build. Large families were common.

In addition to this, infant mortality was very high until the 1920's when good sanitation procedures and antibiotics were introduced. It was not uncommon for a woman to bear eight to 12 children but have only three to five survive infancy.

We have a very romantic notion of babies and children in the 1990's, but research shows that by and large, through man's recent history, children were not viewed with much reverence. In fact, children were treated as second class citizens. They were put to work in the farm fields by the age of four or five. They were not protected by law until the 1920's. And even today there are very few child protection laws. Child abuse— physical, sexual and emotional—was and is rampant. Children were to be seen and not heard.

Until the birth of child psychology in the 1950's, children were not viewed as requiring special developmental needs. It was not uncommon in the early industrial age for children as young as five to work in a factory for 12 hours a day, making half what their parents made.

In the late 1800's, there were so many abused and abandoned children running the streets of New York

IF CHILDREN ARE OUR FUTURE, WHY DO WE TREAT THEM SO POORLY?

City that they would round up these children, put them on a special train and send it out west. Along the train route, local townspeople would come and select children from the train and take them home as part of their family. In many cases these children were nothing more than indentured servants. This is just one hundred years ago!

"Dear Abby" ran a survey asking parents, if they had the choice, knowing what they now know about what it takes to parent a child, would they have children again? More than 50% said no, which is very unfortunate because the biggest losers are the children.

It is time for us to break this cycle. And you can do it by taking the time and making the effort to think about becoming a parent. Once you have made the decision to become one, then pro-actively prepare for it. Take classes, get involved with your children's schooling, join parent leagues. Do it with all the gusto you gave to learning to drive...pass your self-imposed test!

## Making another Life Puzzle: Teaching your children.

It's not likely you were raised by parents who understood about making a whole Life Puzzle. But it is important for you to realize that now that you are aware of making your own Life Puzzle and have decided to add children to your Life Puzzle, you are a vital part of teaching and encouraging your children to create their own Life Puzzle.

Just as the pieces of your Life Puzzle—feelings, thinking, self-responsibility, exercise, sexuality—are an active process for you, as a parent you need to teach your children about their Life Puzzle and its pieces. The next step is to aid them in laying down their pieces throughout their childhood.

I try to imagine how different my life would have been had I been taught about my Life Puzzle and its pieces during my childhood. I know my parents did the best they could with what they knew, and they didn't know about Life Puzzle-making, so there's no reason to be angry or frustrated with them. The picture I had in front of me as a child was that I was to go to school, get good grades, get a good job and get out of the house by the time I was 18. All those other questions—who am I; how do I deal with these feelings of confusion and terror; how do I figure out where I fit in the world, deal with my sexuality, manage my finances, and create a healthy relationship with a man—were not addressed. I crossed my fingers and hoped that when I turned into that magical thing called an adult I would know these answers.

If I had realized instead that it was a life-long process that couldn't be rushed and finished by the time I was 21, I'm sure I would have done many things differently.

How about you? Look at your children. Can you help them to view their life as a puzzle-making process? Could you teach them to draw their own Life Puzzle and put it on their bedroom wall—so they can look at it and realize that each day is another piece to making their Life Puzzle and it can't be done quickly? Can you use the Life Puzzle as a way to keep dialogue flowing with your children during times of growth and confusion in their lives?

Remember all the confusion you had as a child? Your children are just as confused. Can teaching them the concept of making a Life Puzzle help them see that confusion is normal and not a bad thing? When putting together a 5,000 piece puzzle, there are plenty of times you sit and stare at the pieces but aren't able to find one that fits. Then you come back a day later—and boom—four or five pieces are instantly at your fingertips and before you know it another section has started to fill in. Making your Life Puzzle is the same process, and if you teach your children that this is just the way our lives come together they will become more patient and self-loving.

Becoming a well-balanced, whole human being is very difficult work. We need to teach our children this idea of wholeness and balance, and using the Life Puzzle can give them a concrete idea on which they can build. Will you teach them?

## Suggested reading list

There are many wonderful books on parenting, try them all!

| | |
|---|---|
| Chilton Pearce, Joseph | *Magical Child* |
| Berends, Polly Berrien | *Whole Parent, Whole Child* |
| Brazleton, T. Berry, M.D. | *Touch Points* |
| Dreikurs, Rudolf, M.D. | *Children: The Challenge* |
| Gookin, Sandra | *Parenting for Dummies* |

# ACTION PLAN

## Exercise #1. Create a Family Mission Statement

A mission statement for your family is a pro-active process to align all members towards the values and the goals that the group feels is important. This is a group mission statement, so the goals or values are not specific items that each member individually wants, such as 10 year-old Tommy wants to be a great surfer and Mom wants to go back to college for her degree. Instead, it is a statement to which all members agree that they want to live as a union called a family.

Thus a mission statement may read something like this:

> *The Smith family mission: To support each member of our family in developing their most dynamic Life Puzzle through a pro-active process that encourages quality communication among all members through regular monthly meetings.*

The making of a mission statement takes time and starts with getting together to talk about how each person sees the family and how they fit into this group of people. It requires each person to share and appreciate the differences between each other. Despite the wide variety of people who might live together (I come from a family of eight children and none of us is even remotely alike!), a family mission statement can be a wonderful source for pulling this group together while respecting and honoring the differences. This helps the group rise above their unique differences and ties them together through the general, mutually agreed upon mission statement. It's also very helpful to ensure that the children see that they are a valuable and necessary part of the family if the mission statement is to actually come alive. Thus, your 12 year-old may be seeing himself as a self-imposed outcast of the family, but through the family mission statement can discover he is needed. Without his cooperation and support the mission statement will fail. All members must work together to keep it a growing process. Over time, your family may choose to modify your mission statement, but it will require that the entire family continue to communicate with each other. A good mission statement can be the rock upon which your family can return, again and again, especially in the time of crisis.

1. To get started with your family mission statement, try these questions to start a dialogue.
   1. What do we, as the Smiths, want our family to be?
   2. What types of behavior do we value? (for example, honesty, honor and integrity)
   3. How do we want the world to think of us as a family?
   4. What do we need to do to make sure our family mission statement comes to life?
   5. How often do we want to review our family mission statement?
   6. What do we do if we feel that one or more of our family members is not living within the mission statement to which we've committed?

2. After several meetings where everyone shares ideas and thoughts, write up a first draft of your family mission statement. Then continue to work on it until everyone is committed to this vision.

3. Once you agree on the statement, have it written up in large print and posted in everyone's bedroom so it can become a daily process of reading it.

4. Work together to make your family mission statement a living process of your group. Hold regular family meetings. Set up rules that allow all members of the family the right to call a family meeting when they think the mission statement is being forgotten or ignored.

5. Do not be afraid to rewrite the family mission statement if necessary.

*A family mission statement requires effort, but those families*
*that I've seen go through the process say it is worth it.*
*Great families are made, not born!*

## Exercise #2. Create a family journal.

This is an on-going process for all members. Writing the journal becomes a journey that brings all members together and everyone adds to the journal. Thus it becomes a living process.

You might decide to write in the journal once a month or once a quarter at a family meeting. There's no right way or wrong way to design this. You can add pictures, you can center on one member per writing session or you can make a point of writing something down about each family member at every writing.

The joyous part of making this family journal is that you will have it throughout the years to go back to and see what happened.

# Spirituality
*within your*
Life Puzzle.

# *Practice only love: the heart of spirituality.*

**W**ouldn't the world be wonderful, wouldn't your life be easier, if we all lived our lives practicing only love? All the world's troubles would disappear and each human who walked this earth would be operating their lives from the same perspective: LOVE.

All judgement would cease, differences of color, sex, religion and anything else you could think of that sets people against each other, would be meaningless. Regardless of these issues you would approach everyone with the intent of opening your heart to them with love.

At the heart of all spirituality is love. Love is oneness with all. With this comes an understanding that all is one when living in the heart of spirituality: Love for all.

Within the process of your own Life Puzzle, your spiritual development will be a tremendous source of balance for your whole life journey. As within all parts of your Life Puzzle, your spiritual piece is based first in self-responsibility. Thus, spirituality becomes a personal journey as a part of building your whole self—your Life Puzzle.

For most of us, spirituality is intricately tied up with childhood images of watching our parents. By attending churches, synagogues, mosques, or none of these, we are influenced as to the right way to have a spiritual practice. Thus, few of us actually end up developing our own spirituality separate from this process.

That means most of us need to spend sometime within our own Life Puzzle-making to fully explore our spirituality. Now before you jump and get all bent out of shape because you're sure you are completely comfortable with your spiritual development, stop and ask your SELF: in order to reach this comfortable space, what responsible actions did my SELF take to achieve this. Have I examined my early influences, religion, parents, peers and their impact on my Life Puzzle? Have I questioned these influences and truly accepted them or, have I just let them become a part of me because I was afraid, not interested, too confused, felt threatened or didn't want to upset others by questioning earlier beliefs?

And the most important question of all; as a result of my

search and looking within, has my spirituality evolved to such a level that I am busy living it every day by practicing only love?

## Religion and spirituality: aren't they the same thing?

No, they're not the same thing at all. Spirituality is a personal process, while religion is a group proccss. When developing this piece of your Life Puzzle, it is important to keep this in mind.

Spirituality is your personal expression of love for all. It is like no one else's; it is yours and yours alone.

Religion is the organized practice of one's spirituality with like-minded people. However, religion moves beyond the strictly personal relationship and takes it to a group process. This is evidenced by the fact that as a member of a religion you agree to practice your spirituality within an accepted standard of beliefs. Should you, on a personal level, stray very far from this standard of beliefs, it wouldn't be long before you would either leave the religion or the religious group would ask you to leave.

Unfortunately, many people give up their personal relationship with God by confusing religion with their personal spirituality. Often we mask our spirituality by letting a religious group affiliation fill in the blanks, using a religion to do just enough to get by in our spiritual self.

Here's a way to look at it. Religion may be a bridge to the spiritual, but it is not the spiritual. The spiritual is your living relationship of oneness with all. Many people get stuck on the bridge, never realizing that they must cross over the bridge completely and walk off in order to achieve one's personal spirituality. If you get caught up on the bridge—spending all your efforts on building a bigger bridge, more bridges, or fancier bridges, but in doing so you forget to actually cross the bridge—you will never get to the other side, where the spiritual is—love for all!

Why would someone do that? Well, there are lots of reasons. Some of them have to do with particular religions; the leaders are often more interested in the bridge-building process than the spiritual. Oh, they throw in just enough to get members to feel that they are heading toward the spiritual, but when all is said and done these religious leaders are actually nothing more than business folks who have a high stake in the bridge-building process. They are making a very good living from it.

Another reason? It's easier to be on the bridge than it is to cross to the spiritual. For if you are truly developing this part of your Life Puzzle, there will be a time when you will completely cross the bridge and you will have to accept total responsibility for living in the love and sharing in the love that is the spiritual. For many of us, the comfort of the *steady-beneath-my-feet-bridge-of-religion,* is not a comfort we want to leave in order to cross over and step off the bridge. Even though a full, personal spirituality of living love for all promises to bring true peace and fulfillment, it also requires one to completely trust that God will be there to walk with you, hand and hand, without requiring the bridge.

# Okay, this is not exactly what I was planning for my 30th birthday!

That's exactly what I said, while sitting on my bed, looking up at the ceiling and throwing up my hands. Then I started laughing because even though I'd spent the last seven years running my life, working hard on my plans to get ahead and doing what I was supposed to do, well, you know what they say about the best laid plans of mice and men...well, mine had gone completely awry!

And yet, I couldn't help but admit, I was happier, life held a whole new adventure out in front of me, and I had to accept that had all my previous plans actually worked out, it would not have been for the best. So, in the midst of chaos, with very little money in my pocket and my life suddenly turned upside down despite lots of effort to have it come out right-side up, I let go. In doing so, I discovered that the spiritual piece of my Life Puzzle had reached a new level.

Sitting on my bed that evening, I admitted that I was powerless to control, and for once I was going to trust that love would be there for me if I would just accept that love. I said, "Okay, it's all yours. I trust that you have set me on the path and all will work out. I will not worry, I will just let go." That had always been very difficult for me to do. But suddenly, it was very easy.

Paying the bills at that time in my life was touch and go. My salary was smaller than I was used to, and on top of that I had bills that exceeded the paycheck! So I started there. I said, "I'm not going to worry from month to month about the bills. I will trust that they will get paid." When I would wake up in the middle of the night and the panic would start, the little voice inside me screamed out, "Shut up! You promised you'd let go of this, now do it and go back to sleep!" I surprised even myself...and fell back to sleep.

Since those days, I have worked hard to live with love each day, both in trusting that this great force of love will be there to protect me and help me through, and with trying to share this love with others. Some days are easier than others and, oh yes, some days I get caught up in "What if this crisis happens?" and get completely rattled and confused, and in those moments I have forgotten my trust of love to be one with me. It's a great relief to have that love.

• • • • • • • • • • • • • • • • • • • • • •

A friend who reviewed this book questioned this page. She felt it brought into conflict self-responsibility vs. the "let go" concept. How can you do both?

To clarify any confusion: To let go is not to just sit back and let life go by. It means making the most of each day as you learn to accept those uncontrollable events that happen in life. Through pro-active, self-responsible steps, make the most of what you can do with those events even if they're not what you planned. Alas, life's plan for you holds many untold secrets and joys mixed in with many twists and turns. If you spend all your time fighting or controlling life you'll miss so much that is waiting for you.

Awake anew each day, to make the most of your life by accepting responsibility for it, but keep your heart and mind open to new direction. Let go and follow the way!

That's the spiritual and only you can achieve it. Your religion may help you get there, but the religion is not it.

## Does it have to be so complicated?

One's personal spirituality is a vital element in building a healthy, strong and dynamic Life Puzzle. Yet for many of us, developing this section is one of the most difficult. Many of us put it off, never realizing that it can work so positively for us and influence so many other parts of the Life Puzzle.

From talking to many different people, I've discovered that one of the blocks on this issue is centered around their early exposure to organized religions. This has turned off so many people that since they left their childhood religions they've never explored again. The bad taste they received from churches that were harsh and hypocritical and not at all centered in spirituality remains well into their adulthood. This is quite understandable. Some of the horror stories I've heard would make anyone wary of this issue.

However, now that you're focused on building a Life Puzzle that has moved from reactive to pro-active, it is time take another look...not at religion but at your spirituality. You do not need any organized religion in your life in order to strengthen your spiritual self. True spirituality is a singular process, not an organized group function.

"All religions divide man from man, which divides man from God" is one of the truest statements ever said. This is not to say that all religions are bad, but

in and of their very nature one religion is not the same as another religion. Inherently, as people group together under one religious dogma or another, it inevitably sets them apart from other groups. The study of the history of religions is a study about men and women developing the rules and regulations that define the religious philosophy. As a result, many people spend their entire spirituality caught up in defending and "righting" their religion over another. And in that process, the true meaning of spirituality is lost.

True spirituality is being open and loving to everyone. The most enlightened spiritual teachers of history—Jesus, Buddha and Mohammed—were all focused on accepting every human being into the spirituality of love. They welcomed all.

And that is where you can start in your own spiritual quest: welcoming your spiritual self back in your life.

## Love is not complicated.

Love is the center of all spirituality. Living the love for all humans is the process of making your spirituality come alive.

*Can it be that simple?* Yes, and you might ask yourself this question: Why would it need to be more difficult than the process of love for all human beings? It's actually quite the paradoxical thought isn't it? At one level so simple and at another so difficult: Living the process of love for all human beings. So easy to see; so difficult to do.

But when you are focused on building your Life Puzzle and pro-actively developing your spiritual section, this conscious awareness of love becomes a daily process. This allows your spirituality to overflow into the other pieces of your Life Puzzle: relationships, family, work, and communication. And it is fairly simple to see how this overflow improves your entire Life Puzzle. You start from living love for yourself...and everyone else.

### Finding the spirit, even in those who bug us (especially when it's ourselves)!

This is the one of the greatest of challenges to our spirituality...other people. Aren't there days when you're sure some folks were put in your life as a trick? And not a very funny one at that!

One of the interesting outcomes of developing your spirituality by trying to live the process of love for all human beings is the dramatically different view that develops within you: *I am greater than no one, no one is greater than me.* As you remind yourself again and again to consciously choose to live the law of love for all others, you'll discover that it means you have to live the law of love...of yourself.

How can you treat others non-judgementally while your own self-talk is harshly criticizing every step you take? How can you have patience and understanding for others and their foibles if everything you do results in a rash of self-condemnation? It's impossible!

As you acknowledge the humanity in others, despite all the goofy, stupid, mean, ugly and crazy things they may do, you'll also have to accept your own humanity, despite the goofy, stupid, mean, ugly and crazy things that you do.

### The circle of love.

Spirituality is love in action: Love for SELF, you to others, others to still more others, until the circle completes, love for all. It is the process of seeing the light of love in everyone and everything you encounter each day. It is a conscious process of making your Life Puzzle.

### Spiritual growth can start today.

When we are caught up in the reactive victim focus instead of pro-actively building a Life Puzzle, it is very easy for our spiritual piece to fall by the wayside. As you are reading this you may be realizing that spirituality plays a small or nonexistent part in your daily life. Entangled in the stress-filled, mile-a-minute lifestyle that so many of us believed was what we had to do to get by, we realize that we are taking everyone in our life for granted and treating them far outside the lesson of living love. So what to do?

It is never too late to get focused on your spiritual piece. No matter how many people you've offended, no matter how cut off from the world because of your past behavior, you can start again. As long as you are alive, you are living in the presence of love. Reach out to this loving energy and share it with others.

A story a friend told me brought this home quite clearly: It is never too late to renew our spiritual relationship through our loving actions with others.

It seems this gentleman was in his late 30's on the fast track of success and climbing the corporate ladder of a dynamic company. The money was rolling in faster than he could spend it. (Well, almost. He was actually quite good at spending it!)

At the same time, though, his relationships with just about everyone were terrible. He barked and yelled at his employees so much that they resented him. He didn't care though; he had work to get done. His marriage was becoming rocky but he didn't seem to notice because he was rarely home anyway. Even his golf buddies were becoming rather put off by his gruff behavior. After a few drinks he could become quite belligerent. Left and right, his relationships with almost all of the people he knew were breaking down. He was establishing a reputation as quite a mean man. It seemed the more he gained materially and in the corporate world, the less he cared for maintaining relationships with others.

Until, he told me, life was kind enough to intervene. In the midst of all this success this man fell ill. For weeks he ignored the symptoms and kept on charging along at the office. But finally he couldn't get to the office at all. It had gotten so bad that he would get up in the morning, shower and get dressed, but by the time he arrived at the office his body was sweating so profusely that he had to change his entire suit. That finally got his attention.

The doctor discovered a tumor and said they would have to do exploratory surgery. Realizing that he might not ever wake up from this surgery, this man was forced to confront himself. He knew that if he died he would leave behind a lot of people who would be happy to see

him go because of his behavior. He needed to make amends. And so he set about calling everyone that he knew he had offended and asked for forgiveness. This was tough to do. The humbling experience made him realize that despite all the success he'd earned, the only thing that really mattered was the people in his life. To die knowing that he had hurt so many was far worse than dying poor in money.

So he settled with everyone and the day of surgery arrived. They cut his back open, pulled apart his rib cage and looked inside. What do you know…they couldn't find the tumor! Very strange.

When he woke up after surgery they said they hadn't found anything, but after he healed from this surgery they would like to go in from the front. He told them, "Over my dead body!" When they x-rayed him again they found nothing. His symptoms went away and he returned to full health. (Along with this he changed his diet and gave up a five pack a day cigarette habit.)

He made the decision after surgery to get out of the rat race and resigned his position. This greatly surprised the company, but as he explained, he had much more important work to do. He believes that life gave him a second chance and he was going to use it. And he did.

When speaking to some of his friends who knew him before and after this incident, they told me there was a world of change. And that change is mainly spiritual and is focused on caring for people. After retiring for two years he has now re-entered the corporate work world as a high-level manager. But he will tell you that the difference today is that his focus is on helping people grow to be their best instead of using and abusing them just to get a job done. This blesses both him and his fellow employees, and allows him to live his spirituality every day.

# Taking a few minutes to listen: learning to meditate.

**E**ver stop at the end of the day and wonder what happened to it? Running from crisis to crisis, by the time you climb into bed at night is it hard for you to look back on the day and feel any peace and joy in it? And what happened to the conscious awareness of your spirituality? Phew, life is flying by!

We've been so conditioned to be doing something constantly that we rarely take the time to step back and ask ourselves why we're doing it. In this process, *living our higher awareness of the spiritual* gets tossed to the side. We tell ourselves over and over again, "As soon as I get this done and that finished, then I'll take a quiet moment for myself." Alas, that time never comes.

But you can choose to change this in your life. Again, it is a pro-active decision to focus your life towards a more balanced process. It is a conscious act of setting a small amount of time aside each day to meditate. This may be as little as 15 minutes a day, but even this amount of time will produce significant results if you maintain consistency day in and day out.

## Meditation: it's simpler than you think!

Meditation is nothing more than quieting the mind in order to become truly mindful. What? It is a process of mindfulness, being truly present in the moment but without judgement. It's learning to turn off the judgemental brain, the constant self-talk, and listening instead to the voice of silence. This silence is true present mindfulness. It teaches you the ability to live in the present moment even when not meditating!

That's the hard part of meditation: learning to let go of the ever-present noise of the day and just be present in silence. It is a process of becoming completely aware of the present moment, aware without controlling it, ordering it, organizing it or deciding if it is good or bad.

Meditation helps you stop taking life for granted. Most of us let so many moments of the day flow right by us, never even seeing them. That's how we end up living the "get up, go to work, do the day, feed the kids, put us all to bed and get up tomorrow and do it again" lifestyle. Meditation is a way of breaking out of that cycle. In the practice of daily meditation you are able to quiet that fast paced, mile-a-minute self and connect instead to the silence of your inner self and God.

Meditation is simple, yet not easy. The simple act of meditation is nothing more than sitting still, quieting the

## Meditation: your chance to stop being a human "doing" and focus on just being a human.

The simpleness of how to meditate:

Learning to meditate is not about learning the right technique. Unfortunately, when meditation first began making its mark in this country, there was a group that taught meditation for $350 or more with the premise that they would teach you the right technique for doing it. This turned off a lot of people and made meditation a technique to be mastered by the enlightened few. Hogwash!

Meditation doesn't require a guru teacher. You don't have to earn a special mantra (which is nothing more than using a word or sound for concentration purposes). You can start meditating today, wherever you are.

**Here's all you need to do:**

1. Find a private space where you will not be disturbed for 15 to 20 minutes.

2. Find a comfortable spot where you can sit. Then sit in a way that is comfortable for you. That could be with legs crossed 'Indian style' or just simply placed on the floor, straight out. The key here is to make it comfortable so you won't experience a cramp or numbness in your legs, your back or neck.

3. Close your eyes.

4. Begin to concentrate on your breathing. Become mindful of it. Become aware of each inhale and exhale. Feel yourself breathe in and out. You don't have to change it, just be aware of it. It doesn't have to be deep breathing or anything special. Just breathe, in and out with mindfulness.

5. Do this for 15-20 minutes. During this process your brain will be screaming! You'll hear yourself saying, "Am I done yet? This is stupid! I can't believe I'm wasting my time doing this. As soon I finish this, let's see, I've got to put in a load of laundry, then call Ginger..." This is very natural! Don't sweat it. Once you become aware that your mind has raced off to another part of the world, bring yourself back to the breathing. You will have to do this again and again but that's okay. It happens to everyone.

6. Practice, practice, practice! Not to get good at it, but just to do it. Being goal-oriented, many of us get caught up in mastering this meditation thing. We think if we're really good at it then we'll be able to sit down and jump right into the relaxed mindful state. But meditation is not a task to be mastered. It is simply a process of being mindfully aware. As you practice meditating, do it without judgment. You're not practicing the piano! Yes, you expect to get better and better at the piano. But you don't get better and better at meditating. You just meditate and let the mindfulness just be what it is, no judgment.

7. Don't I need a mantra? No, but if you want one, that's fine. A mantra is using sound to help you stay focused. You can make one up, two syllables at most combined in such a way that the sound doesn't make a word that has a conscious meaning to you. For example "ha lem" could be one. Use it with your breath: inhale "ha", exhale "lem".

8. That's it! Now try doing it every day! Live in the moment, feel the spiritual.

mind to an aware mindfulness. But the forces of non-awareness, ("Come on, let's get up and do something") are strong and will work hard to break you away from practicing your meditation. This is why so many people quit trying to meditate because the get up and go voice is so loud and one you are so accustomed to listening to that you do...just get up and go. This is also why living the *spiritual* takes a back seat in our lives—the loud voice says to ignore the spiritual and go do something "real" instead.

But it is up to you to choose to change this. And you can. Meditation is a way to do this. Meditation is not about any religion or belief system. It is, as Jon Kabat-Zinn says, *"Simply a practical way to be more in touch with the fullness of your being."*

## Suggested reading list

| | |
|---|---|
| Kabat-Zinn, Jon | *Wherever you go there you are. Mindfulness meditation in everyday life* |
| Peck, Scott M. | *The Road Less Traveled* |
| Peck, Scott M. | *Further Along The Road Less Traveled* |
| Armstrong, Karen | *A History of God* |
| Berends, Polly | *Gently Lead* |

# ACTION PLAN

## Exercise #1. Practice only love.

Choose a day in which you will consciously focus living in the spiritual for the entire day. To prepare for the day you've chosen, make up little signs that say "practice only love." Make at least 20 of these—about the size of a 3x5 index card. On the day you've chosen, take these cards and place them in areas where you will be able to see them throughout your day as a conscious reminder. So you might tack one on the bathroom mirror, in your wallet, on the car dashboard, on your office desk, etc. Then go about your normal day and see what happens. At the end of the day, go to your journal and write down your experience. How did it feel? When you saw one of your little signs, what happened? How did it affect the day? Did you treat others differently? Did you treat yourself differently? What do you think would happen if you did this every day? How might it change your day to day living? How would this impact your whole life?

## Exercise #2. Learning to meditate.

This exercise is simple. Just start meditating. You can do it once or twice a day for as little as 5 minutes each day. You decide, then follow the direction given earlier in the chapter. Commit to 21 days.

# Financial Responsibility

# *Money...why couldn't it just grow on trees?*

One of the hardest parts in making our Life Puzzle is understanding that someday we will have to manage money and be financially responsible for ourselves.

Money is a big issue for everyone. Though money is only green pieces of paper that move from your pile to someone else's pile and vice versa, for many of us money becomes tied to our self-worth. If I have a lot, then I'm valuable...if I have just a little, then I'm not worth much. This emotional connection to money as a source of self-esteem (remember those outside sources talked about in earlier chapters?) often blocks us from understanding the value of money and its true position in our Life Puzzle.

Another emotion that is often tied to money: fear. Some find it so confusing and frustrating that they live in a continual state of denial. Money then controls them and effectively manages their life. By pretending to not care about money, they often end up in positions of debt and their lives fall into the victim category. Keeping your head in the sand does not work!

● ● ● ● ● ● ● ● ● ● ● ● ● ● ● ● ● ● ● ● ● ● ● ● ● ● ● ● ● ● ● ● ● ● ● ● ● ● ● ● ● ● ● ● ● ● ●

## Where are you on the Financial Choosing Continuum?

Remember, it is not where you are on this Continuum, it is the direction you're headed in that counts. If you're in debt now, but are actively seeking change, that's fine. If you're at 5 but living in denial still, it's time for a change!

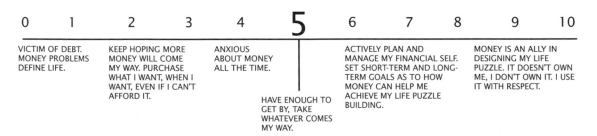

| 0 | 1 | 2 | 3 | 4 | **5** | 6 | 7 | 8 | 9 | 10 |

VICTIM OF DEBT. MONEY PROBLEMS DEFINE LIFE.

KEEP HOPING MORE MONEY WILL COME MY WAY. PURCHASE WHAT I WANT, WHEN I WANT, EVEN IF I CAN'T AFFORD IT.

ANXIOUS ABOUT MONEY ALL THE TIME.

HAVE ENOUGH TO GET BY, TAKE WHATEVER COMES MY WAY.

ACTIVELY PLAN AND MANAGE MY FINANCIAL SELF. SET SHORT-TERM AND LONG-TERM GOALS AS TO HOW MONEY CAN HELP ME ACHIEVE MY LIFE PUZZLE BUILDING.

MONEY IS AN ALLY IN DESIGNING MY LIFE PUZZLE. IT DOESN'T OWN ME, I DON'T OWN IT. I USE IT WITH RESPECT.

Being financially well-off does not mean you are living a successful, healthy, well-balanced Life Puzzle. There are plenty of miserable rich people! Many people believe that when they finally have enough money they will be happy, but this isn't true. Oh, soon after reaching this pinnacle they'll think they're very happy. In time they wake up and realize those old questions of self-doubt are still haunting them. Often these folks become slaves to money and material trappings, only to discover in their 40's and 50's that money hasn't brought them happiness, in fact it has made them a prisoner to it!

Money can be a powerful contributor in helping you build a Life Puzzle, but it isn't money that determines this. Money is but one aspect of your Life Puzzle, and it must be managed just like your daily nutrition, exercise, and family building. When you *manage* this piece, you'll discover that money works to help you attain the goals of your Life Puzzle.

### Why don't we learn to manage money?

Many people believe children should not deal with the harsh realities of money, so we often get launched out into the real world, only to discover we have little or no fiscal management skills. RUDE AWAKENING!

Suddenly we have to figure out how to budget and get the bills paid, while at the same time it seems there are so many things we want, but never enough money. Ah, but here's a charge card! I'll pay that when I get ahead a little bit but...what a mess. Lots of people end up financially crippled in their early

20's. Either that, or they just won't leave the safety and comfort of home because their first excursion off on their own was too scary, and it's easier to not deal with that money stuff.

Money also has a religious tie, and many are taught that money is the root of all evil (actually, the Bible says the *love* of money is the root of all evil). Naturally most of us want to stay away from the evil stuff, so we close our eyes and hope it goes away. It won't!

Putting the role of money into it's proper prospective in making your Life Puzzle will prove to be one of the best steps you can take. Confronting your lack of knowledge (don't be embarrassed by it, this lack of knowledge is rampant in our society) and becoming truly conscious of the role you choose to have money play in building your Life Puzzle is actually a step towards freedom. Because money has such a high priority in our lives, the sooner you determine its place in your Life Puzzle, the better.

### What can you do now?

Even if you weren't taught to understand money and how to make it work for you, begin to change today.

• **Establish a relationship with a banker:** You may think bankers only want to talk with you when you need a loan but that's not true. They are quite happy to get to know you and show you the many programs they have available to help you manage money.

• **Set some financial management goals:** You could meet with a financial planner to assist you, or take advantage of free credit and budget management services available. (Call the United Way for a reference).

- **Meet with a stock broker or financial planner:** Even if you don't have any money they'll develop a relationship with you and assist you in getting your financial house in order. They'll also help you start investing with as little as a hundred dollars in exchange for a long-term relationship with you.
- **Take a class:** Local community colleges and community centers are always offering classes in financial management and planning. Often they're free or close to it. These can be terrific!
- **Read some books on financial planning:** This may not be as exciting as a good mystery novel, but they are great help to take the mystery out of money.

## Teach your children to understand money

To teach the practical realities while young, set your home up as a mini-financial world! Your children, from the age of 4, need to understand that life isn't free or that somebody owes them everything. The truth is, we all have to take responsibility and earn the things we want in life.

Teach your children financial responsibility, just as you have to practice it. Each week you get paid in exchange for work. This money is then divided into three piles: 1) To pay for the necessities of life—rent, food and savings. 2) Taxes and Community: each payday some of your money goes for taxes that help pay for community needs like libraries, roads, and needy folks. 3) Frivolous desires—if there's any left from 1 and 2, then you can treat yourself.

Children think there's a lot of number 3! That's because parents don't teach them about 1 and 2. But you can. Each week give your child an allowance in exchange for work done as part of being a family member: raking leaves, snow shoveling or cleaning a room other than their bedroom. (You don't need to pay children for keeping up their room—that's an accepted responsibility all of us have.)

With their weekly pay have three jars. One third each goes into: #1-saving for future needs; #2 "Taxes"—this is money pooled by all family members for group activities—like trips to Busch Gardens or new video game; #3 Frivolous things—this is money to spend on their desires.

This requires them to learn that money is not unlimited, but must be managed. It also teaches them to put off impulse buying in order to get the things they really want instead of what they see in front of them at the moment.

Doing this will teach your children that this is a natural way to manage money throughout their whole life.

# *Spending our money, our time, our Earth? Creating a sustainable economy.*

If you are going to build a healthy Life Puzzle, you must examine the role that money plays in your life. Is more better? Or is less better in exchange for more time?

Time is money because money is what we exchange our life time for. We've been convinced that we need large amounts of money, therefore we spend large amounts of our "life time" to get it. But is it worth it?

The crisis of our world economy is opening our eyes to the reality that many of us are spending our time making money in ways that leave us stressed-out, sick, and sacrificing our families, marriages and communities because we are so busy working to accumulate those green pieces of paper. Many have begun to examine this relationship between money and time and the value that it has in individual lives as well as the life of our communities, cities, countries and international relationships. And what many have discovered is that we're trading our "life time" for green pieces of paper and not much else. We wake up empty as we watch the world around us in chaotic breakdown.

This can be changed by deciding to create a sustainable economy. This is an economy directed by people who say "enough is enough." They take back their time and discover that everyone— family, marriages, the community, the environment, the world—are better off. It's a conscious choice in building your Life Puzzle.

## For the love of money...

We are a world obsessed with money. We have crossed over the line and let money become the primary value of our world. We have done it at the cost of our humanity: building our Life Puzzle is put on hold for most of our lives while we concentrate on making money. We choose paid work not so much on what we want to do, but on what we think will make a high salary. A recent study shows that doctors and lawyers express high levels of job dissatisfaction. Could it be because many of these people chose these careers for the money, despite the fact that the actual work required is not something they really want to do?

The problem is not with money... money is an inanimate object. The problem is we've placed our love of money (and all the things that money can buy) above all else, and we end up being a slave to money. People spend their entire lives consumed with consuming. Every day is focused on acquiring more money so they can acquire more things. But do we stop to ask ourselves why we want these things? Do we have to have luxury cars, huge houses and designer everything?

Your relationship with money must be confronted if you are going to make this portion of your Life Puzzle work for you. And you will have to do this yourself because our society has already seeded you with the idea that you need lots of money in order to be happy.

## When is enough, enough?

You have to choose or else you will be a victim to the "do what everybody else is doing" attitude that has captured the world.

It's interesting to look at the history of money. Prior to the Industrial Revolution the act of acquiring money for things was not much of a big deal. First of all, there weren't many things to buy. The agricultural society was focused on surviving another farm season with food on the table and a roof over their heads. There weren't any luxury combines to purchase. The rich were a small part of society and this group was usually limited and controlled by history—you were born to it... you couldn't earn your way into nobility. Thus, the grand majority of people were content to live simply because there wasn't much choice.

The Industrial Revolution changed this. The initial surge of the Industrial Revolution allowed an influx of money to flow to a wide portion of society and more people were able to buy a few more things. After this, however, history shows the economy flattened out again. People did buy a few things to improve their lot in life, but beyond this they didn't have much desire for more things. What they wanted after this first flush of extra money was not more money, but more time: Time for family and their community. This, however, did not set well with the industrialists or government which needed a continual buying process to fuel the economy which had just started to grow to levels never seen before. Unknown to most of us, there was a concerted effort by these groups to create an economy of want. Starting in the 1920's, there was a move to create desire/insatiable need in the people. (Even President Coolidge is quoted as saying this!) We have been taught to want lots of things.

Now don't get me wrong...I'm not saying there was an evil group of people trying to trick the masses...instead, it was just a process of the times and the vision (or lack of vision) of people who led us in this direction. There were many benefits, and lots of creative ideas and products that were designed during this time in history. People's lives were improved in many ways. But the problem is that this insatiable desire has gotten out of control.

We've gone past buying things to make our lives easier so we can relax. Now, buying things has become a time consuming process of its own. We work more and more so we can buy more and more but we have no time to enjoy it. And we're not happy. When is enough, enough?

That is the question you must ask yourself when building this piece of your Life Puzzle. This is the process of becoming financially responsible through a pro-active, conscious decision on your part. It will have to be done in relation to the indoctrination of want all around you. There is a pervasive message everywhere telling you that you "have a right to buy...and to buy is right."*

Everything you've read so far about making a healthy, well-balanced Life Puzzle has challenged the old paradigms of doing enough to get by, and doing what everyone else is doing, and your financial responsibility piece will ask the same thing. The current consumption at all costs paradigm that has caught us up in lives based around acquiring money for things must be confronted. There are several reasons to do this: 1) We can't keep consuming things without ruining the earth—things are made from natural resources and these are being depleted.

2) We aren't happy—we are obsessed with consuming— hoping that these things will buy us happiness, and they don't. 3) We've abandoned our health, our children, our society and our earth while running mile-a-minute lifestyles focused on collecting money and things.

There are many forces creating a paradigm shift away from this obsession with money. Choosing to create a healthy Life Puzzle filled with an appropriate understanding of money and the role you choose it to play in your life is the key. Once you have done this you will discover that you are spending your time not on obsessive consumption, but instead on creating a life journey that has value based in conscious choice of how you design your Life Puzzle.

*from *Your Money or Your Life,* by Joe Dominguez, Vicki Robin.

## Suggested reading list

Brandt, Barbara — *Whole Life Economics*

Henderson, Hazel — *Building a Win-Win World*

Eisler, Riane — *The Chalice & the Blade*

Schaef Wilson, Anne — *When Society Becomes an Addict*

Ross, David & Usher, Peter — *From the Roots Up: Economic Development as if Community Mattered*

Durning, Alan — *How Much is Enough? The Consumer Society and the Future of the Earth*

Dominguez, Joe & Robin, Vicki — *Your Money or Your life*

Hawken, Paul — *The Next Economy*

# ACTION PLAN

## Exercise #1. Explore your relationship: journal writing.

Answer these questions for yourself about you and the messages you learned about money.

1. What did you learn about money as a child?
2. What role does money play in your life? Does having or not having it affect your self-esteem?
3. How much of your free time is spent in consuming things? (e.g., trips to the mall for shoes, to the grocery store, the video store, etc.)
4. How often do you wish you had all the money you needed and didn't have to work at your job?
5. What would you do if you won the lottery? What does this say about your priorities? What about your relation to the community?
6. Are you at peace when it comes to thinking about money? Why do you feel this way?
7. How much time do you spend dreaming about acquiring things? (e.g., home, cars, new furnishings, clothes, etc.)
8. How much time do you spend dreaming about improving your community?

## Exercise #2. No shopping allowed.

For one week, except for grocery shopping or vital necessities, try not to shop. No trips to the mall, no runs to the video store, no quick pick-ups of coffee and donuts for a treat or a frozen yogurt for an after dinner trip, and no stops at the convenience store for a soda and chips.

Note in your journal: How does this make you feel when you become more conscious of your buying and spending? How much money did you save this week by not buying a little of this or a little or that? What did you do with your time when you decided not to go to the mall to just look?

# Is *there a* Special Challenge *keeping you from making your* Life Puzzle?

# What is your special challenge?

**A** special challenge is something about yourself that *you* think sets you apart from the rest of the world. A special challenge could be a physical handicap, diabetes, a heart problem, a learning disability, or cancer.

The key in defining a special challenge is *you.* One person with diabetes may consider that a special challenge, and others may not. It is only a special challenge: *If you decide it sets you apart, limits your life or is a central defining factor of your life.*

You may be reading this and saying to yourself, "I don't think I have a special challenge," and that's fine. Not everyone does…but most people do.

Physical special challenges are more obvious, but there are emotional challenges such as depression, being short tempered, abusive, addictions or being a screamer when angry, that can limit our lives and keep us forever tangled up in trying to control, manage or deny them.

It could be your mammoth hips that you're sure is the first thing anyone sees about you. It could be your shortness, your tallness, your thinness, your fatness.

A very common special challenge is the inner belief that you are not good enough as compared to most other people.

## How is your Special Challenge defining your life?

Your special challenge is a product of the re-active pattern mind set. Based in the victim process, we *allow* special challenges to limit our lives or be a central defining factor from which all other accomplishments or potential must take a back seat. For example, suppose you consider having diabetes a special challenge. How is it defining your life? Do you let it control you, as in "I would like to try this, but I have diabetes." Do you use it knowing it will excuse you from taking on new opportunities that present themselves? Is it the first thing you tell a new person about yourself to see how they react to you? Do you spend a lot of time being angry at it, using up valuable energy that could be spent on learning new things or allowing you to participate in other activities? If yours is an emotional challenge such as being an abusive spouse or parent, are you hiding yourself from

MY LIFE WOULD HAVE BEEN GREAT BUT THIS NOSE RUINED IT

the world so no one will know you? Are you telling yourself you are hopeless and useless while your mind is consumed with the fear that it will happen again because you are powerless against it?

Are alcohol, food obsessions and drugs your special challenge? Are they the focus of your entire life, to the exclusion of building your Life Puzzle? If your special challenge is directing your life, only you can choose to change this.

## But I have to scream, I'm Italian, we all scream!

Screaming was Jenny's special challenge. It had gotten so out of hand, it led her to be a verbal abuser of her children and husband. For Jenny, it had begun to define and limit her life because she felt no control over it, it controlled her. She lived in fear that her mouth would just sort of take over.

As we explored how this special challenge had come to such prominence in her life, it became apparent that it was rooted in a misinterpretation from her early childhood.

She grew up in a home with Italian parents and grandparents. Her maternal grandmother and her mother were both extremely vocal, and screaming was the norm. They were always screaming, with fights going on between them, and Jenny had watched, often in terror, as they attacked each other.

Now as an adult, she found herself doing the same thing with her family. As she said, "I hate it, but I have to do it. I'm Italian, we scream!" As we talked she came to realize this wasn't true. To stop her own screaming was to take back her life and resume building a healthy Life

Puzzle based on her own choice instead of allowing the special challenge to own her life.

## Addictions: are they a disease?

Whether it is alcohol, drugs or food* many of us have our Life Puzzle controlled by addictions. These addictions have been labeled diseases in our medical system. As a result, many people walk through life feeling helpless to this disease, and it becomes their special challenge—forever limiting them because they come to believe that they can do nothing about it.

I challenge that addictions are a disease. They are a consequence of the re-active, unconscious model lifestyle that we grew up in.

To look at it from a different angle, what if addictions are a lack of knowledge of how to build a Life Puzzle? This lack of awareness leaves many people confused, scared and unsure of how to build a healthy, balanced life so they turn to their addictions—food, alcohol, drugs or work, to fill the pieces of their Life Puzzle. Our addictions become an all consuming focus of our lives because we don't know what else to do to build our Life Puzzle.

For example, a teenager who is confused often discovers that under the influence of alcohol or drugs he feels balanced, okay, one of the crowd. When he is sober this feeling of balance is removed, so what does he do? Drinks or snorts cocaine again and again. Soon,

---

*Food is the largest addiction in this country—consider that 66% of Americans are obese and 42% of our children are obese, and it is obvious that food and weight issues are a large special challenge for America!

he can't live without this false feeling of balance, and alcohol or drugs take over his life. When will he come to realize that he needs to get back on track and build his Life Puzzle?

Unfortunately, because our medical system is so focused in the disease process, therapy tends to focus on controlling the disease, i.e., the substance abuse, and less time is spent on helping the addict learn about boundary building, self-esteem and building a Life Puzzle.

I think addictions are misdefined as a disease. Since most of us operate from the reactive side of the Choosing Continuum, it is easy to think in terms of addiction as a disease. If most of us operated from the pro-active side of the Continuum, we would look at addictions as a poor choice in making a Life Puzzle. What do you think?

## "I'm the only one who has this problem, everyone else has their act together."

If I could have only one thing come out of your reading of this book it would be for you to understand that you are not alone out there. While you may think that everyone else knows what's going on, each one of them is thinking the exact same thing, *everyone else but me.*

It seems to be a uniquely human phenomenon that we isolate ourselves with the belief that no one else feels like we do or understands the unique special challenge that sets us apart. I call this the "Why does everyone in the world have their act together but me" club. And I've got news for you, just about everyone I have ever had a discussion with has admitted to me that they think they are part of this club! Which means that nobody has their act together! So from this day forward, consider that club closed.

Everyone is searching for answers— the captain of the football team, the prom queen, the guy driving the Porsche, the lady with the three perfect children and minivan who never appears to be flustered, the supervisor who makes the job that takes you half a day to complete look so easy as he finishes it up in 20 minutes, the top salesman, the president of the company, the perfect body model, the successful writer, the 80 year-old grandmother—they're all looking, too. We are all searching for ourselves!

The key factor goes back to self-esteem and the external motivation that drives us. Because so few people listen to their inner voice of self-love, they spend most of their time hearing the critical inner voice that is centered on telling us how we aren't good enough. This critical inner voice creates the "not good enough" special challenge that controls our lives.

The funny thing about this is that studies show other people generally are assuming you are judging them, while actually you are assuming they are judging you. This means nobody is all that concerned with the other person, they're focused on themselves.

For example, as you walk up to a new person you are assuming that she is noticing your big hips, height, acne, or bad hair…you name it. But if you asked her, you would discover that she is assuming that you are looking at her crooked teeth or messed up hair. This misinterpretation skews a lot of lives! We're so busy wondering what the other person thinks of us that we don't spend any time operating our own lives from a self-responsible, self-love base.

If you listen to many movie stars you will find a common theme of "I always felt different, separated from the rest of the world. No one understood me." Every time I hear a movie star say this in an interview I almost can't help but laugh. This feeling is so common among human beings, yet few realize this! Alcoholics, drug abusers, food addicts and plain, average citizens say the same thing!

We can often go back to our childhoods and realize that it was our fear and confusion during this time of our lives that led us to concentrate on our special challenge as the key definition of ourselves. Our culture teaches us to stay private and hide our vulnerability from others. Children, after the age of ten, go inside themselves, not from a point of self-love, but of self-fear. From this comes the terror and confusion that stays with us for a long time. It prevents us from creating a healthy, well-balanced Life Puzzle while we let our special challenge define and limit our lives.

## Meeting your Special Challenge head on: *seeking balance in your Life Puzzle.*

If you look again at your Life Puzzle you'll realize that whatever your special challenge is, it is but one-sixteenth of your Life Puzzle. It is up to you to decide if you want to continue to let it consume you or you want to work on putting it into balance within your whole Life Puzzle.

Many of us choose to stay in the victim model or on the reactive side of the Choosing Continuum because of our special challenge. But now that you've been introduced to making your Life Puzzle and you understand that you are not just your special challenge, you will have to acknowledge your decision to continue to let your special challenge define your life or just be but one part of your Life Puzzle.

If you decide that you want to build your Life Puzzle, go back to the Choosing Continuum and look at it again. Where does your special challenge put you on the Continuum? Are you finding yourself below the five level? Now ask yourself this…What direction am I headed?

Because that is how you turn a special challenge around. For example, if you have cancer or AIDS, you would find yourself at 1 on the Choosing Continuum. And certainly either of these special challenges will define your life. But there is something interesting about how different people operate their lives within this special challenge.

I've worked with cancer patients and there are basically two types of people. One stays in the victim model and this special challenge consumes their life. They act helpless, angry and hopeless.

The other type of cancer patient takes this special challenge, accepts it, and uses it as a source for growth. I cannot tell you how many people have said to me, "Getting cancer was the best thing that ever happened to me." The reason they often say this is because it has forced them to get out of their "doing just enough to get by" lives and shift into a pro-active state.

These are people who are putting their special challenge in balance with building their whole Life Puzzle. They refuse to let the limitations of their special challenge be a controlling factor. They go through their therapy, and yes, they may even die much sooner than they might have without this illness, but they decide that as long as they are alive, to live fully.

Interestingly, research on people with AIDS shows a dramatic difference in longevity between those who become actively involved with managing this special challenge and those who rage bitterly against it and the world. The former group have many people who lived very long and productive lives (over ten years after diagnosis), while the latter group have quickly given up and died.

All of us will likely be challenged with something that we could let limit our lives. But as you build your Life Puzzle, it is important to understand that you have the ability to choose: It is up to you to decide if it will limit, or become but one aspect within, your whole Life Puzzle.

## Suggested reading list

Hay, Louise            *The Power is Within You*

Henfelt, Robert        *Love is a Choice*

Morgan, Marlo          *Mutant Message Down Under*

Roth, Geneen           *Why Weight?*

# ACTION PLAN

## Exercise #1. What is holding you back?

Meeting your special challenge head on.

Journal writing: Acknowledging your special challenge.

Set some quiet time aside to write in your journal. Explore the issues that are controlling your life, but may also be limiting it. What is it in your life that you are sure, *if it was not in your life*, would enable you to become a more healthy and happy person. (This could be a physical, emotional, intellectual or spiritual aspect of yourself...or a combination of them.) When did you first notice this special challenge? How much of your daily life is spent dwelling on it? How frustrated are you by it? How much time do you spend trying to control it and the influence it has on your life?

If you weren't spending your time trying to control it...what would you do with this time instead? [For example, if you didn't have to go on another weight-loss diet so you can get the special challenge of "I'm too fat" under control, what would you do instead?]

## Exercise #2. Ending the limitation of your special challenge: Building your Life Puzzle.

In the first exercise you explored your special challenge. Now it's time to make peace with your special challenge. From this point forward, you need to decide whether you will remain a victim of your special challenge or whether you will put it into perspective with your whole Life Puzzle. This can be very tough to do, and you may want to engage a supportive counselor to help you get started, especially if your special challenge is an addiction to drugs, alcohol, food, gambling, sex, money or some other agent.

**Step 1.** Decide to stop letting your special challenge limit your Life Puzzle from this point on.

**Step 2.** Focus your energy on owning your Life Puzzle. Look at the other pieces of your Life Puzzle—what part has been particularly ignored due to the time spent focused on your special challenge? For example, if weight is the issue, have you not exercised because you don't want anyone to see your body at the gym until after you lose the weight?

**Step 3.** Choose one action to focus on that removes the limitation of your special challenge. In the example above, you might choose to start exercising. If it is drugs or alcohol or some other addiction, concentrate on your fear of knowing yourself. If it is a special challenge due to sexual or physical abuse, choose to work with a counselor. If it's a physical handicap that is limiting you, explore actions you can take to reduce it's limitation (sometimes this action is simply changing a mental attitude towards it).

Start small and choose one or two actions that you will immediately engage in whenever you feel you are becoming overwhelmed by the special challenge. For example, if you have a desire to binge, determine ahead of time that you will immediately take a walk. Or you might choose to repeat an affirmation of self-love to quiet the noise of your desire to binge.

## Exercise #3. Affirming your Life Puzzle: making wholeness a conscious choice.

An affirmation is a verbal statement of what you want to be. In the process of stating over and over the desired condition you want to achieve, interestingly, over time it becomes real.

In this exercise, write down three statements that define how you want to build your Life Puzzle through a pro-active, conscious process.

Example:

1. I am actively choosing to eat well to build my healthy Life Puzzle.

2. I am actively choosing to confront the issues around my childhood sexual abuse in order to build my healthy Life Puzzle.

3. I am teaching myself to be an honest communicator instead of stuffing my feelings with alcohol. I do this to build my healthy Life Puzzle.

Write three affirmations that work for you. Write them in a way that you can visualize yourself doing these actions and as a result you 'see' your Life Puzzle growing in positive ways that you're pleased with.

Once you've written these statements, say them aloud to yourself at least three times a day. This may be when you first wake up in the morning, while you're in the shower, driving to work, before you go to lunch, after an upsetting phone call, before dinner, or before washing your face while getting ready for bed. It doesn't matter when, it's just important to make sure you say them to yourself aloud three times or more per day. Try it and see your life change!

# What does it all mean?

*The whole picture of your Life Puzzle is found among the pieces.*

# *No one gets out of here alive...so why do life?*

**W**hat is the point of going through all the action to live if you're just going to die anyway? What's the point of putting in any effort?

Finding meaning is why you bother living and the most important thing to realize is that in the *process* of living your life, you will find your meaning. But you must determine whether the process of your life is pro-active or reactive. This decision will powerfully impact the meaning of your life.

### Building your Life Puzzle: A decision to actively search for meaning in your life.

Building your Life Puzzle is the journey of finding meaning. As you work and play at filling in the pieces of your Life Puzzle you will discover your meaning at different times throughout your life and in a variety of ways.

Based in pro-active choice, your Life Puzzle is an inner process of building the trust necessary to take responsibility for your life. You learn to live in the here and now. While making the most of today you are aware of the next stage of building your Life Puzzle and you continue to grow.

It is up to each and every one of us to make the decision to either pro-actively build our Life Puzzle or to remain reactive and victim-based throughout our life. This decision will affect the meaning of our lives. Once made, the process of finding your meaning of life begins.

### So, what do you choose?

Death is a reality. You will not achieve immortality. Some day you will die. Yet death is something that few of us are very comfortable discussing. We avoid talking about it and most important of all, we avoid planning for it.

Planning for it? Yes, planning. Whether it is funeral arrangements, writing wills, or discussing our desires with loved ones, we can plan our deaths, with grace.

Instead, avoiding the finality of death leads many people to retreat from taking responsibility for their lives. They exist in reactive lives that have little meaning or commitment. By ignoring the reality of our death we waste our "life time" because we assume there will always be time to do it later. When one acknowledges death, one must also acknowledge that the value, or meaning, of life becomes a function of living respectfully with death. Accepting your death, you live in the here and now and give it meaning, for tomorrow you may not be here to give it meaning.

I remember thinking that when I turned 21 I would finally have it all figured out. As a child I repeatedly heard, "Wait till you're an adult, and then you'll understand," but then I turned 21 and not only did I not understand, I didn't have a clue what was next! I was sure that turning 21 would magically bring the meaning of life to me, and when it didn't, I was lost!

I feel fortunate though that I bumped into Life Puzzle-making. I learned then that life is short, no one here gets out alive, and that if my life would have meaning, it would be because I *actively lived and sought it.*

*If only I could get everyone to just do their part, then my life would be great.*

"Well," I said to my friend, "it's never going to happen, so I guess your life will never be great…sorry." The look on my friend's face was quite clear, she thought I was nuts and that I clearly underestimated her ability to control others and the events around her.

Many of us get caught up in controlling other people's lives as a source of finding meaning in our own. But the truth is, you can't do this. Oh yes, you can spend your entire life doing this, but you will not find your meaning there. That's because no matter how hard you work on it, somebody or something will inevitably upset the control.

In controlling other people or events, you are expecting a desired outcome; for example, after spending all your time making sure they do their part right then your needs will be met. You

believe you will be rewarded (have meaning?) for giving your life over to managing them. And every once in a while you will achieve this, but for the most part your life will be chaotically controlled by trying to manage others who aren't doing their part right. It doesn't work.

Build your own Life Puzzle, not someone else's! If you find yourself caught up and entangled in someone's life (or busy trying to tangle someone else up in yours), you're spending too much time ignoring your own Life Puzzle. Are you managing your husband, children, or family members, and there's no time left for your life? The only person who can change this is you. If you can't see a way out of this, consider short term counseling to help you explore ideas for making a change within yourself. It will prove beneficial for you and those you are busy trying to manage!

## The Only Security in Life is Insecurity…learn to love it!

The first time I heard this statement, I railed against it. How could this be true? At that time of my life I was knee deep into creating my little "boxed life of security." I was organized, on track, and going to get all my ducks in a row as quickly as possible. Yessirree, I was hot on the trail of completing all the things I thought would make me feel like my life was all together and therefore, had meaning: House, cars, career, 2.2 cats (sorry, I wasn't planning on kids at this point). I was working my tail off and doing everything I could in life to make it come out right.

And then, all of a sudden, my world got turned upside down. In retrospect I am grateful, but at that moment I couldn't believe it was happening. I had worked too hard to make sure it wouldn't come to this, and yet issues beyond my control had created havoc in my otherwise secure life.

In the next few months and years, I questioned everything about life. It was clear to me that the only thing you could count on was that you couldn't count on anything, no matter how hard you tried. And after I got over the shock of this, it taught me to stop living so many years ahead of myself, and instead to live in the here and now.

Today is the only moment I have. No one knows what the future brings, and though I have plans for it, I can't control the future with these preparations. I no longer worry about the future, I live for today and try to bring my best self to it, and in this process I find the meaning of my life. Though my long-term goals are important to me, and I hope that time will allow me to complete them, I cannot guarantee it, no matter how hard I work on them. But if I do not live fully in the here and now I will miss the meaning in today's beauty.

## Prepare to die well...

Death is a natural process as it happens to everyone. Yet our fear of accepting this reality prevents us from pro-actively preparing for it. And because today we live longer and longer, the likelihood of becoming incapacitated, mentally or physically, makes it even more imperative that we plan for our deaths.

**"God grant me the serenity to accept the things I cannot change, change the things I can and the wisdom to know the difference. Amen."**

I've always enjoyed this prayer, because I think it does help put into perspective the process of finding meaning to our lives.

Each of us is here for some purpose; each purpose different and unique to each individual. The human species is an ever-growing and changing group, and I think each person can add to this changing process.

From the early cave man to this moment today, every person has added something to the human drama. Each successive generation has brought something to the table of change. Change has been going on and on, and within all these changes is the meaning of life.

It is hard to imagine why some things haven't changed yet—like child abuse—so we can see there is still much to do. But we can look at something like space travel, that is awe inspiring, and see the positive results of people making changes. More change is coming. Even though it is sometimes hard to determine what each person adds to the total picture, I'm sure we all do, and that includes you.

Be patient with yourself!

There are steps you can take to prepare for dying. These are pro-active steps that bring forth your desires for the future that will continue after you die.

**Prepare a living will.** If you don't want to be hooked up to all sorts of life saving equipment after an accident or illness, you need a living will. Taking this step is an important part of your self-responsibility in creating your Life Puzzle. Don't put this off. Remember, nobody plans to have an accident!

**Prepare a regular will.** Don't assume others know how you want things divided up after your death and that all your relatives will act respectfully. When money is involved people can get very funny (and downright mean!). Avoid creating a legacy of hate and ill-will among your heirs by taking the time to write a quality will while you still can.

**Discuss death with others.** Death remains fearful because we so rarely talk about it. Remove this fear by talking with others you respect, take a class on the subject, or read a book. You may be surprised to discover a tremendous amount of peace with this topic once you have fully explored it. It is when we are in confusion that fear maintains control over us.

## Let's take a walk to the cemetery.

Death has always played an important part in my life. Unlike many people, death came early to my life journey and it has been a topic I was forced to deal with whether I wanted to or not.

My mother died when I was seven. Of course it was a shock when it first happened, but when you're that young you

don't really understand that she's never coming home from the hospital. Add to this the fact that my father was a doctor and she was a nurse, and it just never occurred to me that she wouldn't be fixed up okay and sent home. (I also learned quite early that doctors aren't Gods; they're human.)

My mother was buried on the top of a small mountain that overlooked the little valley town she grew up in, a one-street coal mining town. From the cemetery you could see her house, her church, her school. Every summer I, my sister and brother would spend a month with my grandmother in this sleepy little town. With no TV in the house, we were forced to get creative to fill up our days (a blessing in disguise, I assure you!). We took many walks to visit my mother's grave. It wasn't that far, but it was all uphill. Though no stone marked her or my grandfather's graves, we knew where they lay and we would leave wildflowers when we found them. Mostly we just visited. Death and life merged as one for me, for though she wasn't alive, in my heart she always would be.

My father died when I was 24, and the reality that death and life was an ongoing process was reinforced. It taught me that life and time are precious and to make the most of them. Not by filling them up with all the things you're supposed to do to please others but by being aware that time will not wait for you to get all those things out of the way so you can do the things you really want to do. Experiencing death so early in my life taught me to pay attention, to look, listen and learn fully, today. It also taught me to accept full responsibility for my life because no one else was there to do it for me.

## What about you?

If you've never encountered death, are you living life without the balance of death?

## If not me, who? If not now, when?

Your life is just that...your life. The value of your life, the meaning you give to it, will be found in the process of putting together your Life Puzzle pieces.

Meaning of life is found in the simple processes, not the "big bangs." It is found in the daily learning we acquire and the growth this creates.

Many of us think that meaning is some end point, some big accomplishment such as becoming the CEO of a corporation, making ten children instead of two, getting the next promotion, accumulating more money than most people, receiving some big award, or becoming famous. Yet if you ask most

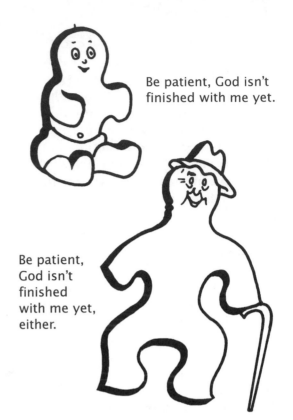

Be patient, God isn't finished with me yet.

Be patient, God isn't finished with me yet, either.

people who have accomplished any of these things they'll tell you that it isn't the end all, be all. After they've managed these feats they still have to get up the next day and do something else.

Throughout this book you have been challenged to look at all the pieces of your Life Puzzle—from feelings and thinking to special challenges and financial responsibility. It is the merging of all of these parts that will become the meaning of your life. The question renews itself every morning: Will you pro-actively work on your Life Puzzle or just let it happen?

If not you, who? If not now, when? Ensuring that your life has meaning starts today, through the simple act of living with the awareness of your Life

Puzzle and your responsibility in creating it.

Our society tends to be very youth-oriented, looking at old age as a negative to be avoided at all costs. This adds to our intense fear of death and leads people to believe that they must rush their lives and accomplish everything possible in their young years. This rush is unnecessary and produces very poor results.

At birth you are handed your Life Puzzle box filled with 10,000 pieces but there's no picture on the cover. As you go through your life and lay those pieces down, the picture of you will begin to form.

The rush to get it all done contributes to Life Puzzles that are all jammed together. Busy trying to get all the pieces done quickly, we avoid laying pieces that actually have value to the meaning of our lives. This results in a picture that is fragmented, not merged into a wholeness.

There is no rush to get it all done quickly. As long as you are alive you will continue to add pieces to your total Life Puzzle. Realizing this, your older years are as important to your Life Puzzle as are your younger years. As a 65 year-old, feelings, thinking, community and the environment, sexuality, spirituality…are as important as they are at 25.

Take it one day at a time!

## The art of the mundane, a meaning in every moment.

"There's just nothing exciting in my day to day life," James said as we started another session. "When it gets especially dull and I'm staring out the windows of my house I just have to get out and go to a bar to get a drink. Once I have that first drink, even though nothing has changed, at least I don't feel the dullness any more. A few more drinks and I get a little crazy and can laugh with the other people in the bar and I finally feel alive. It gets me through the night at least, although the next morning I am hung over and mad at myself for having succumbed to the fear of being alone with myself in the house."

James has been an on-again, off-again alcoholic for twenty years. He's gone for long periods of time without drinking, and this usually happens when he's especially busy working on a project that he's excited about. When the project is finished, it isn't long before alcohol returns to fill his life because as he says "It helps me feel like I'm alive when the rest of my life feels so dead." For James, life is a series of either/or's…either he's high with life or he's low on life, there is no in-between. Since life can't always be a fantastic, highly energized, accomplishment-filled daily process, for James, it left far too much time that was bland, dull and usual. This he couldn't tolerate, so he used drugs and alcohol to mask the day-to-day process of living and kept an eye out for the next high moment that would break him away from the ordinary.

I said to James, "It sounds like you have never learned the art of the mundane and as a result you are looking for the highs of life in all the wrong places." With arched eyebrow, James looked at me and I knew he had no clue what I was talking about.

James is like so many people—

spending their entire lives busily looking for the great "Ah ha, that's it!" feeling that will make them feel alive and valuable. But those great moments come only a few times in anyone's life, and if you pin your existence and joy of life on those moments you will miss most of the true joy of living, because those great moments are achieved through all the little moments of life...all the dull days of doing a little here, a little there. Reading this book, taking this class, keeping your house in order, paying the bills, going to church, synagogue, or mosque, taking time to volunteer on a community project, calling a friend to wish them well on their new job. As I said again to James, the people who enjoy truly great lives are those who have learned the art of the mundane.

These people are not waiting for the Academy Award day of life, they focus their energy on the little bits of life and make them a joy. They make an art out of daily living. Every little task can become a joyous process if one decides to make it so. Because, let's face it, no one just wakes up one day and receives an Academy Award; to get to that day takes lots of work.

Actors will tell you that it's great to have the moment of the award, but it has to be put into perspective. In order to achieve it, they sat on sets and waited for hours on end to do the acting. They had lots of boring hours, watched directors ranting and raving to make them repeat the same scene over and over again. Though it looks great when the film is all put together, the individual moments of getting it in the film can were not nearly as vibrant and dynamic as it looks on the screen. And it is the same with real life.

But if you asked the actor or actress if all those hours sitting around waiting were dull and useless they would say no, they were all necessary. And what if they hadn't won the Academy Award...would it still have been worth it? I bet the answer would still be yes. They have made an art out of the little moments.

The art of the mundane is teaching yourself to see the beauty, joy and value in the little moments of life. It's as simple as cooking breakfast with consciousness, and the joy of creating a nourishing meal for yourself. It's as simple as cleaning your home...not just to get it done and over with, but in a way that makes it joyful to see the accomplishment while you incorporate an exercise routine into it (vacuuming is aerobic!). It's as simple as working to create a peaceful, joyous environment in which to raise your children—no matter that you're not living in the picture perfect house you'd always dreamed—you create perfection in the space you've got.

You don't focus on what you don't have because that gets you caught up in the "it would be good if" and prevents you from enjoying the very moment you have in front of you.

The art of the mundane is driving to work and making a point of smiling at the guy in the next car over who looks grumpy and tired (and discovering that your smile made him smile, too). It's getting to work and telling someone how nice they look, or how much you appreciate their help in getting the quarterly report out. It's the joy of deciding to go to the gym two days a week instead of eating a junk food lunch and being happy that you've made this pro-active choice in making your Life Puzzle. It's the call from your children at 3:00 p.m. as they arrive home from school to talk about their day, and you give 100% attention as they tell you about the star they got on their spelling test.

For these are the moments of our mundane lives. In and of themselves they're just rather ordinary lives, but they are what we are about. If we forget to live fully in each of these moments we will miss them, or even worse, we will not see the wonder in them because we're focused on waiting for the next "Ah ha, that's it!" moments which are few and far between.

I learned the art of the mundane, one evening in the middle of making a salad for dinner. I had all the veggies out and was quickly washing and getting them ready to cut. I started chopping the carrots with an irritation that said "This is so boring, I hate making salads every night." And then some little voice inside me said, "Well, let's see, you're 32 years old, you'll probably live until your 85, which means you've got another 53 years of making salads. Are you going to make them all with a growl on your face?"

In that moment, I knew it was up to me to make a choice. I was choosing to make myself irritable, I could just as easily choose something else. I did—the art of mundane living!

That was my last irritable salad! I learned to change that boring, dull salad making into a pleasure filled time. I poured myself a glass of wine, I turned on some music I enjoyed, and I slowed down. I stopped chopping with anger and started slicing with a smile on my face.

The shift has been incredible, but not just in salad-making. That lesson taught me that every little mundane thing that I can do—the dishes, the laundry, running errands, producing the monthly report for the umpteenth time—can all be turned into a joyful slice of life…if I choose to do so.

## Celebrating the process of making your Life Puzzle.

Happy Birthday…another year gone by and we're going to have a party to celebrate. But what are we celebrating? The fact that the sun and moon came up 365 times since the last party? Whose accomplishment was that? If you really stop and think about it, except for surviving all the ups and downs of the sun and moon, what do we celebrate at a birthday party? Time? Doesn't time go by whether we sit on our behinds or we do wonderful things? Why do we make such a big hurrah over 365 moons?

Marla Morgan, in her book, *Mutant Message Down Under*, highlights this issue and makes a wonderful point about celebrating the passage of time versus growth in a life passage.

She tells the story of traveling with an Aborigine tribe in the Australian outback. Aborigines don't celebrate yearly birthdays; instead, an individual chooses for him or herself when to throw a celebration party. They celebrate growth and accomplishment throughout their life journey. Thus a 12 year-old boy may go three years without asking the tribe to celebrate with him. But now he asks them to acknowledge his growth as an arrow maker. Through all the trials and hundreds of arrows that weren't quite right he has developed his skill. He knows there's no point in rushing it because it isn't getting tasks done fast that are valued in this society, it is truly learning a task to its fullest and finest that is important. Through this boy's journey, as is true for all members of the tribe, it is the learning process that is important and never-ending.

Thus the 50 year-old member is just as honored for the accumulated wisdom and learning that has made him a valued elder. Now his party to celebrate his mastery of teaching arrow making is just as important as the young boy's. Of course, this could not have been accomplished unless he had learned many years earlier to master the art of making them himself.

This mastering of life through the process of learning is the journey of an Aborigine's life and it makes so much more sense than the way we celebrate time and our birthdays.

We are so focused on time...by the time I'm 21 I should have or be this...by 30 it should be this...by 40...50... We spend much less time on mastering and living the process of learning, and much more on a time line of *doing what everyone else is doing so we'll all look the same at about the same age.* So many lives are caught up in this that when we don't meet the 21 deadline, then we focus on the 30...yeah, when I'm 30 I'll have all that...ooops, didn't quite make it at 40 so—ah, time is running out.

## Just because you haven't, doesn't mean you can't.

A terror that reigns over so many of our hearts is the feeling that we haven't accomplished something that we're supposed to do within the time-line. This is the life that is on the left side of the Choosing Continuum—reactive and unconscious. It's when we get our lives caught up in hoping that if we get all the external issues—money, job, spouse, kids, house, and cars—then we'll feel okay. It's not a life spent building a healthy Life Puzzle, but one that's in competition with the sun and moon...it must be done by this time. When we don't hit the time clock, we panic as if we have failed. The true failure is in not realizing the artificiality of this clock. Accomplishing tasks to meet a "by 20, 30, or 40" time line usually results in lives that have very little conscious creation to them. And in that, we often wake up in our 60's, to discover that life is passing us by, and we don't really know who we are.

But you can choose to break away from the clock, shift to building your Life Puzzle and celebrate growth, not time. Call your friends together to celebrate growth in the individual pieces of your Life Puzzle.

For example, when you've achieved mastery in your exercise piece by consistently exercising three days a week for more than a year, throw a party to celebrate! When you've given up a negative thinking rut by realizing that you don't react using judgmental thinking every time you meet a new person, celebrate!

For aren't these the things, once

mastered, that are truly the valuable accomplishments of a meaningful life? Isn't it the laying down of small pieces of your Life Puzzle each day that is more important than getting a big house, car, trophy spouse, and waking up with the realization that you don't know why or who you are?

The meaning of your life is a daily process of living, loving, growing, and building a healthy Life Puzzle. As you fill in the pieces your life will merge into a balanced whole.

There is a story told about natives from the island of Fiji that I think drives home the point of living within the moment and making the most of what is right in front of one. Fiji was dominated by the Europeans and natives were looked on as lazy. The story goes like this: The Colonial comes upon a Fijian lying on a hammock with a fishing line on his toe, drinking from a coconut.

"Get up!" says the Colonial.

"Why?"

"Because you've got to go to work and earn money."

"Why?"

"So you can make investments, educate your children and establish a retirement fund so you can go to a South Pacific island and lie in a hammock with a fishing line on your toe and drink from a coconut."

—from *National Geographic*, October, 1995.

## Suggested reading list

Kubler-Ross, Elizabeth          *Death is a Vital Experience*
                                *The Wheel of Life*

Kabat-Zinn, Jon                 *Full Catastrophe Living*

Sankar, Andrea                  *Dying at Home*

Nuland, Sherwin B.              *How We Die*

Colgrove, Melba, Bloomfield,
Harold and McWilliams, Peter    *How to Survive the Loss of Love*

# ACTION PLAN

## Exercise #1.

Write your own obituary. In it, go through the 16 pieces of your Life Puzzle and note the accomplishments and/or quality you achieved in each of these pieces.

## Exercise #2.

Volunteer at a hospice or other similar situation where you can work with and support those who are in the process of dying.

# Let's get to it…

*piece by piece to find peace in your Life Puzzle.*

# *Piece by piece to find peace.*

**W**ell, here we are at the last chapter. I've shared quite a bit with you about creating your Life Puzzle through choosing a pro-active process of living. But this book is just a starter. In truth, if this book included all the information you'll need throughout your life it might be 5,000 pages long!

Believe me, I've contemplated writing that book, but I know you would never read it. Besides, the learning you'll be doing over the years will come in increments. Nobody needs all 5,000 pages, you can't use them all at once. Making your Life Puzzle is done a piece at a time, and only you can decide which piece is the most important one to work on at a particular time in life.

I hope you will use this book as a motivation to become much more conscious about your Life Puzzle and your responsibility in owning, developing, and creating it in the way that is right for you.

## Which piece is most important?

That depends on you and where you are right now. One of the people who read a draft of this book felt I should highlight the spiritual section as being the most important part of one's Life Puzzle. I agree with her that the spiritual is very important, if not the most impor-

tant, but I reminded her that she felt that way because she had already done so much work on the other pieces of her Life Puzzle that she had arrived at that knowledge. Had she read this book at an earlier stage of making her Life Puzzle, she might not have reached this same conclusion.

And so it will be with you. Only you can listen to your inner voice in developing your Life Puzzle. You need to assess where you are right now and then listen to your inner heart to tell you what piece you should focus on next.

If all of this is very new to you, then I encourage you to begin with the nutrition and exercise pieces. These are very tangible areas of one's Life Puzzle, ones that you can look at, see where you are out of balance, and do what you need to do to adjust.

After those two areas have become part of your Life Puzzle as a daily lifestyle, then listen again to your inner heart. Confront your thinking process and your feelings. Work with a counselor, read a lot of books, take classes and learn everything you can about opening yourself up to all the possibilities within these areas to improve and build your Life Puzzle.

There are many books available which will help you in all the areas of your Life Puzzle. Keep reading and you will keep growing.

### Find like-minded friends!

Choosing to create your own Life Puzzle by creating a conscious, daily lifestyle is a wonderful decision. However, at first, you may feel like a loner out there! That's not to say there aren't others who are also doing it. It's just that you're more likely to run into people who aren't. (Remember the victim model...most people convince themselves it's easier to be a victim than to empower themselves).

If you commit to building your Life Puzzle you will discover other people who are also trying to take full responsibility of their lives. Stick with them and help each other. There are actually a lot of us that are doing this, we need to speak up a little louder to find each other!

### Ready...set...go!

There are no magic signs that will happen when you start making your Life Puzzle... you've just got to commit to yourself and realize that "if it's to be, it's up to me!"

When I was first introduced to Life Puzzle-making, I remember thinking, "Why wasn't I taught all this stuff?" It seems it's something every human being needs, so why don't we learn it at home or in school? At first I was really angry, but I've since come to understand that the only reason it isn't taught in most homes or schools is that our parents and teachers (and preachers and just about everybody else!) don't know it either, because no one taught them.

So I turned that frustration into energy...the energy to learn what I needed to do to create a balanced self. It's been a lot of work, and it will be for you too, but it is the only way to do it. As more and more of us do it, in time it will become the normal way. At this point we all have to have the courage to do it ourselves. Hopefully your grandchildren will begin to learn it in school, but that's only going to happen if you teach your children yourself. Then we can hope that when they are adults they will get involved in changing the school systems to create healthy classrooms (self-responsibility and empowerment as the key!) that encourage children to build a balanced Life Puzzle.

But that's a long way off. If it's ever going to happen, it will be because today you choose to commit yourself to making your own Life Puzzle—one day at a time, piece by piece. Remember, your opportunity to add to your Life Puzzle is not over until you die, so you've got a lifetime to work on it. Good luck and keep growing!

AS LONG AS YOU LIVE

KEEP LEARNING HOW TO LIVE

*~ Seneca*

# *Index*